FRED GIPSON

FRED GIPSON — 1908–1973

FRED GIPSON
Texas Storyteller

By

Mike Cox

Introduction by
Joe Austell Small

Jacket by Vic Blackburn

SHOAL CREEK PUBLISHERS, INC.

P.O. BOX 9737   AUSTIN, TEXAS 78766

Copyright © 1980 by MIKE COX

First Edition

Lithographed and Bound in the United States of America

Jacket from *The Trail-Driving Rooster*, by Fred Gipson, pictures by Marc
Simont. Copyright, 1955, by Fred Gipson. Reproduced by permission of T.
Beck Gipson.

Jackets from the following reproduced by permission of Harper & Row,
Publishers, Inc.: *Curly and the Wild Boar*, by Fred Gipson, illustrations by
Ronald Himler. Illustrations copyright © 1979 by Ronald Himler. *The Home
Place*, by Fred Gipson. Copyright, 1950, by Fred Gipson. *Hound-dog Man*, by
Fred Gipson. Copyright, 1947, 1949, by Fred Gipson. *Little Arliss*, by Fred
Gipson, illustrations by Ronald Himler. Illustrations © 1978 by Ronald Him-
ler. *Old Yeller*, by Fred Gipson, drawings by Carl Burger. Copyright © 1956
by Fred Gipson. *Recollection Creek*, by Fred Gipson, drawings by Carl Burger.
Copyright © 1944, 1945, 1946, 1947, 1948, 1955, 1959, by Fred Gipson.
Savage Sam, by Fred Gipson, decorations by Carl Burger. Copyright © 1962
by Fred Gipson.

Photographs on page iv (frontispiece) and page 195 by Mike Cox.

Library of Congress Cataloging in Publication Data

Cox, Mike.
    Fred Gipson, Texas storyteller.

    Bibliography: p.
    Includes index.
    1. Gipson, Frederick Benjamin, 1908–   2. Authors,
American—20th century—Biography.   I. Title.
PS3513.I79Z58   813'.54   [B]   80-18146
ISBN 0-88319-054-0

CONTENTS

ILLUSTRATIONS

PREFACE

Sociologists have labeled those of us born shortly after World War II the "War Babies." They could just as well have called us "Walt Disney Babies." I don't know anyone near my age who did not wear a coonskin cap and play "Davy Crockett at the Alamo," watch the Mickey Mouse Club on television, or cry at the end of Disney's movie *Old Yeller*.

Several years went by after the movie before I began to suspect that Walt Disney did not actually write *Old Yeller*. While in high school, writing a three-times-a-week teenage news column for the Austin *American-Statesman*, I finally got to meet Fred Gipson, the man who did write *Old Yeller*. He was in Austin to give a speech, which I covered for the newspaper.

A couple of years later, as a cub reporter for the San Angelo *Standard-Times*, I was sent to Mason to talk with Fred and find out what writing project he had planned next. We hit it off, and after that, anytime I came through Mason and he was there, I went out to his Llano River ranch. He liked to talk, and I liked to listen. Unfortunately, I didn't have sense enough to tape record him until the spring of 1971, when I interviewed him for a couple of hours, getting his basic life story down on tape.

"I think you ought to think in terms of some sort of autobiography," I said near the end of the tape.

Fred replied: "Well . . . who is going to do the work? It is going to take a long time and everybody's memory is skipping and you have to type it, and sort it, and write around it, and everything like that to fit it in. I won't attempt to do it. I can't do the work any more."

When Fred died a couple of years later, I decided to write his biography. How had this man, whom Walter Prescott Webb compared to Mark Twain, developed from someone whose earliest ambition had been to be a muleskinner or coon hunter into a writer whose most famous story has sold millions of copies in dozens of languages? I think I have found the answer to that question, but Fred was right, it was a lot of work.

Fortunately, a great many people made the job easier. Tommie Gipson North, Fred's first wife, provided much information, though at times it was a painful experience for her. The same can be said for Beck Gipson, Fred's son, who always took the time to answer my questions and who let me live on the Gipson ranch for a couple of weeks while I added finishing touches to the manuscript. Cookie, Beck's wife, also filled some important gaps and pours a bourbon and water that "makes the cows come home."

Fred's closest friend, Joe Small of Western Publications, provided much insight into the man, as did several other good friends, including Frank Wardlaw, Allen Maxwell, Margaret Hartley, and Holmes Jenkins.

Stella Gipson Polk, one of Fred's sisters and a writer herself, told many helpful stories about the family's early life and fixed some fine country meals when I visited her ranch outside Mason. Charles Gipson, Fred's brother, taught me the difference between a "go Devil" and a "section harrow" and helped me, a city boy, to understand what growing up on a dry land farm in the Hill Country was like.

The late R. Henderson Shuffler, who never knew this book was in preparation, did much for Texas letters by urging people like Fred Gipson to give their papers to the University of Texas. The thirty-nine boxes constituting the Gipson Papers, administered by Ellen Dunlap of the Humanities Research Center, were extremely important to the development of this book. The correspondence between Fred and his agent, Maurice Crain, and the letters to and from Evan Thomas, his long-time editor at Harpers, were very revealing.

Many other friends of Fred's and several close friends of mine helped me in an assortment of ways.

And finally, a recognition that reads like a cliche, but is true: My wife, Rosalyn, helped so much with the tedious editing of draft after draft and with the typing that without her there would be no book. More important even than this, she put up with me for the years that this book has been in the making.

To her, I dedicate this book.

INTRODUCTION

The following is going to be far from a formal introduction to a book. It is more of a talk with friends and admirers of a man who I was as close to as I have been to any person outside of my family in my lifetime.

We were coming home from a trip on which we had bared our very souls to each other and found that we were suddenly engrossed with the feel for a total honesty pledge. Sensing that we might be toying with something that wouldn't work, we decided to test this all out honesty business on the spot. As a starter, what was the biggest fault that we saw in each other? I asked Fred to lead off.

"Well," he said with short thought, "you are always introducing me as the famous Fred Gipson, author of *Hound-Dog Man*, *Fabulous Empire* and other notable books. People appear properly impressed and there I stand with my mouth hanging open and nothing to say. I wish you would just say, 'I want you to meet my friend Fred Gipson,' and leave off the sugar topping."

I was astonished. Fred had often spoken of his constant need of a well-fed ego. Perhaps I didn't know my "gut-honest" friend as well as I'd thought.

Fred then asked for my criticism. I mumbled that his fighting life too hard would make him an old man before his time. I voiced surprise at his revelation relative to my cake topping. We agreed that there were probably still things we needed to learn about each other and promised to work on it. We did—and the more we opened ourselves up, the closer we became.

It got to be a regular thing. Every other weekend the Gipsons and Smalls would get together. The goer would stop by Fredericksburg and pick up a jug of its well-known wine. In the beginning, I think we paid a full 75¢ a gallon! After a couple glasses of this stimulating nectar and some polite conversation about what had happened in the interim, we started thrashing out problems of the world and invariably ended up independently rich. Upon those occasions wherein we had some trepidations relative to the wine remaining in an uncontaminated condition overnight, things got progressively merry. Almost invariably they would begin with, "I remember one time . . . ."

After a while, our frequent visits got more and more into sessions complaining about life and less fun and storytelling. I decided to bring this to Fred's attention. Walter Webb was giving one of his parties at Friday Mountain Ranch. The Gipsons had come down for the weekend, and Fred and I were on our way out to the ranch when Fred started talking about how bad things were. When he got to his first "starve to death," I interrupted. I reminisced a bit on how much fun and satisfaction we had derived from knowing each other, and then I made a suggestion. "Fred, our visits are turning more and more into profound analyses of our grievances against life and less and less on the good times we used to have. Why don't we bitch hard and deep for the first thirty minutes, then get back to a constructive line of thinking?"

To my surprise, Fred readily agreed. "You start," I invited. Fred didn't hesitate. He tore into Tommie and her constant spending with vehemence. It had gotten to be his most familiar line of late. When he finished one episode, I interrupted with, "Fred, Tommie doesn't throw around money like many women I know. I've never known her to spend any big money at all."

"Yeah," Fred's brow furrowed, "but she can nickel and dime you to death!"

Fred was the best bass fisherman I have ever known. We fished from deep within the interior of Mexico throughout most of the West. I could hold my own with him fairly well until we hit his own stomping grounds: There he was king, and Fred knew it.

One afternoon we were fishing his favorite stream, the Llano. Fred had taught me how to fish the various creeks that flow into this small river as well as the main stream itself. I was constantly amazed at the thoroughness of his knowledge of bassology in this particular maze of potholes, rock-studded shallows and deep, still-running water. We took turns at lead fishing. The follow-up man was playing the cleanup role since he was working just-fished waters.

Fred had given me first turn as lead man and I came up with a nice bass in less than ten minutes. This was always the signal to cross over, so Fred took the lead. Our kidding while fishing was merciless. "I always like to get the first one," I remarked. "Looks like this is going to be my day."

"Accidents happen to even the worst of us" was Fred's dry comment.

Shortly, I had another strike and played in a spotted native bass. I have always felt that if a man really enjoyed his sport, he should show it—like being quite vociferous on landing a fish. My celebratory mood was not lost on Fred. When I held up the fish and asked him to look, he barely glanced back and did not bother with the forced smile he sometimes displayed, even while fishing seriously and in a highly competitive mood.

When I caught bass No. 3, it really started getting under Fred's skin. This had never happened before. We both knew it could change suddenly. I was always slow in starting and consistently came in a poor second. Even though it might mean nothing in the long run, this early lead plainly rankled Fred. One thing we both knew without bringing it up—never let up on rawhiding each other. It would have been a definite show of weakness that neither would have approved of.

"Biggest one yet!" I chortled. "Say, Fred," I said as a sort of afterthought, "maybe you ought to change places with me. Looks like they're hitting better back here . . . ."

This little nicety brought exactly what was intended. "Oh, hush!" Fred said, and continued fishing feverishly.

He caught one finally. It wasn't a big fish and he didn't even call it to my attention—just strung the bass hurriedly and continued in his up-front position. I mumbled, barely loud enough for Fred to hear, "Makes company feel a shade bad playing follow-up man all the time . . . ."

It was getting late when we came to the big hole. Fred's mood changed. He became talkative again. "Best fishing hole on the Llano," he explained. "More fish in this hole than on a mile of regular water." Fred moved into position and cautioned, "Let's fish this one right." He cast completely across the hole and reeled in slowly. "Look!" Fred pointed about half way across the hole after he had cranked in his lure. "Four of them just setting there. Nice ones too!"

I saw the four bass. They had followed the lure a ways and were lying at attention as if they had been disturbed from a siesta and were just now beginning to take notice of what was going on. I caught Fred's spirit of excitement. He cast again, quickly. I think that was the second time I had seen Fred backlash in years. His language was highly descriptive as he plucked at the crow's nest. I was showing weakness in our fishing competition. I was hesitating to cast. "Go on!" Fred admonished. "They're not going to sit there forever!"

I dropped my lure about two feet ahead of the outside bass on my left and it struck immediately. This was a good one and I played him carefully. Quickly stringing the fish, I glanced at Fred. He was still pulling and fuming at the backlash. I felt sorry for him then, but I simply couldn't afford to show it. Even now I hardly know what it was, but it would have actually weakened something close between us if either had displayed compassion at a time like this. I cast into the hole again and the strike was vicious. It was a beautiful fight. The aerial display was impressive. When I finally got my thumb in its mouth and held that fish up, I knew it was the biggest bass I had ever caught on the Llano.

I glanced at Fred. He had crocheted the wrinkles out of his backlash and was fishing that hole as if his very life depended upon catching a fish fast. We both knew that my snagging the second bass was mostly luck since a fish that big is nearly always spooked by landing another fish nearby—my first one. The commotion the big fish made had put the others on guard. They had gotten the message that we were not passing out free chow.

Fred looked at the sun. "Time to go home," he said flatly. Then he glanced at my string of fish. With a genuine ring of sincerity in his voice, Fred said, "You're not *that* good, you little bastard—and you *know* it!"

One afternoon I got a phone call from Fred. "Let's just haul off and do some of these things we are always talking about and never do. Why don't we go down to that spa in Mexico you are always talking about and soak some of the nicotine and alcohol out of us?" I generally had an excuse for such impromptu trips since I was ever-busy trying to make a bare living in those days, but to the last day I live I will be happy that I replied, "We should be half way down there by now—what's holding you up?" Fred came to Austin and we got an early start next morning.

Somehow smoking was one of the few vices that never attracted me. I would bum one off Fred now and then as we sipped our drinks and it actually tasted good, but as for regular smoking, it held no appeal whatsoever. Fred got a thing going about how many cigarettes I had bummed off him, and when he brought it up around a group (sometimes I asked him for a cigarette just to get him started), I would sit there in deep admiration of his descriptions of the shameless bum that I had become and how my constant need of tobacco was all but sending him to the poor house.

As we pulled out that morning, Fred mentioned that he was about out of cigarettes. I stopped at a little drive-in and said, "Sit still, I'll be right back." I noticed the quizzical look on Fred's face. It turned into downright astonishment as I threw a cartoon of cigarettes into his lap with a brief statement: "Now, that ought to take care of some I've bummed off you during the past ten years!"

Fred didn't say a word. It dawned on me then that I had made a gross error. I had stabbed one of his choice bantering subjects and ruined a pot full of fun. Sure enough, Fred didn't mention bumming again. It took me almost a year of persistent bumming before Fred seemed to feel free to dwell on this subject again. I made sure this time that I wouldn't dirty the water.

I have never enjoyed long trips in automobiles. This one I enjoyed thoroughly, going and coming. We took it leisurely, stopping anywhere at any time that we saw something interesting to explore. In order to make sure that we got our full money's worth, we sipped on Scotch and water and Fred would offer me a cigarette every time he took a pack out of his pocket. "We need to store up as much impurity as possible," he said. "No telling when we'll get such a chance to clobber so much poison at one time again."

We stayed in Monterrey that night and got off to a leisurely start the next morning. We both agreed that this was the way to make a trip—enjoy anything that looked enjoyable. About two o'clock in the afternoon we started getting hungry and decided to pick out a good-looking eatery and partake of some Mexican food. We had hit that lonesome stretch between Monterrey and Valles where you see nothing but pavement and mesquite for long, monotonous hours. Finally, we pulled into a place that read "Food" even though it might not have met our standards two hours earlier.

A Mexican woman and her daughter appeared and we were having quite a hassel with our ordering until a lanky Texan strolled up and let it be known that he owned the place, that this was his wife and daughter and he would be glad to help out. We settled for *wavos con carne*, which turned out to be pure delight. We invited the man to have a beer with us and he accepted. As the half-cool fluid found its mark in empty stomachs, we grew fascinated with talking to this particular person. It became evident that he didn't intend to return to Texas for some good reasons. He had bought land down here in the semi-wilderness and was content to raise a family and run his little business far away from any rat race. We asked him about the country and got a good history of it and that whole part of Mexico. We spent nearly three hours in this place and suddenly realized that we would arrive at our destination a couple of hours after dark.

There is a fascination to this type of travel that most Americans never discover. Most trips are laid out with timetables almost as strict as an airline's. If there is anything interesting in between to see—too bad. Sometimes the in-betweens and the unlooked-fors prove to be more interesting than the main course.

We arrived in Valles, and it was only a short drive to Tanninuel, where we got a good night's sleep. We were ready for our first steaming bath next morning. I'll never forget it! It was a scenic thing—a big pool of naturally hot water that boiled up out of the earth at a temperature that I do not recall, but I do know it was *hot*! The pool was surrounded by tropical growth and a great cave that formed a miniature amphitheater in which an orchestra played to the customers on various occasions. You could stand shoulder deep in that water and pretty soon the sweat was rolling off your head right down into your eyes and you could just *feel* the poison seeping out of your body!

We were warned against staying in too long and withdrew to our room after about forty minutes. I could tell that something was on Fred's mind. He would get up and go to the bathroom, pace around the floor and look out the windows. Finally, I asked him, "All right, Gipson, what's gnawing on you?"

He replied, "I'm worried about our health. I think we lost more poison than a man's body can stand at one time. Wouldn't be surprised if we had some reaction. It might be that we ought to mosey over and get a bottle of good Mexican rum just to make sure we taper off gradually."

So we went and got a bottle of rum. In fact, we got two just to make sure.

One morning while we were eating breakfast a distinguished looking man walked up to Fred and exclaimed, "Fred Gipson! Why you old hound-dog man!" This person turned out to be an executive from New York. I still don't remember how he knew Fred personally, but it really doesn't matter in the long haul, as Fred would say. The man (of course I have forgotten his name, too) told us that he was leaving with a party in an hour for his place on the Panuco and that we simply *had* to see his river estate. He promised fishing that we would never forget. That sold us.

The trip out there was a story in itself. Even with writers' imagination it was hard for us to fashion a road in our minds out of what we were going over, but it was worth the trip! There was an absolute mansion on a high cliff on the Tamesi that looked like all of the ''get away from it all'' places you have ever dreamed about in your life. It came complete with servants, every type of drink you could imagine and incomparable food.

We were surprised after supper that night when the man told us he had to rush away the next morning and get back to New York but that we were welcome to stay there as long as we wished. Surely we should remain a week, a month or just stay there until he got back if we wished and use the servants and everything he had as if it was ours. Now a chance like that comes maybe once in a lifetime and maybe only once in five or six lifetimes. We stayed and we fished and we were waited on hand and foot.

One incident will never fade from my mind. We started fishing downstream and Fred got a couple hundred yards ahead of me. I got fascinated with a certain part of the river and was making slow time. I heard Fred yell and saw him motioning for me to come on. After two or three yells and motions, I quickened my pace and noticed what could best be explained as an ''I can't believe it'' look on Fred's face. ''Just hit that spot of water right over there at the swirl with your lure,'' Fred said. I looked at him and there must have been a question mark on my face. ''Cast into that swirl.'' Fred pointed to a spot below a waterfall that was both picturesque and noisy. I did. There was a small explosion. All I saw then was a streak of silver and a broken line. ''Tarpon?'' I asked incredulously. ''Try again,'' Fred said.

After the fourth cast, I quit. They were tarpon all right. I succeeded in getting a small one into shallow water, but he made a run for it, then threw my plug in a leaping arc. Fred laughed. ''I've had so much fun that I've about run out of plugs. Never thought I'd hang onto a tarpon in fresh water.'' They had migrated upstream from the Gulf, and that pool below the falls was full of them. We never landed even one. They were too big for our light tackle, but what an outstanding experience!

We fished upstream from then on to avoid the tarpon and climbed back up to our little mansion with heavy stringers. The head man met us with a smile, asking how we would like the fish prepared. Fred and I sat out on the veranda overlooking the river and sipped on our drinks.

''I have always heard of paradise,'' Fred said, ''and I suppose this is as close as I will ever get to it. Couldn't a man stay here for the rest of his life and write and fish and drink and flat *live?* Don't see how anybody could ever get tired of this, but isn't it just like life—my friend can only spend one night and he's got to rush back to New York. Looks like if you can *afford* something like this, you can't afford not to use it.''

I couldn't believe it next morning when Fred said we ought to be getting back to Tanninuel so that we could think about starting the trip home. I tried to talk him out of it, reminding him that this might be our last and only chance to live like barons, but Fred persisted and we pulled on out of paradise and back into the world of reality.

This was a part of Fred that I finally became accustomed to: He simply couldn't be away from home long at a time. Never a homing pigeon could have had a stronger and more emotional desire to return than Fred Gipson. It would come at the oddest times.

We were making a long-talked-about trip up into what we called the real West. I was publishing *Western Sportsman* then and had a lady reader who was a fishing writer and quite a fisherman of note herself. She promised us some of the best trout fishing in the West if we would come up to Montana. We were about half-way through Yellowstone Park headed for Montana when the homing desire hit Fred. I could always tell when the urge for Mason County grew strong within him. I learned not to fight it since it did nothing but grow stronger. I turned the car around and headed for Mason County . . . .

Who of us that could be called a writer of any sort could ever forget Dee Woods and the Southwest Writers Conferences? Dee would make up her program, put some of our names on it and then inform us that we were to be there at a certain time and perform certain tasks. Dee was a lovable person who got things done. She never incited our resentment by presuming that we would attend her Writers Conferences every year.

I remember one conference in particular—I think it was in May 1952. J. Frank Dobie made this one and was the head honcho. A part of the schedule was a day at the King Ranch. Somehow Fred and I managed to miss the bus, and the other writers went on without us—a considerable blow to our ego in itself, although Fred reasoned they probably didn't notice that we weren't aboard. At any rate, we got in my old Plymouth and broke some speed records trying to catch that bus. We caught up about twenty miles down the line and when they saw us, our fellow writers directed the bus driver to pull over. He did, by a little beer stop. We locked up my car and joined them.

A day at the King Ranch was always interesting. It ended with barbecue but no beer. In those days alcohol in any form was prohibited on the King Ranch. On numerous occasions Fred and I would allow ourselves to be persuaded to entertain certain individuals or even a small gathering with our questionably melodious refrains of "Crawdad Hole" or maybe something like "Red River Valley." Fred had a high nasal twang that lent just the right note to off-key singing, and I was strong on volume and short on just about everything else. Nevertheless when the beer started flowing and people got in a gay mood, invariably they would ask for the two troubadours to give forth with our God-given vocal talents.

But this was one time we didn't want to perform. After a long day and a heavy meal we were muchly content to listen to Dobie relate some stories and do his thing. When he announced that next on the program would be Fred Gipson and Joe Small singing "Crawdad Hole," we tried to melt behind a convenient log. I believe that was one of the most embarrassing moments in our respective lives. As we were walking up to the loudspeaker, I reminded Fred that he had always said, " 'We don't sing good, but we sing loud' and, for God's sake, sing loud NOW."

I think it was the first time we had heard ourselves sing while we were cold sober. It was horrendous. For the first time, in a cold sweat, we fully realized why people wanted us to sing—we were so bad that we *might* have been actually good. Anyhow, we sang five cowboy songs. We both learned something that night that we hadn't thought much about in the past—if you can't be the best at something, do it with such a will, so strong and determined that you might just get away with it after all.

By the time we got back to my car that night everybody was so dry a wet floor could have been mopped clean by using any one of our shriveling bodies. Everyone on the bus started getting out when we took our leave. It was evident that an old worn-out Plymouth couldn't carry a bus load of people, so we played elimination games and finally got down to ten people.

We walked into the little beer joint and Gene Arrington, who started out in the magazine publishing business with me in 1936, ordered three beers for each of us. I'll never forget the look on that waitress' face as she stacked three beautiful, cold, sweating bottles of beer in front of each of ten people. We had a reorder, of course, and then wedged ourselves into that car of mine. There was barely enough working space left for the driver to move his elbows. Everyone was singing by then. It is probably just as well that I do not have a tape of that particular ride back to Corpus Christi.

There has been much speculation as to what mark Fred would have left on the world of writing if the latter part of his life had evolved without so much pain, sorrow, complications and tragedy. I believe that Fred was just hitting his stride with *Old Yeller* and could have had fifteen to twenty more years of productive writing. We talked often about goals, ambitions and possible writing projects. Books such as *Hound-Dog Man* and *Old Yeller* will remain very much alive even as our lifestyle changes in the future. They portray vividly a life that no longer exists and could very well be valued as history as well as top-class entertainment. I believe Fred would have written more books of this caliber and some even better.

Inevitably, he has been compared to Mark Twain. I believe Fred would have ranked with Twain if he had been able to continue his writing career, uninterrupted by the tragedies that he suffered. In my opinion, some of the things Fred wrote are as good as the best of Mark Twain. One thing for sure, Fred Gipson could get into the very inside of a little boy and his dog perhaps as no other author ever has. He could make you live, and think and feel the story as if you were the central character yourself—and that is one of the things that puts the ''great'' into authors. In my estimation Fred Gipson *is* a great author. Just how great he will be rated by future generations is a question I am not going to try to forecast right now. I'd rather relive one of those days on the Llano with him, followed by a fireside session beginning with ''I remember one time . . . .''

JOE AUSTELL SMALL

FRED GIPSON
Texas Storyteller

Fred's parents, Beck and Emma Gipson. (Courtesy Beck Gipson.)

1

The Home Place

Fred Gipson sat on his patio, a hand-rolled cigarette in one hand, a glass of Scotch and water in the other, his feet propped on the railing. He looked out on the Llano and wondered whether he wanted to walk down to the sandstone rock of the river's edge and see if the bass were hungry.

Beneath the wooden decking, a bullfrog was croaking, its sound mingling with the splash of water from the artesian well-fed creek that trickled down to the river nearby. A rooster bobwhite quail called in the distance and on the place across the river wild turkeys gobbled. The breeze was walking around in the big cottonwoods in front of his ranch house, kicking the brittle leaves.

He felt absolutely alone.

Gipson knew he ought to feel well off. His simple story of a boy who had to kill the dog he loved had sold more than two million copies and was still making him a living. Friends assured him he had written a classic comparable to anything Mark Twain had done.

He never thought things would turn out like they had. Yet, who should know better than the man who wrote *Old Yeller* that a good story does not always have a happy ending?

West of Llano, Fred's parents, Emma and Beck Gipson,[1] could see the high, bald hills beginning to turn a bluish gray in the fading light. "We'll never get across those mountains!" Emma fretted.[2]

Beck reined their team and studied the situation. Compared to the scenery they were both used to back in East Texas, the uplift stretching across the horizon before them did look like a hard pull. But he figured they would make it. That was about their only choice, considering what the doctor had said.

The trouble had started when they lived in Hunt County. Though he was a relatively young man, Beck came down with cripplingly painful rheumatism. His doctor suggested a move to a drier climate, but there was another problem: Emma was pregnant and could not stand a long trip. The couple decided to go to Devers, in Liberty County near Beaumont, to stay with Emma's parents until the baby was born in August 1899.

As soon as Emma was able, the Gipsons, their newborn and their oldest child set out for the West Texas town of Mason. En route, Beck stopped in the cotton fields to earn enough money to keep his family in food. Soon after arriving in Mason in November 1899, Beck's appendix burst. It should have killed him, but a doctor there told his anxious wife the appendix apparently had ruptured inward instead of outward, an unusual occurrence that had saved his life. He was so sick for a while he almost wished he had died, but he eventually recovered.[3]

As he grew stronger, Beck began to collect his own farming implements and look around for some cheap land.[4] Neither he nor Emma had ever seen any prettier land than the country around Mason. Bluebonnets sprouted bigger and bluer and with a sweeter fragrance in Mason County than anywhere else in Texas. Huge masses of ancient gray granite—some bigger than a barn—dotted the hilly, mineral-rich landscape. Oldtimers even claimed the high mineral content of the soil had something to do with their longevity.

The Llano River, full of places to swim and fish, flowed between granite banks, over sandbars and small rock islands. The river and the creeks that fed into it were lined with native pecans, elms, and hackberry trees. Dewberry bushes and catclaws grew in the protection of granite ledges. In the hills were agaritas with their yellow berries, black persimmon, and wild plum.

Cattle and sheep, deer, and other wildlife thrived on the seas of native grass. Wild turkeys, fat on such native delicacies as wild onions, weighted down the limbs of their oak roosts. Wolves were a serious threat to livestock, and an occasional mountain lion wandered through. The stream beds were homes for skunks, possums, ringtail cats, coons, and bobcats.

It was easy to get involved with the land and possible to live off it if a person worked hard enough. And when the work was done or

2

could be put off, it was a land a man could hunt and fish or enjoy a basic satisfaction just looking at—especially if it was his own land.

Beck Gipson was able to afford 81 acres northeast of Mason. Ben Gooch had owned the land—and more—first. He died in 1872. By the time the Gipsons arrived, the Gooch land had been divided and was being sold piecemeal for small farms.

Originally, the area east of Mason had been covered with aged oaks and juniper. But with the increase in farming, the trees were being cut to make room for more cotton. When Beck bought the land, it was still "new" in the agricultural sense, and if the weather cooperated, the family got by.

By now, the Gipsons had four children, all girls. At first, the family lived in a red, clapboard two-room shack on the side of a rocky, prickly pear and catclaw ridge. It was the only improvement on their new property. The front room was normal sized, but the back room was like an enclosed lean-to.

Fred was born in the old picket house on the Gooch land on February 7, 1908. In a way, he actually had five mothers, his natural mother and his four older sisters—Jennie, Bessie, Stella, and Ethel.

Mrs. Gipson was a stern, hard-working woman who worried about everything. Life was a serious matter to her, not to be taken lightly. When she did laugh, she almost seemed embarrassed by it, covering her mouth shyly with her hand. But she loved her children and had an abiding sense of fairness. She built wooden boxes for her daughters to keep their things in. The boxes, however, did not have latches or locks; Mrs. Gipson told the children they were honor-bound not to touch the contents of the others' boxes.⁵ She loved to read and had even managed to teach her husband to read. But she felt she could only afford the indulgence of reading while busy churning butter.

As a young boy, Fred had a knack for getting into the kird of situation that had the same familiar ending: a paddling. When he was seven, he overheard his father telling his mother that someone was buying live rattlesnakes at San Antonio. The venom, Beck Gipson explained, was taken from the snake and used as a medicine to counter-act snakebite. He said the snakes were caught by men using a loop of string tied to a long stick.

That was all the ambitious Fred needed to hear. He would become a millionaire. One commodity Mason County had no shortage of was rattlesnakes. Catching a snake was easy. But when Fred arrived

3

home, pulling the snake along as the writhing rattler tried to plunge its deadly fangs into his bare heels, his mother became hysterical. Beck grabbed a hoe and, with one hit, destroyed forever the snake's potential sales value. By this time, Mrs. Gipson had recovered from her scare sufficiently to take out after Fred with a barrel stave. With just a couple of licks, she quelled her son's ambition to be a rattlesnake seller. But she did not stop there. When she was through, Fred had decided it would be all right with him if he never saw another rattlesnake.[6]

Sometimes Fred could get in trouble just by the way he looked. He might feel perfectly fine, but if he looked bilious to his mother, she brought out the hated bottle of castor oil. As a measure of preventive medicine, Mrs. Gipson sometimes lined up all her children for a dose. Fred ran away once rather than face that doctoring. But when he came back, he got an even bigger dose.[7]

When Fred was really sick, his mother brewed him a special medicinal tea of peach leaves or made a concoction of sulfur and molasses.[8] Serious illness in the Hill Country was a matter of deep community concern. As soon as word got around, neighbors would head to the stricken person's place to eat his food, drink his whiskey, and stand around outside offering support to the worried kin.

The Gipson children fretted a lot about the health of their neighbors because when one of them got sick, Mrs. Gipson would go help out. Nothing was wrong with that but when she got back, just as a precaution, she insisted on giving her children a half cup of water and Black Draught. Hiding did no good, and they had to drink the medicine slowly. If they tried to get it down with one big gulp, Mrs. Gipson rinsed the cup and made them drink the leavings.[9]

As soon as they could afford it, the Gipsons built a bigger house. It had two bedrooms, a kitchen, a dining room, a front gallery with wicker furniture, and a back porch. Beck and Emma had the largest bedroom, with the children divided between the other bedroom and the back porch. Over the fireplace hung a photograph of a raven-haired Beck Gipson with drooping mustache and his serious-looking wife.

A big liveoak with spreading limbs that kept the gallery cool in the spring and summer stood in front of the small white house. Beneath the liveoak was a poke bush, and morning glories climbed the tree's trunk. Hollyhocks grew high in each corner of the fenced front yard, which was made bright with phlox, touch-me-nots, four-oclocks, marigolds, and petunias. And somehow, Mrs. Gipson had found room in the yard to plant dozens of rose bushes. The only bare ground in the whole yard was the walk from the front gate to the gallery. Around back, a big mesquite provided the Gipson children with candied wax for chewing gum and kite repair. Near the back porch was a windmill, which had led to one of the more serious quarrels Beck and Emma ever had. Beck wanted a windmill to pump the water from the well. Mrs. Gipson thought pulling up the water was a job for the children. But the windmill went up. Mrs. Gipson was not pleased, but her children were delighted.

Outside the kitchen door grew a Mexican rose bush, which in the spring was alive with hummingbirds. The smokehouse stood just north of the kitchen. Behind the house to the northeast was the cow pen, the horse and mule lot, and the corncrib. South of the house was the grape arbor. To the Gipsons, it was the home place.

The Gipsons raised cotton and corn, grew their own fruit and vegetables, milked their own cows, butchered their meat, and baked their own bread. A few of the rich folks in the area had tin lizzies, but when the Gipsons went to town, they rode in a wagon. The children walked the two miles to school, and at night they did their lessons by kerosene lantern.

Life was hard but simple and good, too. The Gipsons had made it through the national financial panic of 1906, and they would continue to get by as long as the Good Lord gave them the strength to work and rain enough to make their crops.

When their work was done, the Gipsons spent time together, usually on the front gallery where they could enjoy the south breeze, or in the winter gathered around the fireplace in the "front room." Beck and Emma were good storytellers, and the children grew up hearing hunting and fishing yarns, tales of Indian raids, and animal stories.

The Gipson children hated to go to bed on family storytelling nights, especially Fred and his younger brother, Charles. For the boys, the evening's end meant leaving the comfort of the fireplace for their bed at the back of the house. On cold nights, their only warmth was each other and Old Ring, providing Mrs. Gipson did not spot the dog before they slipped him under the covers.[10]

Many winter nights, as sleet splattered down on the corrugated metal roof over the unscreened back porch, Fred went to sleep thinking about his parents' adventure tales and thirsting for some excitement himself. Some day, when he grew up, he would be a mule breaker like his father, or a bronc buster, or a cattleman with a big ranch. Or maybe he would be a hound-dog man, running coons in the winter and catching catfish in the summer.

The Gipson children. *Clockwise:* Jennie, Stella, Bessie, Ethel, Fred, and Christiana *(center)*. Fred's younger brother, Charles, is missing. (Courtesy Beck Gipson.)

2

Barefoot Boy

The boy in the overalls walked down the lane, swinging the yellow lard bucket and trying to be brave. This was the day he started first grade—and he was two months late. The Gipsons had raised a better than average cotton crop, and Beck Gipson, like many other cotton farmers, had been forced to keep the children out of school to help him get it in.

Now Fred had reached the old swinging bridge across Comanche Creek. As she had packed his lunch in the lard bucket that morning, Mrs. Gipson had warned Fred not to look down as he crossed the bouncing span of wooden planks.[1] Gamely trying to follow her advice, the seven-year-old made it across.

When Fred reached the school, a two-story red sandstone building with bats and honey bees in its belfry, the children were already marching inside. Stella gave her little brother hurried directions to the first-grade room and then ran back to her place in line. As he walked into his classroom under the stern gaze of his teacher, Fred tripped. The lard bucket hit the floor with a clank, and his lunch spilled out. The other children laughed as he picked up his biscuits and put them back in the bucket.

Fred could tell right off that his teacher did not like the idea of a cotton farmer keeping his children out of school to help with the crop. It looked like she was going to take it out on Fred. The only thing that helped him get through the morning was the prospect of the lunch in his lard bucket—bacon wrapped in biscuits, and biscuits smeared with mustang grape jelly.

7

After the superintendent struck the iron triangle beneath the mahogany stairway to signal the lunch period and the students went outside to eat, Fred noticed a fat boy and the teacher's son giving him a hard look. As Fred started his lunch, one of the boys called him a "country SOB." Fred bent his lunch pail beyond further use on the head of the teacher's son and then whipped the fat boy. He got a hard spanking at school, but he had earned respect and had no more trouble with his classmates.[2]

Fred's lunch was always hearty, but a farm family did not have money to waste on delicacies like peanut butter and potted ham. Fred did without such fancies unless he could figure a way to swap with some of the town boys. Lunchtime under the oaks in the school yard was as exciting as market day in some exotic, far-off port. If food was not the object of the trade, deals could be cinched for a marble, a battered top, or a pocketful of twine that could be used to make a baseball.

One day, excitement whipped through the school like a blue norther. A classmate of Fred's electrified his friends with a device made from a penny match box: A piece of wire held a spool of thread in the box; attached to the thread was a live locust. When the box was opened, the locust leaped out and headed for a tree, only to be hauled back by the thread as the boy cranked the spool with his thumb.

A boy clever enough to figure out something like that soon noticed that Fred was getting interested. He baited him with numerous demonstrations. By noon, though Fred was hungry, he was more interested in trading for the locust kite than eating. It cost him all of his lunch to get possession of the magic match box. After school, Fred rushed home and into the kitchen, a bit less excited about his retrievable locust. He wanted something to eat.

"Didn't you take your lunch this morning?" his mother asked.

"Yes'm," Fred replied.

"Didn't you eat it?"

"No'm."

"Well, what did you do with it?"

He might have pulled off a lie, but Fred told the truth because he was genuinely proud of his locust kite and the sharp deal he had made to get it.

Mrs. Gipson looked scornfully at the captive locust. "You turn that poor bug loose right now," she ordered. "And you can wait till supper time to eat!"[3]

Fred might trade his lunch but never his hat, which he wore with the brim upturned and a red feather in the headband. He would not go anywhere without it if he had a choice. But one morning that first year he was in school, Fred could not find his hat.

"Stella, have you seen Fred's hat?" Mrs. Gipson asked.

Stella said she had not, and a search of the house turned up nothing. Fred's mother was sorry his hat was missing, but she said he had to go to school, regardless.

"Without my hat? Mama, I just gotta have my hat. Guess them ole girls . . .," he trailed off. He clearly suspected that one of his older sisters had had something to do with the disappearance of his beloved hat.

"Get your books and don't you back-talk me," Mrs. Gipson said sharply.

As Stella and Fred walked down the bluebonnet-laced lane toward school, Stella felt sorry for Fred for a reason other than his missing hat. She had a feeling Fred would not be the good student her parents expected. Ethel always made 100s on her report card; Bessie got good grades in deportment; and Jennie had already been to normal school and was teaching. Fred would not get a report card until he was in the second grade—the thought almost made Stella shudder.

About a week after Fred had first missed his hat, Stella and Bessie were sitting in a favorite tree when Stella happened to look down into an old barrel near the foot of the tree. The hat was in the bottom of the barrel. Stella scrambled out of the tree to retrieve the hat, but Bessie stopped her.

"Better let him see where he put it," she counseled. Stella wanted to get the hat for her little brother, but in the Gipson family you were supposed to mind those older than you.

Earlier that day, a bareheaded and embarrassed Fred had gone with his father on the weekly Saturday wagon trip to town. They did not get back until late, but as soon as Fred heard where his hat was, he rushed to get it. He reached down into the barrel, pulled out the hat, brushed it off, and set it on his head.

"Guess them ole girls hid it," he said.[4]

In feeling naked without his hat, Fred was taking after his father who owned two hats at a time all of his adult life. He wore a black felt John B. Stetson for everyday use and kept the other one in a box for Sundays. When his everyday hat wore out, he started wearing his "old" Sunday hat and bought another one for church.

Mrs. Gipson did not mind her husband wearing a hat—practically every man in Texas did. What did worry her was how the heat built up under his black Stetson—she had heard that caused baldness. Beck Gipson was a handsome man, and Emma did not want to see all his hair disappear.

With that in mind, Mrs. Gipson tried to convince him he needed to wear one of those high-topped, Mexican straw hats in the summer. He would not hear of it, however. The argument stretched over a period of years. Finally, Mrs. Gipson had enough. She hitched a wagon ride to town with a neighbor and bought her husband a straw hat. When she gave it to him, he was not happy about it but put it on.

Fred watched as his father went to the lot, wearing the new straw hat and looking like another person. Fred could tell by the way he walked that he did not like the hat and was struggling hard to contain his anger.

Tied to the back wheels of a wagon, two mules quietly munched corn spread in the bed as Fred's father entered the lot. Six months before when he had bought them, as Mr. Gipson liked to say, they had been as wild as mad snakes. But now they were fairly gentle. Still, so they would not get spooked, he called to the mules. They recognized his voice and kept eating, casually looking in his direction, as if to be polite. Suddenly, the mules went wild. They began snorting, whistling, and pawing the air with their forefeet. In a few seconds of explosive fury, they overturned the wagon, righted it again, and started pulling it around the corral.

Beck Gipson was perhaps the best mule man in West Texas, but all he could do was stand there and yell "Whoa!" as the mules raced around the lot. They only stopped when they had pinned the wagon against the fence and could not pull it free.

Whirling around, Mr. Gipson stormed to the house, brushed past his worried wife, and marched into the kitchen, the straw hat crumpled in his white-knuckled fist. As Mrs. Gipson watched from a respectful distance, her husband crammed the hat into the wood stove and looked down grimly as it burst into flames.

From his hiding place, Fred heard what his father had to say: "Now, Emma, let's get this straight. I'll just be damned if I'll wear a hat that a mule can't stand the sight of!"

Mrs. Gipson never again tried to get her husband to change hats.[5]

Almost as important to Mr. Gipson as his hats was the weekly wagon ride to Mason on Saturdays. Sometimes he took only Fred along; sometimes he and Mrs. Gipson went by themselves. But more often, the whole family went. As it was for most farm families, the ride to town was the highlight of the week, a chance to shop and catch up on talk about the price of pecans, watermelons, cotton, or cattle, rain or the lack of it, and politics.

Some Saturdays, Fred was allowed to go to Otto Schmidt's theater, an old corrugated iron building on the west corner of the courthouse square. The screen was a big sheet stretched across the wall. The audience, ever careful of splinters, sat on long pine benches. Fred and the other moviegoers cheered the heroes and sucked in their breaths when a speeding locomotive, spitting steam, seemed to be heading right out into the audience.

When Fred got a little older, he and little brother Charles would go see Tom Mix movies on money earned from the sale of possum and coon hides. Fred admired how Mix, chased by men in black hats, could leap from his horse onto an overhead tree limb to outsmart his pursuers. After carefully watching how the celluloid cowpoke did it, Fred figured he could, too.

Back at the farm, he saddled an old pony and trotted off toward a chinaberry tree. He effortlessly leaped from the saddle onto a limb. Thirsty for an admiring audience, Fred made Charles stand and watch him do it again. This time, for the sake of showmanship, he rode the pony a little faster to make sure Charles realized just how talented a horseman his older brother had grown to be. That was a mistake. The horse reached the limb before Fred had time to jump. Fred woke up to see the old horse standing over him, bending his neck to look straight down into his face with mild curiosity.[6]

When the whole family went to an old-settlers reunion and fair at Katemcy to see the aging Herman Lehmann put on a one-man exhibition, Fred got a taste of the old west far more realistic than anything he ever saw in a Tom Mix movie. Lehmann's show was to be staged a short distance from the schoolhouse in an open field bounded on one side by a barbed-wire fence. The spectators stood under the pecan trees, leaving a narrow strip of unoccupied space between them and the fence. That area would serve as Lehmann's arena for his one-man Wild West show, a demonstration of how he had killed buffalo with the Indians who had captured him when he was a boy and forced him to live with them for nine years.

By the time the Gipsons reached Katemcy, a good-sized crowd had already gathered. Fred cut out on his own, trying to make his way to a ringside seat. But the gangling boy with the blue eyes, long upper lip, and hay-colored hair was not making good progress. Grownups, he realized, were not much inclined to make way for a barefoot kid. Dropping to his hands and knees, Fred began to crawl through the legs of the adults—a forest rooted in dusty boots and high-topped shoes.

There in the arena on horseback was the old German, dressed in buckskin. Lehmann wore a hat made from a buffalo head, the curved black horns jutting out just above his ears. Around his neck hung a breastplate fashioned of bones; a white sash decorated with flowery designs circled his quirt-thin waist; white fringe hung from the full shoulders of his buckskin blouse. Lehmann's mouth curved downward. Folds in the sagging, leathery skin on his high-boned cheeks made a triangle topped by his prominent nose. For a man his age, the skin under his neck was taut.

Just after Fred reached the edge of the crowd and stuck his head out to see what was happening, Lehmann cut loose with an Indian whoop from another time—a human panther's scream that would make a grown man break out in a midnight sweat. At the scream, the frightened steer—the substitute buffalo—let out a bawl and charged down the fence line. Lehmann galloped behind the steer, bow and arrow in his hands and his old, experienced legs wrapped tightly around his saddleless horse. Leaning under his horse's neck, as he had done many times before on real buffalo hunts, or when the target had been a man, Lehmann overtook the steer.

He drew his bow, the arrow pointing at the wide-eyed crowd. A miss might send the deadly shaft whistling in the direction of some spectator's heart. He probably did not even see Fred; but just as Lehmann, the steer, and Fred were lined up on an axis as straight as a war lance, Lehmann let fly with his arrow.

Fred heard a "thunk," and a bellow of pain and pink foam blew from the yearling. A bloody arrowhead ripped through the steer's thick hide, just inches from Fred's astonished, horrified face. The steer made it a few more yards, running on impulses from a dying brain. The animal's knees buckled, and it dropped in a spray of dust as Lehmann wheeled his horse and let out another yell.

Lehmann dismounted in an effortless movement and plunged his knife into the belly of the fallen yearling. To the horror of the crowd, he thrust his hand inside the steaming cavity and, after some quick knife work, yanked out the steer's glistening liver, holding it up for the crowd to see. Spectators gasped and gagged. Some were overcome by a sudden interest in the clouds overhead or just closed their eyes. They had come to see a steer killed by a man who once had been an Indian captive, but they were not ready for this.

Those who still watched then saw Lehmann begin to eat the raw liver. The Indians, and Lehmann because he had learned from them, considered it a delicacy. Fred was not around for that part of the program. The bloody arrow had been enough for him. As Lehmann ate the liver and wiped blood and bile from his aged face, Fred scrambled back through the crowd to the safety of his family.[7]

By the first of April, when the bees were in the myrtle and the bluebonnets were perfuming the air, Fred had already forgotten where his shoes were. He was proud that the soles of his feet were almost as tough as cow hoofs and claimed he could kick up sparks just walking barefoot across a bed of granite.

It took a little time each spring, though, for the toughening-up process to finish. That was the best time for a favorite sport of Mason County school kids: seeing who could run across the widest stretch of needle-sharp grass burrs. What Fred did was run full speed, moving so fast he did not have a chance to feel the spikes of the burrs sinking into his flesh.

Rusty nails and mesquite thorns did present problems. Mesquite thorns were especially bothersome since they were prone to break off in the foot. The only way to get them out was with a sharp pocket-knife and a bottle of hot water after the wound festered. Once the tough part of the hide was cut away, a person stuck the bottle to the wound, and the suction pulled out the thorn. It took some hard teeth-gritting to get through that. Red ant stings on bare feet were doctored with ragweed or a mixture of dirt and spittle packed on the bite.[8]

Eventually, a country boy's thoughts turned to matters other than going barefoot. Fred's first love came in the fourth grade when a little blue-eyed girl ran off with his heart. But she had to share Fred's affection with something even more dear to him than she: his Barlow knife. Fred spent half his time honing that knife; the rest of the time he was shaving hair off his arms to show how sharp it was.

A knife was mighty important to a Hill Country man, no matter his age. He could not get along without one. He skinned his coons, marked his cattle, shaved kindling, sliced his meat, whittled, and occasionally settled his political or social disagreements with it. A man was expected to keep his knife oiled and sharp. A rusty knife was a disgrace.[9]

Naturally, it was a serious moment when the little girl asked to borrow Fred's knife. She needed to sharpen her pencil with it, she said. Fred spied her pencil, however, and saw it did not need sharpening. He knew her asking to borrow his knife was just a subtle female ploy to get his attention, which was all right with him.

But the love story came to a sudden, bloody end. The first stroke of the knife slipped and slit Fred's sweetheart's thumb to the bone. She screamed as blood splattered on her desk, the pine benches they sat on, and all the children around her. When the teacher finally got the bleeding stopped, Fred no longer had a girlfriend or a knife. Maybe the teacher felt sorry for him. In time, she gave Fred his knife back. But the little girl never spoke to him again.[10]

3

I Reckon He'll Just Be a Hound-Dog Man

Beck Gipson surveyed the bluish-gray cloud to the northwest and took a deep whiff, hoping the smell of rain would reach his nostrils. His land needed water. If he seriously thought it would do any good he would get his shotgun and blow open the belly of that cloud to bring down the rain.

When enough rain fell on Mr. Gipson's land, he could grow a third of a bale of cotton an acre and sell it at a nickel a pound—$25 a bale. During the First World War, cotton jumped to 42 or 43 cents a pound, but that was only temporary. By the 1920's cotton was back down to 5 to 20 cents a pound.

Mason County farmers liked to break their land before Christmas if they could. That gave more time for the earth to soak up valuable winter moisture. Even in a dry spring, if the land had been plowed early, it usually had enough moisture in it to plant. Early March was the time to plant corn, the second biggest crop on the Gipson farm and most others in the county. Cotton could not be planted until the weather got warm, generally around the first of May. Then after the first good rain, the weeds seemed to grow more heartily than the cotton. The more rain, the more weeds. Fred, Charles, and their father had to chop the cotton. When that was done, the Georgia Stock was used to lay back the corn. The blade was set so it would not sink too deeply into the earth, which would waste precious moisture.

By his early teens, Fred knew how to use a "section Harrow," which had teeth that could be staggered according to the size of the crop and was used to plow up the weeds. He also was a fair hand with a ''go-devil,'' a row of disks with fenders, used to work cotton if the weeds were particularly thick. It took longer to use the ''go-devil,'' but it did a good job.

In September, the corn had to be gathered, a chore most families liked to finish before cotton-picking time. Corn was not ready to harvest until it made a nice snapping sound when popped off the stalk. If it did not snap, the corn was still too moist and had to ripen longer. The best ears were kept for cornmeal, seed corn, and family meals. The rest went into the crib for the animals.

The cotton bolls were usually open by October 1. The picking lasted until the first frost. Most of the time, the Gipson family picked cotton twice; occasionally, three times. Fred dreaded the picking. He crawled on his knees until they bled. Even cotton-pickers' knee patches cut from Model T tires did little good. Cotton burrs clawed at his young fingers. When he was not crawling, he stood bending over, back muscles screaming, eyes clouded and smarting from sweat as he dragged along a bag that seemed to weigh a ton.

He longed for adventure . . . he wanted to stand on a mountain of granite looking at the beautiful country, not at the monotonous parallel world of row after row of cotton. The faint prospect of discovering a plowed-up Indian arrowhead was small consolation, but it gave him something to think about.

When he was fourteen, Fred hired out to chop cotton on a neighboring farm. As he moved from plant to plant, Fred noticed a man with a wooden leg beating his son, dressing him down for working too slowly. Without thinking, Fred ran toward the man and dropped him with a wild swing of his hoe. Seeing blood gushing from the man's head, Fred ran to tell his father that he had killed a man. Mr. Gipson grimly got his rifle and took his son back to the nearby field. The ''dead man'' had gotten up and dusted off; he and the boy had quit on the spot and were gone by the time the Gipsons arrived.[1]

Fred's parents and most of the farmers in Mason County had never known any other way to make a living, but Fred could not see himself spending the rest of his life worrying about too little or too much rain, boll weevils, or how much money some buyer in Dallas was willing to pay for a bale of cotton watered with some of his sweat.

Life seemed a little better to Fred during late fall and early winter. Sometime during the third week of December, Mr. Gipson cut a full-bodied juniper for the family's Christmas tree. On Christmas

Eve, the family rode in the wagon to the Methodist Church for the special Christmas service. The children huddled in blankets against the cold and occupied themselves looking at stars and picking out constellations until their father reached Comanche Creek, which was as close to the church as he dared get in a wagon—the mules did not like loud singing. Back at home after church, the Gipsons enjoyed fresh fruit around the fire until the children went to their cold bedrooms for the night.[2]

Winter, when the hair on a mule's flank got thicker and the range hogs and cattle began to bunch, was also trapping time. Fred and Charles earned their spending money by setting traps along the trail to school. All fur-bearing animals were legal for trapping except red and gray fox, beaver, and otter. But in Mason County, that did not make much difference. Catching coons was hard enough—they were getting scarce from overhunting. Still, Fred once got five coons in one day at $6 a pelt. As far as he was concerned, it was like striking oil. Thirty dollars was big money.[3]

On the way to school, the two boys ran their traps and tossed whatever they had caught up in the closest tree. Usually, it was a skunk or possum, but a skunk was the most prized. At Mason Grain and Produce, a skunk skin brought $2 to $5. Possums brought anywhere from 50 cents to $2.

Pulling a dead skunk from iron jaws was a precarious job. If Fred and Charles were not careful, they ruined clothes worth more than the skunk pelt. It did not help their popularity any when the Gipson boys went to school smelling like what they had caught. After school, the boys followed the same trail and skinned their morning catch.

Trapping was not nearly so much fun as hunting with dogs, which is what Fred preferred. The ideal time to hunt was a misty, foggy night with no wind. Dogs trailed best when there was plenty of moisture to hold the scent, and animals moved around more on that kind of night.

Some Mason County men liked to hunt fox, but Fred and Charles never had a fox dog. They stuck with a hound that would sniff out skunks, possums, or coons if any were around. They never went hunting without an axe or grubbing hoe because the dogs could not do it all. Once they had something holed up, it likely would take some digging to get to the animal. A skunk could run fast, especially with a snarling dog at its heels. It headed for the closest hole.

Fred learned that just because a skunk went into a hole, it would not necessarily be the first thing pulled out. One time when he and Charles started digging after a skunk, they unearthed an unhappy rattlesnake. They kept digging and found a possum. But it was a skunk they had seen dash into the hole. Sure enough, they finally reached the polecat. How rattlesnakes, possums, and skunks got along in the same den was always a mystery to Fred. But he saw it happen too many times to believe it was a fluke of nature.

If he did not know what was in a hole, Fred poked a hoe handle inside and then put his ear to the ground. A skunk could be heard angrily patting its feet. If a rattlesnake was inside, it would rattle. Many times he heard both in concert. Maybe the snake appreciated the warmth of the skunk's fur or maybe the snake took one end of the hole, the skunk the other.

Fred and Charles always knew when they got home from running their traps or hunting that Mrs. Gipson would have a good supper waiting for them. Sometimes she piled a platter a foot high with fried ham, gravy seeping down through the stack to mix with the melted butter. The red-checkered tablecloth would be weighted down with bowls of fresh green beans, just picked from the garden, potatoes, hot baked yams, watermelon preserves to go on the hot cornbread, and a bright yellow baked cushaw, with brown spots where the sugar had candied. All of it they washed down with buttermilk.[4]

Behind the Gipson home was a smokehouse full of bacon, ham, and sausage. The sausage was stuffed down in the oak bins where it would stay cool and last until summer. Fried chicken was the Sunday staple. When there was time for fishing, the Gipsons enjoyed catfish and during hunting season, they had plenty of venison. They also raised turkeys.

One of Fred's jobs around the home place was turkey tracking. Mrs. Gipson raised the domestic variety, but they went out into the pasture to lay their eggs. Fred's chore was to follow the turkeys to their nests and recover the eggs so a hen could set them in the safety of his mother's turkey yard.

One old hen always outsmarted Fred. She led him down false trails for hours before finally eluding him and slipping off to her hidden nest. When the eggs hatched, she led her babies back home. Once when cornered, the old hen squatted in the middle of a trail and laid an egg in front of Fred. As Fred scurried home with the egg, she slipped off to her secret nest—the "decoy" egg never hatched.[5]

Fred learned early in life, though, that a man had to work for what he ate. Sometimes it seemed to Fred that he had just gotten comfortable in bed when his father yelled: "Get up. Get up and go get them mules and calves in . . . ."

18

As the predawn light began to silhouette the mesquites along the ridge east of the house, a still sleepy Fred headed for the pasture in search of the mules, who were smarter than some people Fred knew. The mules waited until they figured it was about time for Fred to be looking for them and then moved into a shadowy thicket where they stood still, not even twitching a tail.

The hunt could take a good while, which seemed even longer on an empty stomach. When finally discovered, the mules usually snorted and trotted off across the widest grass burr patch around, knowing the barefoot Fred could not follow very fast. This mule trick made Fred so mad he did not feel the tiny thorns lancing into his feet as he gave chase, slowing only to gather rocks. A few solid hits would convince the mules it was time to head for the barn.

Fred still had to find the cattle before breakfast. Most of the time when he started looking for them, it was well after sunup. And there was always something to distract him from his search. One time he found where a possum had dragged its tail in the dirt along a cow trail and set out in search of its den. Another time he ran across a giant red ant battlefield and crawled up on a granite boulder to watch hundreds of ants biting each other in two.

When Fred found the cows, he had to be careful how he acted. If they got excited, his mother warned him, they would not give down their milk.[6] Occasionally it took two hours before Fred, trailing behind the cattle, finally got back to the house.

His father would be waiting for him, sometimes with a razor strap, wanting to know what had Fred meant by chunking rocks at a $200 mule. Worms could get in a wound, or Fred could have knocked out an eye. And what had taken him so long when there were other chores to be done, Mr. Gipson would ask.

Most of the time, Fred could handle the situation with a couple of lies: The mule had gotten scared by a striped polecat and had run into a dead tree limb and cut itself. The last time he had picked up a rock, he said, was to throw at a jack rabbit. He was late, he continued, because he had had trouble finding the cattle.

Mr. Gipson would put up the strap, promising to warm his son's bottom if he ever caught him tossing rocks at a mule again. Then they went in for a big breakfast, and everyone forgot all about the incident.[7]

Each spring, the Gipson children were given their own garden patch between the fruit trees. Fred found a fascination in watching things grow. After his garden was planted, he spent hours every day hoping to catch a glimpse of a bean sprout at the instant it peeked from the soil. Mrs. Gipson thought that was a waste of time, but

Fred's father seemed to understand his son's preoccupation. He told Fred to check his garden just before sunup.

The next morning as the sun began painting the eastern sky orange and pink, Fred was at his garden, lying on his stomach and staring intently at the row he had planted in beans. There was no telling how long Mrs. Gipson had been yelling for him to come eat before Fred finally heard her. But he could not move. He kept staring at the spot where he knew there were beans. His mother called again. Fred was risking a strapping if he kept stalling, but just as he started to give up and head for the house, it happened: A tiny, green shoot pushed through the earth. He had witnessed the moment of a bean's beginning. Only then did Fred realize he was hungry.[8]

Growing up in the country on a dry land farm, Fred found out a lot about life—and death—an education not provided in the schoolhouse. And he met the kind of people, Charlie Sanders for one, who were not written up in the history books.

Fred could not remember a time when he had not known Charlie Sanders, a tall, stringbean-like bachelor who lived in a shack along the creek bottom a few miles from the Gipson place. His father had died when Sanders was a baby, which left his mother, Kate, to raise him and seven other children. Sanders struck out on his own early in life.

Being single, Sanders did not work unless he felt like it, which was not often. His cotton patch was a disgrace—the weeds grew taller than the cotton. But to his neighbors' disgust, Sanders seemed to make more money, with far less effort, than they did. What Sanders did best was fish, trap, and hunt, though he was not a bad hand at drinking whiskey and romancing Hill Country womenfolk. Everyone knew, however, that he never planned on getting roped into a wedding. Most times, he preferred the company of his dogs.

Since Sanders did not have any offspring of his own, the Gipson children were special to him. Somewhat to Mrs. Gipson's dismay, Sanders seemed to consider her children his. Sanders showed up regularly at the Gipson place. Fred marveled at his ability to appear just about the time Mrs. Gipson was getting ready to start the next meal. She saw right through Sanders' visits but tolerated them because her husband liked to talk hunting and fishing with him.

One day Sanders sauntered up to the Gipson place with a fox peeking from under his arm. As usual, he was there just before the noon meal and was invited to stay. To the wide-eyed amazement of the children, Sanders kept the fox tucked under his arm as he ate.

Neither the fox nor Sanders seemed concerned about the other. Only when one of the children reached out to pet the fox did Sanders acknowledge its presence with a sharp warning that touching the animal would be a good way to lose a finger. The fox's small sharp teeth posed no danger to Sanders, though. He had an almost mystical way with wild animals—they became tame around him.

Mrs. Gipson thought Sanders was a bad influence on Fred, who liked to tag along on his rambles through the countryside. Especially worrisome to her was Fred's avid interest in dogs.

"Beck, you've got to help me with that boy," she said.

"Why, Emma, there's not a thing wrong with Fred only he's a boy—all boy," Mr. Gipson replied, ending the discussion before it got started.[9]

What terrified Mrs. Gipson was the possibility her son would be content to spend the rest of his life roaming Mason County with his dogs, just like Sanders. She wanted Fred to amount to something and did not think he could do it the way he was headed. At one time, Fred owned five flop-eared coon dogs. The way he saw it, a dog was a man's natural companion in the Hill Country. You got your dog in a trade, raised it from a pup, someone gave it to you, you took it in as a stray or stole it. But you did not buy it—that was bad luck.

One of his hounds, Old Misery, was probably the best coon dog in Mason County. Fred liked to brag that the dog's sorrowful voice could knock acorns out of the blackjacks as he trailed a coon down a misty creek bottom. Most of the time, Old Misery could be found snoozing under the kitchen steps, occasionally scratching a flea behind his ear. He looked so innocent that no one thought anything about leaving a full slop bucket on the back porch until they returned and found it empty. Old Misery would be lying on the porch like he had never moved, his stomach swollen like he had eaten a dry sponge and washed it down with a bowl of water. When a neighbor missed meat out of his smokehouse, Fred noticed Old Misery always seemed to look very satisfied.

Fred never let his dog get away with stealing food without a whipping, but he did not hit him nearly as hard for that as he did when Old Misery chased a jack rabbit. A good coon dog was not supposed to take out after rabbits, but Old Misery had a hard time understanding that, despite Fred's efforts. When Fred found Old Misery dead, hung in a barbed-wire fence, he knew what he had been up to. Old Misery had chased one last rabbit and paid for it hard.[10]

Seemed like every dog Fred owned liked to do two things: dig up his mother's flower beds and eat anything it could beg or steal. If Fred had his way, his dogs would have eaten better than his family.

Once when Fred and his sisters got home from school, Mrs. Gipson had big slices of hot, buttered bread covered with hog plum jelly waiting for them. Fred got the heel, the best part, which he took outside to the grape arbor. A few moments later, Mrs. Gipson looked out the window and gasped. Fred was feeding the whole piece of bread to Old Ring, his hound dog.

"I wanted him to be somebody, but I reckon he'll just turn out to be a hound-dog man," Mrs. Gipson sighed.[11]

Fred always figured jack rabbits were just about worthless. But he learned their true value from Sanders on one of the family's annual fishing trips to the Llano, an overnight adventure equal in importance only to Christmas.

Sanders had shown up early that morning with a flour sack of clothes hanging over his shoulder, a .22 rifle in his hand, and a pack of dogs trailing behind him. The Gipson children never understood how Sanders knew when their father was planning to take them fishing, but they never questioned his right to go along. After breakfast, Sanders even helped load the wagon. Enough equipment went into the bed of the wagon to outfit a trail drive—corn and fodder for the mules, cooking gear and staples, bedding, fishing gear, and a couple of ripe watermelons.

Mr. Gipson and Sanders climbed into the front of the wagon, and the five kids scrambled onto the back. The ride was rough, but no one complained. When the wagon rumbled past the front of the house, Mrs. Gipson waved from the front door. She would not go fishing because the memory of what had happened to her father was still bitter in her mind. Grandpa Deischler, too deaf to hear the roar of approaching flood waters, had drowned when his mail hack washed downstream in the Llano years before.

As the wagon rolled down the river road, Sanders told the children: "Now, you younguns keep a sharp lookout for jack rabbits and wasp nests. Can't tell—the minners might be skeerce in that river this time of the year, and we sure want plenty of fish bait."

Sanders had just finished a tall tale when Jennie spotted a jack rabbit, the sun shining through its pink ears and illuminating the tiny blood vessels. "Hold it, Beck," Sanders said, and Mr. Gipson reined in the mules. Sanders whistled, which piqued the rabbit's curiosity. Instead of using its long legs to get to other parts in a hurry, the rabbit stood still, looking at the wagon. Its big ears never heard the crack of Sanders' .22.

When Fred hopped off the wagon, the rabbit was still in the air. It hit the ground dead, but was still twitching when Fred got to it. Sanders, pulling out his skinning knife, was right behind him.

"Put a batch of jack rabbit liver on your hook, and you can't hardly keep an old channel cat off it," Sanders explained.

Mr. Gipson had not driven his mules much farther when Sanders spotted a wasp nest. He got out of the wagon, and Gipson moved the mules out of range, in case things did not go exactly as Sanders planned. If a swarm of wasps charged those mules, they would not stop running until they got to the next county.

Sanders headed for the wasp nest as the children watched breathlessly. The nest was the biggest one Fred had ever seen. One mistake and Sanders was in bad trouble. Casually, Sanders snatched the nest from the bush, shook it to get rid of the wasps still clinging to it, and slipped it inside his shirt. A black swarm of wasps appeared but were confounded when they could not find their nest. Sanders did not get stung once as he walked off with the nest.

By the time they got to Honey Creek, the hound dogs were traveling under the wagon to escape the sun. The Gipson kids were soon swimming in the cool and clear Llano, where you could lie in one of the pools and feel the pull of the river at your clothes as the sun burned your face. The hidden rocks, though, claimed a lot of skin and toenails when the play got too free-wheeling. For country kids who had never been outside the county, the Llano River was as good as the ocean they had read about in school.

They ate dinner beside the river as a south breeze working up the canyon dried their clothes and kept them cool. Under the oaks, the mules ate their corn, and Sanders' hound dogs sat waiting for the leftovers. As the shadows stretched from the canyon walls, the fishing began. Cane poles and lines were baited with the wasp grubs, which Sanders had dipped in a bucket of boiling water to make firmer.

Before nightfall, a tow sack tied to a willow branch was full of catfish and perch. No one saw the water moccasin slither up, intent on enjoying the fish before the Gipsons got them into the frying pan. The muddy-colored snake thrashed in the water, its big white mouth tearing at the sack of fish. If the kids had not heard the commotion, the snake might have gotten away with the theft. But by the time Fred and Charles were finished with it, its fish-eating days were over.

When Charles hooked a big catfish a few minutes later, the battle with the water moccasin was forgotten. Everyone thought the five-year-old was too young to fish, but his father had let him bait a hook anyway. Now, as the family looked on, Charles fought a fish that seemed to be winning the battle. Fred, fearful his little brother would lose the big-tailed monster, lunged for Charles' cane pole.

Then Charles had two battles on his hands. He would not let Fred get all the glory landing that fish, but it was pulling him harder than he was pulling it. As he screamed at Fred to stay away, Charles disappeared under the water, his fists wrapped tightly around the pole.

Seconds passed. Fred could practically hear his mother's anguished sobs at the sight of her youngest son stretched out dead in the bed of the wagon—drowned in the same river that had claimed her father. Just then Charles' hand, still clutching his pole, popped above the water. Mr. Gipson waded into the water and lifted his son out of the river. Sanders rushed up and grabbed the pole, but the five-year-old would not let go. The little boy finally surrendered the pole when Sanders reminded him that he had almost got eaten by a catfish.

Sanders worked the cat into shallow water. Then Mr. Gipson reached down and pulled the fish up on the bank. It would go thirty pounds for sure, he guessed. What his father said next stuck in Fred's mind: "It don't take a big feller to catch a fish. It just takes one that'll hang with him."[12]

That night, stuffed with fried fish, the children went to sleep as their father and Sanders swapped tales around the campfire. Mr. Gipson realized his youngest son had grown a little that day and his oldest son had learned something, too. There was still plenty more to teach both boys. Come fall, it would be time to take Fred deer hunting.

Deer were not as plentiful in the Hill Country as old-timers said they used to be, but some mighty big bucks could be found in Mason County and Beck Gipson knew where. Every fall, he earned money guiding hunters, which amounted to getting paid for something he would have done for free. When deer season started, he headed for the woods, his friends said, like the law was after him.

Fred was fourteen that November 16, the first day of deer season in 1922. Well before sunup, he was stationed by a post oak in a creek bottom. Frost coated the grass in the opening he was supposed to watch. It was cold enough for the deer to be moving, and when they started, likely as not a big old buck would walk right through that clearing.

Fred clutched an antique, octagon-barreled, lever-action Winchester he had borrowed from one of his teachers. The night before, he had noticed the two paying hunters in his father's party winking at each other as he cleaned the old .30-.30. They had more modern, high-speed rifles. Maybe his Winchester did not have a long range or cannon-like knockdown power, but Fred knew the rifle he held had layed over many a deer and maybe a few men in its time.

As it got lighter, Fred took in the country, keeping his mouth clamped shut so his teeth would not chatter. The Winchester had not seemed too heavy at first, but now it began to feel like a wagon axle in his hands. The barrel was cold and his fingers were numb. His feet hurt, his nose was running, and his watering eyes clouded his vision.

His father and the two hunters had moved over the ridge leaving Fred to face the biggest moment of his young life alone. Fred could hear wild turkeys leaving their roosts in the distance and was still thinking about how nice it would be to kill a long-bearded gobbler for Thanksgiving when he saw the buck. The deer's head was down, but Fred could see a fine set of horns above the grass. The tan-coated buck was apparently trailing a doe. Every few feet it stopped and sniffed the air for danger. For some reason, it was not smelling the creek bottom intruder with the Winchester.

Fred raised his rifle. He looked down the sights but everything blurred. Buck fever. His father had told him about it, and even though forewarned, he was its victim. He could not even hold the rifle steady, much less see the deer. Thoughts crowded into his mind: Here was his first deer and all he had to do was squeeze the trigger. But what if he missed? That would be a humiliation. How could he face his father? Or younger brother Charles?

Wildly, Fred swung his rifle, jerking the trigger when the barrel pointed in the general direction of the buck. The big deer leaped in the air, but the first shot missed. When the buck landed, it froze, staring at Fred. A second explosion ripped the cold air. This time, the buck did not stand still. When its black hoofs hit the ground, it was running toward a stand of timber. All Fred saw the third time he pulled the trigger of his Winchester was a white tail.

Tears came to his eyes. Three shots at a big buck almost close enough to throw rocks at and he had missed! Fred ran in the direction he had fired, hoping maybe for a miracle and the chance at a fourth shot. He almost tripped over the dead deer.

There it was with a small hole behind the shoulder right where the heart was. In its desperate death run, the buck had crashed into a hackberry bush, catching its hind leg on the branches. It fell and never got up.

When Fred looked up, he saw his father walking toward him through the trees. "That's bringing 'em down," he said. "I knew that third shot got meat. I heard it spat from where I was. Son, that's a good 'un. It sure is."[13]

Two men, father and son, stood there a minute admiring the buck. Then Mr. Gipson got out his knife and told Fred to do the same. Another lesson was about to be learned: When a man kills a deer, he cleans it.

Fred fishing on the Llano River. (Courtesy Beck Gipson.)

4

"Seize the Opportunity"

The smells and sounds of a fall evening settled over the Gipson home place like a comfortable patchwork quilt. Smoke from the mesquite logs in the fireplace mingled with the aroma of a distant cedar chopper's fire, while the cool air carried the lowing of a neighbor's cattle. The mules crunched on their corn and the hogs lolled in the mud. Old Rose was bedded down in the cow pen, her calf romping in the pasture. The hounds were lying down, their bellies bulging from scraps collected after the Gipson family's evening meal.

A new sound intruded. The ears of the mules shot forward, the calf stood still, the hounds got to their feet, and even the hogs looked up. Fred, strumming a guitar and singing "On the Sunny San Juan," was sitting on the cowlot fence.

Mrs. Gipson had banished her son and his $4.98 mail-order guitar from the house until he got better or gave up his foolish notion of becoming a cowboy crooner. Fred had not been too bothered by that—the cowlot was one of his favorite places anyway.

When Fred began "Swanee River," he did not notice the hounds, sitting on their haunches, gathered around him. Only when they started wailing their accompaniment, their noses pointed to the sky, did Fred realize he was being insulted. He interrupted his playing long enough to gather rocks and try to teach the dogs better manners. But when Fred returned to the guitar, the hounds slipped back and began howling again. The session ended when Mrs. Gipson yelled to remind Fred that there was school in the morning, which her son would just as soon have forgotten.[1]

Fred was in high school, and Mr. Gipson, though without a formal education himself, served on the school board of trustees. If Fred had a choice in the matter, he would rather hire on as a cowboy somewhere or spend his time hunting and fishing. High school had not proved to be all books and business, however. There were "Kodaking" trips, picnics, and parties, like the Halloween get-together at Koock's Hall, where Fred and his classmates enjoyed roasted peanuts and popcorn.

Fred's body took a few licks during his high school years. Trying to show off at a school picnic near the river, he did a graceful dive off a bridge, only to land nose first on a hidden concrete piling. His nose was what broke. That nose was to take further abuse when Fred misjudged a fly ball during a baseball game, and not long after that, Fred had a disagreement which quickly turned into a fist fight that he lost. Thereafter, every time Fred looked south—and he was the first to laugh about it—his nose veered to the southwest.[2]

Though not a star athlete (his name did not even get in the local paper's game stories), Fred played a rough game of football. Mrs. Gipson did not care much for Fred's being involved in football, but she eventually went to see him play in one of the home games. In the middle of the game, someone hit Fred harder than he figured he should have been hit. It made him mad. As his mother looked on aghast, her son landed a solid blow to the stomach of one of the opposing players. Fred was ejected from the game, and Mrs. Gipson never went to another football game.

Fred was living the life of a rough and tumble country boy, but was not without traces of refinement. When he was a sophomore, the students of Mason High produced their first annual, *The Branding Iron*, and Fred became a published author. Writing his short story "Luck," a tale of two boys who help catch a cattle rustler, had been work. Fred had a hard time finding the right words to put on paper. But when he was finished, he had a western story good enough for his teacher to read in class and to be printed in the annual.

At the end of the school year, though, Fred easily picked up where he had left off the summer before, spending as much time as he could fishing and roaming with his dogs. He did not miss having writing assignments.

Fred's junior year in high school was a mixture of pleasant social activities and terror. "Tanned and freckled the famous 'Thirty' [there were thirty juniors] trooped back from vacation sports to resume the

The snow-covered home place where Fred grew up. (Courtesy Western Publications.)

ever-present and waiting studies and confinement of M. H. S.'s grey walls,'' was the way someone described the return to school in volume II of *The Branding Iron*.

Twice each month getting up and going to school was almost unbearable for Fred. Every other Wednesday, the Lone Star chapter of the school's literary society was responsible for the morning program. That usually meant Fred had to give a speech or read a prose selection in front of the student body. He would rather have punched an angry wild hog in the nose than make a talk.

Fred admired the school superintendent, S. N. Dobie, but sure wished he had not come up with the idea of splitting the high school students into two competitive groups: Fred's Lone Star chapter and the rival Woodrow Wilson chapter. The Wednesday performances were judged by Dobie, who tallied points and at the end of the year, declared an overall winner. His motive was to provide students with "practical experience in speaking."

The fighting spirit between the two groups was high. "*Defeat* is an undefined word" was the motto of Fred's chapter; "Build for character and not for fame" were the guiding words of the Wilson chapter. By the end of Fred's junior year, however, the Lone Star chapter found there was a definition for defeat. As the annual put it, "At the end of the session . . . Wilson . . . won by a large majority of points."[3]

Eunice Green, a member of the victorious Woodrow Wilson chapter, was one of Fred's closest confidants. They both were from the country which gave them a certain kinship, and both worked in the school library. It was not a romantic relationship—they were just close friends.

"Dear Eunice," Fred penned on March 10, 1926, "It is with great pleasure that I write in your memory book. I'll never forget the good times we've had together ever since you have come here to school. I don't know how I'll ever get through any other school without you to show me how to do things. Hope you good luck through everything. Frederick Gipson."

Although there were plenty of good times in high school, Fred was a much more serious student than he had been in grade school. His report cards never showed a failing grade, which qualified him for membership in the Alpha Beta Gamma Club. He was a polite, formal young man, well liked by his classmates. But shyness was a problem, and not just before the literary society. When Fred needed to ask something in class, he waited for the chance to walk to the teacher's desk, stoop, and whisper his question so his classmates would not think he was stupid.

Fred liked the quiet of the school library which contained more than eight hundred volumes. His main job was helping place orders for new books; Eunice handled the checking out of books. The collection grew by about sixty books during his senior year, but if Fred had had his way, there would have been more books of romance and high adventure. For that kind of material, he had to rely on the newsstand at the Mason Drug Store.[4] Fred had always had a taste for pulp magazines and novels. When he was younger, he slipped Zane Grey westerns and Buffalo Bill story magazines behind the cover of his large geography book. His teachers marveled at his interest in the many countries of the world but could not understand why he did not do better on the tests.[5]

Fred's interest in romance went further than wanting to read romantic tales. Not long after Stella married Jack Polk, they bought a Model T Roadster. Fred finally prevailed upon his older sister to let him borrow the car for a date.

Although Fred had never driven a car, everything went fine until he had to back it up and realized no one had told him how. The situation was critical: Next to him sat a girl and it would be a tremendous loss of face to admit ignorance on a thing like backing a car. Trying to look like he knew what he was doing, Fred frantically experimented with the gears until he found the right one. Inwardly he was delighted, but he could not show his elation in front of his date, who was quite impressed with his car-handling abilities. She patted him on the head and said he was doing some wonderful driving.

The Class of '26 had thirty-eight graduates. Seven of them, including Fred, had gone to school together since the first grade. When the senior class picture was made outside the school, Fred sat in the first row, elbows resting on his knees. He wore a white shirt, a tie loosened around his collar, and well-shined black shoes.

"Seize the opportunity," was the class motto. Fred figured it was time to get out on his own and look for that opportunity.

He found the first prospect in an ad in the weekly Mason County News. "Success begets Success" the advertisement by Draughon's Practical Business College of San Antonio guaranteed. Fred studied the ad: "Let our 'Big School' train you for success. If you are ambitious to succeed, clip and return this coupon." The "Big School" offered training in bookkeeping, shorthand, and typing.

Fred clipped the ad and mailed it, an investment of two cents toward a career that could offer a lifetime income. Within a couple of weeks, a representative of the school offered Fred a "scholarship." It sounded like a good deal. Fred decided to take up instruction in bookkeeping, which would be a heck of a lot easier than working on a farm.

In 1926 no commercial transportation was available from Mason to San Antonio, Texas' largest city with a population of 161,000. However, trucks from J. J. Johnson's grocery store in Mason made regular runs to San Antonio. Fred caught a ride on one of the trucks; when he needed to go home, he would travel the same way or hitchhike.

In San Antonio, Fred boarded with an elderly couple. Before long, he was miserable, missing the farm, his dogs, even his sisters. And studying bookkeeping turned out to be far from exciting. Within a year, he was back in Mason.

On the plus side, he had learned some bookkeeping, which helped him land a job as Johnson's bookkeeper. Fred did not have to worry about dealing with large figures. By late 1926 and early 1927, the economy in Mason County was beginning to slow: jobs were scarce; money was tight. The way it looked to Fred, everything a person wanted to buy was too high; everything he tried to sell, no one was willing to pay for.

Even though Fred learned bookkeeping, he had always wanted to be a cowboy. Fortunately, Fred's brothers-in-law, Ned and Jack Polk (married to Bessie and Stella, respectively), were ranchers and usually needed help.

In the fall of 1927, Ned hired his 13-year-old nephew, Duke Polk, and Fred to help drive a herd of goats from the Black Ranch in Edwards County to a new lease on the Jeffrey Ranch on the James River in Mason County. As Ned pushed the herd out, Fred marveled at the sight of the long line of white goats, their coats shining in the afternoon sun. Ned decided to move them along an oil pipeline that recently had been laid from Rock Springs through the Mason area.

But trouble was ahead. The oaks were full of acorns and the weather looked like it was about to change for the worse. The downpour began about three o'clock the next morning. Then the goats stampeded. It took the Polks, Fred, and a couple of Mexican hands to get the herd under control. The rain kept falling and hardly let up during the rest of the ten-day drive.

Every few yards, the goats got so bogged down in the mud that they had to be pulled free. The mud built up around their hoofs until they looked like they were walking on big black mushmelons. Despite the mud, the tough goats cut out on their own looking for the tasty acorns in the live oaks and shin oaks; the less hardy goats hid in the timber, shivering under their soggy coats, bleating miserably. Whatever the goats did or wherever they went, Fred and the other hands had to get them back in line.

One of Fred's jobs was driving the chuck wagon, a Model T truck, that carried the food and bedding. Even in the best of weather, as Fred liked to say, it would not pull a man's hat off on a windy day. On this drive, the truck got stuck about as easily as the goats; it was just harder to get it unstuck.

Good grub sometimes made a trail drive easier, but the continuous rain mostly meant soggy food. Trying to build a cook fire with wet wood was not worth the trouble. The bread, covered with fuzzy green mold, had to be trimmed before being eaten. The trail hands at least had a little variety in their meals until some range hogs got into the back of the truck one night and ate everything except a few cans of pork and beans and the moldy bread. So for the rest of the drive, Fred ate pork and beans, goat meat, and smelly bread—three times a day.

Fred and Duke thought nothing worse could happen until some of the goats, looking for a dry place, climbed into the truck and bedded down on their blankets, leaving the Model T full of goat droppings. The other hands tried to sleep in their wet, cold blankets. It had rained so much that the soles of their boots had soaked off and curled back. The men wrapped baling wire around their boots so they would fit in the stirrups.

The goats seemed to hate water more than the herders. They would not voluntarily cross a shallow stream. Fred and the others had to rope about forty head and pull them over, hoping the other goats would follow before the ones they had just roped decided to run back to the main herd. When the South Llano was forded, the reverse happened. The main bunch of goats must have worried they were about to be abandoned and stampeded to join the goats that had just been dragged across. Fred and Duke ended up in the river.

By the third day of the drive, "trail fever" set in. Ned was under a lot of pressure. He pushed himself and his mount practically to the point of exhaustion and began snapping at his men, including Fred and Duke. Ned's outlook did not improve any when he found Duke chunking rocks at the goats. The trail boss sternly told his nephew not to do it again and took the time to explain why—he could ruin a goat that way. When Ned caught Duke throwing a tree limb at a goat a short time later, he was not as polite.

Fred found Duke crying after Ned rode off. "Fred, you know, damn't if I knowed the way home I would just quit right here." Fred agreed but he did not know the way home, either.

When the trail crew reached the big Liveoak Ranch on the Little Devils River, they were invited to stay the night and eat some hot food. But before Fred and the others could sit down and enjoy a good meal, they had to go back and get the truck—it was sunk to its bed seven or eight miles up the road.

Fred, like everyone else on the drive, was wet and muddy but too shy to ask where he could clean up. No one seemed to notice his discomfort, either. Fred felt a trace of guilt when he crawled between those warm, clean sheets with mud caked between his toes that night. He was too tired to worry about it long.[6]

The hardships of goat herding did not cure Fred of wanting to be a cowboy. His brother-in-law Jack gave him the chance to take part in a fading western institution, the cattle drive. Shortly after the Civil War, Texans began herding cattle up the trails to northern markets. By the late 1920's, though, most ranges were fenced and cattle were shipped mainly by rail. Since Mason was not a railhead, some of the last trail drives in Texas were staged in Mason County. This gave Fred an opportunity to "hire on" as a hand for $4 a day.

Although twentieth-century trail drivers did not have to worry about Indians or rustlers, pushing several thousand head of cattle thirty miles to the railhead at Brady was a hard three-day trip. And Fred soon learned that being a cowboy was not quite the romantic adventure the Tom Mix movies and the pulp magazines made it out to be.

A cowboy was usually in the saddle at daylight, blistered by mid-afternoon, and hungry by sundown. He rode hard through thick brush that boxed the ears, daubed medicine into a cow brute's bloody, worm-infested wounds, worked a loading shoot in the summer, and breathed the dust and the odor of sweaty men and thirsty cattle. In fact, a lot of cowboying boiled down to ugly sights and nasty smells . . . the spurting blood veins when horns were cut off a cow, the burning hide at branding time, the bellowing and blood when a yearling was made a steer.

Maybe someone from the city who had never been a cowboy would think it an exciting way to make a living. But Fred quickly found cowboying was as hard work as plowing or picking cotton; he decided the kind of cowboying he was cut out for was bronc busting, the glamor end of the business. A good horse-breaking man was always in demand on West Texas ranches. It was not a bad way to make a living if a man did not mind fracturing a bone occasionally.

When Fred was young, he had practiced bronc busting on Old Rose, the milk cow, and later graduated to tame mules. About the time Fred got out of high school, he got his first shot at an outlaw horse—a sorrel broomtail with its own ideas about what it would have on its back. Fred climbed on the horse and tried to sound nonchalant as he yelled, "Turn him loose!" He felt the tension in the horse, wound up like a mainspring about to go haywire. When the horse shot from the chute, he headed for the moon. A few seconds later, Fred made one last, desperate grab for the saddlehorn before flying off. When he hit the ground, it knocked the breath out of him and left him with a skinned nose.[7]

Eventually, Fred got a little better at bronc busting, but it never seemed any easier. When the glamor faded, it was just another way to make a dollar.

Mules could be as cantankerous as a walleyed bronc, but like his father, Fred was a fair mule man. For years, Mr. Gipson supplemented the family income by breaking the pack animals that could walk faster than a horse and do more on less food. He would buy several big mules in Kimble County and take them to use in the fields. By planting time, they would be fairly gentle, and by fall, they were well-broken mules. A good span of mules brought $350 to $500.

Mule breaking was tricky work that required skill not many men took the time to develop. The least thing could set a mule off as Fred had learned the time his father wore the new straw hat into the corral. And once mules got skittish, only the most experienced mule man could handle them, something seldom worth the effort.

By the time Fred was twenty, he had his own span of hard-tail mules and went to work for the county as a mule skinner. Using a Russell "Bull Dozer" pulled by a two-mule team, he earned $2 a day scraping dirt roads in Mason County. He spent a lot of time on the Fredericksburg Road, then known as Highway 9, fighting the "Johnson bar" of a fresno. Later Fred learned to operate the first motorized road machinery in the county, an Atlas Tractor, used instead of mules to pull a road scraper.

Working with Rudolph Martin, Fred helped survey the road between Mason and Menard. He kept the field notes while Martin, a Texas A&M graduate, took the angle and degree readings. At night in a tent by the roadway, Martin went over the readings to make sure they were heading right. Although not paid for it, Fred helped with the mathematical work.

Fred in early-day tractor when he was doing road work before going to the University of Texas. (Courtesy Beck Gipson.)

In the winter of 1929, Fred and another man were camped on Beaver Creek, just south of the Llano River. They had been having trouble with a mysterious night prowler. Fred figured it was a wild hog. No wild animal was much smarter or meaner than a domestic hog gone feral. A wild hog could eat up a cornfield, a kid goat, a chicken, even a rattlesnake—it did not seem to care. It could take a good chunk out of a man, too. The fence had not been invented that would keep out a wild hog, an animal that could outrun a horse, smell almost as good as a coon dog, and fight anything.

As Fred and the other man slept one night, it began sleeting. When they woke up the next morning, everything was frozen. To their surprise, an old boar hog was snoozing next to the coals of the fire, steam pumping from its snout. Fred realized the hog was the culprit that had been raiding their camp and immediately went into action. He quietly built another fire and put a kettle of water on it. After the water had boiled awhile, Fred splashed it over the sleeping hog. The big-tusked hog noticed a difference in temperature right off. It was last seen headed down the creek, steam rising off its scalded side. One thing for sure—that hog had raided its last camp.[8]

Seemed like everyone who grew up in the Hill Country knew a wild-hog story. There were plenty of hogs around in those days and they were always trouble. But mean as they were, Fred had always sort of liked wild hogs. He appreciated their tough, independent ways. Still, one of the scariest things a man could come up against in the Hill Country was a bunch of 400-pound hogs cornered by a pack of dogs. Fred had seen it: gleaming six-inch tusks, small eyes blazing hatred and defiance as the bristling hogs snapped tiny teeth and pawed the dirt with their forefeet.[9]

Like a cornered hog, Fred was beginning to feel trapped. The country was edging toward a depression, and the Gipson family was barely getting by. Mr. Gipson was forced to hire on with a road crew and worked with Fred on the first concrete bridge in Mason County. The work was done on a day-by-day basis, and the competition for jobs was fierce. Men who did not work hard enough did not have a job at the end of the day; a waiting list of men stood ready to take their places.

One Friday afternoon, after a hellish week, Fred and his father went to the road crew foreman for their pay. They needed the money to buy food for the family. The foreman said he could not pay them until the following week. Fred exploded, grabbing a sledgehammer handle. He and his father had been working ten-hour days in weather so hot they blistered through their shirts. They were going to get their money now, Fred said. And they did.[10]

In 1931 when Charles graduated from Mason High School with top honors, Fred was without a job. That fall, Charles left Mason to enroll at The University of Texas in Austin, but Fred stayed behind, still hopeful some job would develop. By the summer of 1933, no work was to be had in Mason County. At the urging of Charles, who was now a sophomore, Fred decided to go to the university. He had $60 in his pocket when he left for Austin.[11]

Fred (*right*) and his sister Bessie's husband, Ned Polk, with Birdsong. (Courtesy Beck Gipson.)

5

"One Thing and Then Another"

The first problem that Fred and Charles faced in the fall of 1933 was finding a place to stay. University of Texas students who did not live in dormitories had to take rooms in university-approved boarding-houses, which cost about $40 a month including meals.

The brothers were routed from the first place they picked by bed-bugs. But while buying groceries in a Red and White grocery store at Nueces and Guadalupe, they overheard the old man who ran the store mention that he had an apartment for rent in his house. The price sounded right, and the old brown-trimmed yellow house was con-veniently located on the streetcar line. The Gipsons arranged the deal and shared the apartment with Clyde Wilkinson, a graduate student from Coleman, Bevil (Doc) George, and John (Hooky) Ingram, both from Fredonia.

The apartment was a refuge where Fred's country ways did not bring embarrassment. Since all the boarders were "country boys" and short of money, they depended mostly on home cooking. Fred be-came the main cook and, as the oldest, unofficial "dorm mother." When any of them went home, they returned with all the home-canned goods, preserves, potatoes, and cured meat they could get off with. When the larder was empty and there was not much money, they "haggled with the grocery man like a boarding-house lady."[1]

During his first year at the University of Texas, Fred had a job in a New Deal program offering students a chance to work two or three hours a day cleaning up the grounds. It seemed like easy work to

Fred, who jumped at the chance to earn some money. While most of the others in the program were eighteen, Fred was twenty-five and the age made a difference. He was interested in working—the other boys had just as soon toss a football on the intramural field as pull weeds.

The program was not well supervised and it did not take long before someone saw the freeloading and reported it. The committee handling the job program decided not to pay the students, which did not seem to bother those who had been goldbricking. But Fred had worked hard. He stormed into the official's office and demanded his pay. He got it.

Still, money was hard to come by. Charles applied for a $100 loan established for a deserving student, qualified, and was sent to collect the money. However, the person in charge of the cash was worried about Charles' ability to repay the loan. The official asked whether Charles' father was good for the $100. Beck Gipson could not have come up with $10, much less $100. He had already seen some of his farm land auctioned for unpaid taxes. Nevertheless, Charles got the loan which covered the tuition for both brothers.

In February 1935, offered a well-paying job he could not turn down, Charles quit college and went to work for Humble Oil Company as a seismograph operator in New Mexico. By August, he had saved enough money to pay back his student loan plus some extra to help Fred stay in school.

For freshman English, Fred discovered he could translate the stories he had heard as a boy and around campfires during his road-work days to the written word and not lose anything in the process. Fred's professor liked the stories so much that he read them to the class and gave Fred good grades.

Still, English was tough and no one knew that better than Joe Small. One of the first friends Fred made when he entered college, Small was a thin, dark-haired, brown-eyed fellow from Burleson County. Fred was older, of course, but the two men had common interests in writing, and both understood country ways since each had been raised on a farm.

Small had been writing successfully since he was fourteen. By the time he enrolled in the University, fifty of the fifty-three articles he had submitted to magazines had been published. Small was thinking about publishing his own magazine, and he and Fred talked about Fred's doing some writing for the publication if it got off the ground.

At the beginning of his sophomore year, Fred decided to try some journalism courses. It seemed a natural step, given the results he got from his freshman theme writing. His name appeared for the first time in *The Daily Texan* as a by-line on a column highlighting radio programs.

Fred took a feature-writing course taught by DeWitt Reddick, who encouraged Fred to write about things he had experienced or knew about. The two would talk about a story before Fred wrote it, and after it was handed in, Reddick would critique the effort. Fred was required to write five feature stories and made an "A" on each one.

Fred's work was once again read aloud in class. He was developing a following, but more importantly, he was beginning to believe he actually could write. Before, writing had been a dream, something that would beat working for a living. Now, as his stories began to get attention in *The Daily Texan* and the admiration of his classmates, the dream was becoming a reality.

Inspired by Small's free-lance writing success, Fred tried his hand at western fiction, but to his dismay, the stories kept coming back from the magazines. "I wonder why I don't just swear off this writing business and go back home to farming, or coon hunting . . . something that couldn't be such a bother to a man," he wrote in *The Daily Texan*.[2]

On October 12, 1935, *The Daily Texan* published "On Account of a Girl, Maybe," the first in a long string of personal stories by the UT student from Mason. Fred wrote:

> He's in a sad predicament, poor fellow; and such a promising young writer, too. He has drifted out upon a sort of literary plateau, a dreary, barren plain indeed, stretching out to illimitable distances, unbroken by the slightest convolution that might arouse and stimulate his flagging genius. Search as he may, he can find nothing to write about.

But he had found something: his dealings with the opposite sex. He blamed his latest "experiment in love" for causing the "destitute young writer . . . his present loss of creative ability." The relationship had gone just fine for a while, he wrote, but then the "lady grew indifferent." It made him so mad that he wanted to go out and toss rocks at a mockingbird. Instead, he smoked a cigarette and went out and gorged himself, ignoring the cost.

Toward the end of the story, Fred grew more sanguine and indulged in a bit of fortune-telling:

Now I predict that this poor baffled writer, who has had so much trouble of late, will . . . spring out of bed some morning, his head whirling with a sizzling hot idea. To the typewriter he will dash and, in a few minutes, slap out a piece of work that will startle the world. Then he will become famous and grow a dinky little mustache for the women to admire and microbes to inhabit.

On November 3, 1935, the cowboy boot wearing writer had a story in *The Daily Texan* that showed his developing powers as a writer. He called the piece "Monarch."

Out of the eerie blending of moonlight and shadow, where the rocks rose stark against the skyline, there came a strangled cry. A moment of silence; then—low it was at first, and soft, barely distinguishable from the usual noises of the night. Then rapidly, swelling in volume, it rose higher and higher, ascending the scale in one full sweep of undulating sound. At its peak it held for a moment, loud in its defiance, awesome in its portent; held until the echoes among the rocks broke into wild clamor; held while the canyons reverberated with hollow roars; held majestically; broke; and quickly died away.

Six paragraphs followed, describing the reactions of animals to this noise: The buck flashed its white tail and ran, the owls quit screeching, the quail huddled closer together.

Beyond the flats, where the woods began, two sleepers lay under a lean-to. And they started up from their blankets as one; scarce awake, they started up, each feeling a chill clutch his spine, yet hardly convinced of having heard a sound. But their dogs, hackles erect, tails between their legs, crept under the shelter with them. And though the dogs bared their fangs until they gleamed in the moonlight, yet the dogs uttered no sound. Nor could the men discern any sound in the night about them; nothing but the soft play of moonlight and shadows—and silence.
"What was it, Paco?" whispered one.
The other shivered.
"El Lobo, Senor. The grey wolf; he keel another calf!"

Fred sometimes practiced more conventional journalism, as in a glowing book review of *The Texas Rangers* by Walter Prescott Webb.

He praised Webb's use of color which "raises it above the plane of a dry and factual textbook of history." Parts of the book would be dull to the average reader, he wrote. "But, apparently, to have left out these parts would have been to deprive the book of one of the things it has above nearly all of the previously published historical books of Texas, whether textbook or novel—a convincing ring of authenticity."[3]

As the Christmas holidays approached, and with them a welcome trip back home, Fred wrote "Hard-Pressed Sam," which appeared in *The Daily Texan Book Review and Literary Supplement*. The story was based on a real-life Mason County character, the county tick inspector, whose job was to travel from ranch to ranch making sure livestock were being properly dipped.

Someone suggested that Fred send the story to *Southwest Review*, a quality literary quarterly, published at Southern Methodist University in Dallas. After the magazine's editor accepted the story, Fred wrote his mother to announce his first free-lance sale:

> A certain Fred Gipson received a ten dollar check for his first feature story. This made him so reckless that he spent one dollar of it Sunday afternoon taking a brunette to a picture show, which was very foolish considering he may never sell another feature story for even one dollar . . . .[4]

February 22, 1936, was a beautiful, warm day and Fred was stirred to write about it:

> It's days like yesterday that really try a man's soul—that is, the man bound to the campus by the laws of Higher Learning like a serf to the soil. A warm day, with fleecy clouds overhead and a south wind blowing a promise of spring. And, yet, what can you do about it?

The water was too cold for swimming, and a dip in the indoor pool would not be any fun for a man who grew up swimming in creeks and a river. "So you sit and chew a germy pencil and think how you'd enjoy just taking up a .22 rifle and prowling around in the woods, and maybe shooting a cottontail and roasting it over a mesquite wood fire . . . ." Fred was suffering from spring fever. The good weather made him turn his attention to other things, mainly "to call up that little coed you met the other day and walk her off out somewhere where you can get some really serious wooing done for a while. You've been getting behind in that respect here lately . . . ."[5]

Although Fred was as interested as the next "ed" in getting in as much wooing as he could, pitching woo was closely related to economics. He enjoyed long walks with coeds—around campus or downtown because they did not cost much. Once he spent hours exploring Shoal Creek with a coed who needed to find a fossil for a geology class.[6] The dark stacks in the University of Texas library or the back of the streetcar provided inexpensive places for a little necking. When there was money, the back row or balcony at a movie was nice, too.

One way to romance a girl was to take her to a dance in the Texas Union. There were Saturday night "Germans," organized by the German Club, and afternoon "tea dances." Going to a tea, Fred wrote in *The Daily Texan* involved dressing up "like a sore toe," sitting in a soft chair, and sipping tea "out of an eggshell cup." He would "crook [his] finger in the daintiest and most proper manner and swap scandal and flattery with the ladies and smoke their cigarettes—all this, for hours at a time . . . ."[7]

The proper social affairs at the University of Texas were not like the Hill Country dances Fred knew. A schoolteacher in Austin once asked him to take her to such a country dance but Fred turned her down. He wrote a column explaining that city folks "are just not built up right to stand such carryings on." There were dangers everywhere for a city-raised person:

> One good swallow out of a fruit jar of Hill Country drinking-whiskey that's been aged in gasoline barrels and flavored with a couple of mountain boomer lizards or a handful of wasps or whatever else might take a notion to crawl into it—one drink of that, and a city dancer's eyeballs would pop out till you could rope them with a grapevine and his toenails would turn black and curl up backwards.

Also, Fred continued, there was the danger of falling through one of the large cracks in the floor and being attacked by a wild hog nested under the dance hall.[8]

But no one had to coax Fred into taking a coed to a movie—if he had the money. He took a certain amount of kidding about his cinema preferences. It got so bad that he wrote a column in protest of "those people who make fun of the sort of movies I like." He explained:

> I like pictures of primitive romance and action, pictures with their settings deep in dark jungles of far-away places, where there's death and wild animals stalking about, where

While a UT student, Fred established a reputation as the cowboy boot wearing writer for *The Daily Texan*. (Courtesy Beck Gipson.)

the booming of tom-toms is relayed from one grass hut to the next, where black-skinned, half-naked natives go in for orgies of feasting and dancing by flaring lights of their campfires and don't mind roasting and eating a couple or three people to appease the wrath of their gods.

Fred should have had the foresight to see such movies alone, but instead, he went with friends and was "brought back to realities every few minutes with cracks such as: 'Now, the hero is registering rage . . . Ah, Sex rears its ugly head . . . Funny how a native princess like that just naturally knows to wrap herself up in a printed piece of calico.' " That ruined the show for him, and Fred vowed in print to go to the next one by himself.[9]

Fred had plenty of things to do, or things he should have been doing. His by-lined features appeared regularly in *The Daily Texan*. He wrote about a zoologist who specialized in flies, a feature on paper boys (his roommate had a morning route), a fashion story on "bright colored, unmatched suits," and a story on final exams (". . . everyone is seriously and conscientiously worrying . . . about not really giving a hoot whether he passes a course or not"). And he was still trying to sell some of his stories to the pulp magazines. At the end of the day, after whatever studying he might have done, Fred sat up writing, sometimes into the middle of the morning.

He was now living in a $25-a-month apartment with three other Mason County boys, including Stanford Leach, who had grown up in the community of Fredonia. One day, Fred came in looking like his best coon dog had died. Leach asked what was wrong, and Fred confided that one of his professors, J. Frank Dobie, who taught a course in southwestern lore, had told him to get the notion of writing for a living off his mind. He did not think Fred had the ability.

Fred helped change Dobie's mind not long afterward. He entered a writing contest sponsored by the Texas Book Store and won first place for a story called "Because of a Maverick Sow," a tale about a henpecked husband who found his courage by going wild-hog hunting in defiance of his wife. First place meant a $15 prize, but even sweeter than that, Dobie had been one of the judges.[10]

Despite that success, Fred felt that fate was intent on slapping down his every attempt at getting somewhere in life. A deep depression settled over him. At least it gave him something to write about:

I'm pretty muchly down on the world and sad and dismal
and with a feeling that there's not a whole lot of use in anything
. . . . That's the way people get to feeling about it all when they
commit suicide. Don't get excited, though—or hopeful. I
wouldn't commit suicide.

He discussed how messy self-destruction would be but added, "just stopping to think about how much nerve it would take makes life look a
whole lot better to a man."

This was not the first time Fred had felt so despondent, and he
continued:

I . . . wonder—vaguely, of course, and without a great lot of
interest—just why these spells of gloom, all uninvited, get upon
a man and start riding him.

I don't think it's anything I've eaten, because I'm about
broke and the eating has been light. And I'm usually broke, so
that shouldn't cause any troublous change either. I'm not particularly lucky in love affairs. But then, I was never used to
being lucky in love affairs . . . . How sad and frustrated I am![11]

Depressed or not, Fred was becoming a "Big Man on Campus,"
at least among the 320 journalism students. He had pledged Sigma
Delta Chi, the national journalism society, in January 1936 and was
elected president of the SDX chapter the following fall. He also began
writing a regular column, "One Thing and Then Another," that appeared on *The Daily Texan* editorial page. The title came from a
figure of speech constantly used by Fred in his columns.

The first column appeared on September 18, 1936, but did not
have a by-line. It was about "Uncle Hurry," one of Fred's brothers-
in-law in Mason. Around the supper table, Fred and Uncle Hurry had
had a parley and agreed "between ourselves that ranch life was
mighty straining on a man's constitution and anatomy and one thing
and another and that life would be a whole lot more worth living if
we went aristocratic and cut out so much hard work."

Then, too, we think there ought to be more aristocrats than
there are anyway, providing, of course, we are two of them.
If everybody were aristocrats we figure there wouldn't be half
the labor trouble we are having now and there wouldn't be
any use in the New Deal or having to elect Landon to get rid
of it.

Fred listed the things he would do if he were an aristocrat, like having an automobile with an ice box in it "to keep our drinking beer in."

There is one little point of the matter, though, that we are going to have to take time and consider one of these days as soon as we get around to it. And that is how to manage to get rich enough to become aristocratics in the first place.

In his column on Saturday, September 19, 1936, Fred wrote about a discussion he had had with his father the week before about the Spanish Civil War, which was getting headlines in the newspapers. Sitting comfortably on the gallery of the home place, Fred and his father concluded: "War is sure a terrible lot of trouble and bother . . . . It messes up the lives of people like you and me way off over here, where there isn't any fighting going on and isn't likely to be any . . . ."

The war and the ensuing argument about it, Fred reasoned, indirectly "messed up the lives of people" and caused social tragedy. "Dad didn't get to town all afternoon—which will ruin him socially, I guess, because in country places like we live, everybody goes to town on Saturday afternoons." His father had not missed going to town on a Saturday afternoon for twenty years.

"Along about six o'clock, Dad and I came to the conclusion that the best way to get rid of war was just to abolish it altogether, tell everybody to forget about it, and holler up their coon hounds and go possum hunting."[12]

The Spanish problem was not the real reason his father did not go to town. For several months Beck Gipson had been waging a one-sided fight with cancer. By October, Mr. Gipson was losing ground rapidly. He had been looking forward to deer season, when he would make good money as a guide. But on Monday, October 19, just nine days after he turned sixty-four, Beck died on his farm. The funeral was conducted from the Gipson home the following afternoon. He was buried in the nearby cemetery named for Ben Gooch, the man who first settled the land the Gipsons now owned.

Before his death, Beck Gipson was aware of his son's hope to make a living as a writer. It worried him. Shortly before he died, he confided in his daughter, "Stella, Fred can't make a living writing unless he earns $100 a month."[13]

6

"All Newspapermen Are Crazy"

Gipson sat in a dance hall on Corpus Christi's North Beach, nursing a cold beer. The nickelodeon was knocking so hard he expected it to walk right out the front door after another couple of records. Oil field roughnecks danced with the taxi dancers at a dime a whirl. The drunker ones danced alone and did not seem to be able to tell the difference. His mother would never have approved of his being in such a dive, but this was the night life of Corpus Christi. Since he had been in town less than a month, Gipson intended to get a feel for the place.

A big-bellied man with beer roses blooming on his cheeks sat across from Gipson and every few minutes shouted, "Is there a chiropractor in the house?" Then the man would laugh and start pounding his beer bottle on the table. At the other end of the bar, a little man was trying to balance someone's 200-pound wife on a beer bottle atop a table.

Gipson watched the taxi dancers operating and soon had the system figured out: You sit at a table alone but with two bottles in front of you. Before long, the girls in the rustling dresses sashay by, offering a sly, sweet smile of encouragement. You get one to join you for a drink, and then it is a dime a dance, not counting the money you spend on her drinks, cigarettes, and her favorite song on the juke box. If the money held out, he learned, a person could get even better acquainted with the dancers—rough girls in a rough town.[1]

Corpus Christi was booming, despite the Depression. Gipson worked for the city's newspaper, the *Caller-Times*, which was growing in circulation just as fast as the seaport of fifty thousand it served. Nueces County's wild growth was being fed by oil and cotton; the year before, 1936, the county had had the biggest cotton crop in Texas. Gipson would not have picked Corpus Christi for his first newspaper job. He preferred Austin or the Hill Country. But the same thing that drew others to the coastal city drew him: money.

Grady Kinsolving, publisher of the *Caller-Times*, who said he had admired Gipson's *Daily Texan* stories, personally hired him.[2] For a college journalism student—which most hard-nosed newspaper men did not have any use for—Gipson's copy was surprisingly good. Kinsolving liked Gipson's vivid descriptions and his sense of humor, which seemed to come through in everything he wrote.

Of course, Gipson realized, Kinsolving might have just been buttering him up before bringing up the matter of salary—$25 a week. Still, Kinsolving's intentions seemed good. After Gipson accepted his offer, the publisher pulled a bottle of whiskey from his desk and poured the young writer a shot. Then he filled a jigger for himself. To Gipson's amazement, the publisher exposed a surgical tube that had been concealed under his clothing and emptied the bourbon into it. Kinsolving explained that after his operation he had found that when he wanted a drink, it was easier to let the whiskey get straight to the place it did most good. Gipson knocked down his drink the regular way and felt like he could use another. He had just been hired by a man who had cancer.[3]

At the end of the fall semester in January 1937, his friends on *The Daily Texan* had put together a farewell dinner in his honor. DeWitt Reddick sat to Gipson's right at the head table, cracking jokes as his former student wrestled with his old enemy—fear of speaking to a group. He got a good-natured roasting from his colleagues and professors. Harry Quinn praised Gipson's cigarette-mooching abilities. Journalism instructor Granville Price spoke at great length on the one headline Gipson had been able to write in his class during the fall semester. Toastmaster Joe Belden elaborated on Gipson's accomplishments on the *Texan* staff. Then Gipson ran out of rope—it was time for him to talk.

"I'm scared," he began. He forgot what he had intended to say and tried to ad lib. "But if anybody tells you I fell over in a faint, it's a lie," he wrote in one of his last *Daily Texan* columns.[4]

A few days later, Gipson started work on the *Caller-Times*, and on February 7, 1937, his twenty-ninth birthday, his first by-line story appeared. It must not have made a big impression on the copy desk, which two days later awarded him a second by-line but misspelled his name "Gibson."

Gipson and his fellow reporters on the *Caller-Times* had no shortage of news. "Things Are In Terrible Shape From a Standpoint of Vice/Corpus Christi is the Worst City in Texas, Says Lawyer Who Was First DA This District Ever Had," moaned a banner headline on January 24, 1937.

Texas Rangers were busy raiding gambling dens like the Dragon Grill, Jimmie's Plantation, the Harlem Grill, and the Marine Bar. The most common targets were marble machines—pinball machines that paid money to winners. All the commotion led to Gipson's first page one story which appeared March 3: "Acme of Amusement or Instrument of Iniquity? Marble Machine Player Analyzes His Emotions."

Gipson set out with a pocketful of nickels to see if the marble machine was "an instrument of exhalted and unquestionable pleasure or . . . a device of the devil, breeding sin and vice and iniquity." The machine did not look particularly sinful, all polished ". . . with colored pictures of race horses' heads on the tote board and a whole bunch of numbered holes for the ball to fall in, only the holes were pretty closely hemmed in with metal springs to keep the balls out."

Gipson was reluctant to drop a nickel in the machine but dismissed the hesitancy as the sadness he always felt when he parted with money. His first shot was lucky. It paid off "like a cow giving down her milk." The take was sixty cents which encouraged him to drop another nickel. The tote board showed horses number one and six would be the winners.

He pulled back the spring handle and launched the shiny ball, which was heading straight for the number six hole and a sure win. But right on the edge of the hole, the ball hit a spring and rebounded to the number five hole, and the "also ran" light flashed. After losing the sixty cents he had won plus six nickels of his own, Gipson concluded, ". . . there was never a device more definitely of sin, more degrading and degenerating and deteriorating to human morals."

The editors on the *Caller-Times* found Gipson could come up with a story on almost anything—from pelicans to how to buy a Valentine. For the 29-year-old man from Mason, the job in Corpus Christi had become a feast of new experiences and new friends.

The boardinghouse Gipson lived in was run by a Mrs. Prince, who said she believed her newspaperman tenant would someday be a famous writer. She came to that conclusion, she said, because Gipson suffered from insomnia. "I read in a book where nearly all the great authors are troubled with it,'' she offered. ''It seems that their minds are so keenly alert, flitting from one thought to another, that they just can't control them enough to go to sleep.'''

Gipson agreed he must be bound for fame. When he went to bed at night, his mind wandered worse ''than a coon hound when the folks are all gone.'' His first thoughts at bedtime would be about how happy he was that another day was over. Then . . .

> I lie quietly until I hear that single footing, 89-cent clock of mine break rhythm to gain a beat and I get irritated because it doesn't seem exactly fair for a cheap clock to rob a man of his time like that because a man gets old and dies quick enough like it is—lots of men without ever getting rich, too.

That led to his next succession of thoughts, which dealt with money and how nice it would be to have some. He could have all the fishing gear he wanted, three blonde cooks, and a redhead ''. . . to help catch bait when the fish wouldn't bite flies or plugs.'' Too, he would have enough money to go fishing in the cool north in the summer, and the warm south in the winter.

''It's a great comfort and satisfaction for a man to know that his insomnia is an indication of an artistic mind,'' he wrote.[6]

To avoid routine work, Gipson tried to stay away from the office as much as possible. Outside was where the stories were, anyway. Sometimes, like the day he was standing on Leopard Street just watching traffic, a story walked right up to him.

''Tiene callos?'' a man asked.

Gipson turned to see a drunk Mexican man, about fifty years old, stooped, unshaven, and dressed in worn, dirty clothes. He carried a leather case under his arm. Gipson knew the man had asked, ''Do you have corns?'' He answered in English: ''Never had but one corn, and a bull yearling stepped on it one day and mashed it off so now I don't have any.''

The old man said he could fix corns, ''Lift them out just like that,'' and snapped his fingers. Gipson was intrigued. He had always liked Mexican people and wanted to know more about how this man cured corns. The man said he had many customers and could make $12 to $15 a day.

''Think you'll get a customer soon? I would like to see you operate,'' Gipson said.

"I like you, let's go get a beer," the old man said. "I'll find a corn in a minute."

He led Gipson to a dark saloon with a sawdust-covered floor. They walked through a shattered screen door, and Gipson wondered how long ago someone had been hurled through it. Beneath a row of crudely done paintings of female nudes was the drunk proprietor, leaning against the low bar, which had nails driven through it to discourage loafers from leaning or sitting on it.

"Two beers," the corn doctor said.

"Got any money?" the proprietor asked.

The doctor looked apprehensively at Gipson, who fished a dime from his pocket. Four or five hard cases looked on.

"See that gun over there?" the doctor asked, pointing to a .45 on the counter behind the bar. "That bartender can really use that gun, he'll take care of us. Needn't be afraid."

The doctor had a couple more beers before Gipson coaxed him back onto the street in search of someone needing treatment. In front of another bar, the doctor finally found a willing patient. The only problem was the price, which was finally set at two bits. Gipson and several of the patient's friends followed the doctor to the hovel that was his home. The doctor marveled at the size of the corn on his customer's foot. From his leather case, he pulled a bottle of dark liquid and a swab of dirty cotton stuck on a board splinter. He daubed the fluid on the man's corn.

"What kind of medicine do you use, Doc?" Gipson asked.

"That's my secret. An Indian showed me . . . while I was a boy."

Whatever the preparation was, it worked. The old man lifted the corn away without hurting his patient.

"Let's get a beer," the doctor said.

Gipson followed him, letting him get farther and farther ahead. Finally, he darted around a corner, losing the doctor. He was halfway back to the newspaper office before he remembered something else the doctor had offered: He was going to introduce him to Juanita, the girl he said had the most beautiful legs in Corpus Christi.[7]

That might have been helpful. Gipson was having trouble finding the right girl. He figured it might be his country ways, which he had not been able to shake. He still thought beans should be eaten with a spoon and that women ought to wait on the menfolks before they ate. Still, he had a rugged, tough body that was in good shape, despite his time at the typewriter.

But when it came to females, something embarrassing was always happening, like the time Gipson and three girls stopped at a drive-in restaurant. Each of the girls ordered a bottle of beer while he ordered a bottle of sweet milk. The girls giggled at that and the carhop looked amazed. When she returned to the car, she handed in the three bottles of beer and gave Gipson a bottle of milk with two straws punched through the cardboard cap.

"Do you guess you can suck it through these straws?" she asked.

Gipson drank his milk and the girls downed their beers, laughing at him and calling him a sissy and trying to singe the hair on his arms with their cigarettes. They even insisted on paying for everything with their money.

"City girls don't seem to think I'm much of a man, and it's getting on my nerves," he wrote. "Mama warned me against city women when I left home."[8] The story was written lightheartedly but had more truth in it than most people knew. Gipson was uncomfortable around women, even though he craved their companionship.

By the end of summer, Gipson had written a story on scorpions, and on cabbages; he had toured an oil refinery, made the rounds of the bay with a state game warden looking for poachers, and covered a fishing visit by the President of the United States, Franklin D. Roosevelt.

Typically, Gipson found the feature angle to develop. The first day of the President's visit, Gipson and most of the other reporters on the *Caller-Times* staff tried to get close enough to Roosevelt to talk to him and take his picture. Leaving the straight news to his colleagues, Gipson wrote, "I guess about the most strenuous of outdoor sports is that of President hunting. I spent a whole day at it yesterday and I'm all worn out."

The reporters had gone to Port Aransas and tried to learn what the President was up to by asking around, but no one had seen the President or knew if he had caught any tarpon. Visible out in the bay, however, was the President's yacht, the *Potomac*. The reporters got Captain Hugo Mueller of Corpus Christi to take them out on the water in search of the President.

The Gulf was rough. Gipson told the others on the boat he wished he had his spurs. The boat, he later reported to his readers, ". . . would rear back on its hindlegs and start climbing a swell until it got nearly to the top and then get mad and just ram its nose through the top of it and drop about ten feet into the trough into the other side where it would waller and pitch and roll and do everything a sun-fishing bronc could think of and more and then start up the side of another swell.''

Two gray destroyers, bristling with guns and torpedoes, rode the waves more gracefully as Captain Mueller maneuvered the reporters in search of a President. By noon, they had not found any Presidents; so they went back to Port Aransas for lunch at the Tarpon Inn. The hunt resumed when Governor Jimmy Allred showed up to visit Roosevelt. The governor was taken to the *Potomac* in a Navy launch, followed by the press boat. Doc McGregor, the newspaper photographer, braced himself against the hull of the boat and started taking pictures.

Gipson and the others were so busy looking at Allred that they did not notice that Roosevelt had finally appeared on the deck of the yacht. As Allred went aboard, Gipson got his first glimpse of FDR: ''There he sat—just a nice looking man, maybe a little nicer looking than most men—dressed in a white sports shirt and shaking hands with the Governor of Texas, in a regular Texas fashion.''

McGregor was busy sliding another film holder in his camera when the launch put out from the yacht and headed in their direction. The Navy men asked, in what amounted to a command, that the photographer destroy his film. McGregor reluctantly complied, ''. . . a disappointed man.'' Gipson, however, was not too disturbed about losing the pictures. He had at least seen the President of the United States. What did bother him was a bad case of sunburn.[9]

Gipson's stories were becoming increasingly personal. He was writing a feature column though it did not have a standing head or consistent play. The material was popular and the powers in the Harte-Hanks newspaper chain decided they could get more mileage out of Gipson—literally and figuratively. They sent him on the road, traveling from Corpus Christi to San Angelo, home of the *Standard-Times*, the flagship paper of the chain.[10] Occasionally, he would go to East Texas and do stories for the Paris *News*, another Harte-Hanks property.

Gipson was happy with the traveling job. He did not like sitting in the office, putting up with the things that made newspapering at times tedious—rewrites of news releases, obituaries, the little old ladies who wanted a story about their cat in the paper, fielding calls from people infuriated because they did not get their paper, and the ''crazies'' who walked in off the street, claiming to be someone they were not.

Fred Gipson, newspaperman, while he worked for the Corpus Christi *Caller-Times*. (Photo by Doc McGregor, Corpus Christi *Caller-Times*.)

"Any day now I look for somebody to catch me walking down the road, bareheaded, barefooted, and talking to myself," he wrote. "Of all madhouses, a newspaper is the maddest. Of all nuts, newspapermen are the nuttiest . . . . All newspapermen are crazy. I think I'm the craziest of the lot."[11]

He turned that pronouncement into a readable column. He could take a day when nothing was happening and make something of it. All it took was time. Three lines written, two marked out; three lines written, two marked out.[12] He labored to perfect stories,[13] a troublesome trait in a business whose ownership wanted a lot of copy in a hurry. Occasionally, Gipson resurrected his *Daily Texan* stories—an essay on spring, fall, a boyhood fishing trip or some other tale. With minor editing, he could make one of the old stories suitable for publication again.

He prowled West Texas like an itinerant cowhand, driving from rodeo to rodeo, political barbecue to political barbecue, oldtimer interview to oldtimer interview. He received a lot of mail and enjoyed a good readership.[14] His "mug" shot became a regular addition to his column, which went from three times a week to daily.

As a columnist, Gipson dished out philosophy along with entertainment. A column on short skirts led to his definition of morals: ". . . mostly just things that everybody but yourself ought to be governed by, anyway, and usually are directly opposite to nature and are always a great bother to a man whenever he runs into them."[15] Sometimes the philosophy got more serious: "Life's a funny thing. A man doesn't know what it is, or why. All he knows is that it just drifts along, century after century out of one body and into another, ever changing in form and yet ever remaining the same thing—life."[16]

Gipson found one of the main obstacles to enjoying life was work. A truly happy man, he believed, was the man who took time out from his work to enjoy nature—to watch a bean sprouting, or to lie under a tree and gaze up through its foliage searching for one dim star in daylight, or to watch a deer wag its white tail as it lowered its head to drink, or to sit and soak up a West Texas sunset.

"Show me that man," Gipson wrote, and "I'll show you a happy man, a man that's living . . . . But he's not the man that snatches at life on the run. He's not the man that tries to crowd a week of living into the space of two or three hours, that he may give up the rest of his time to work. Work is an abomination to man. But I guess I had better get back to it."[17]

In columns about work or nature, Gipson was writing about himself. Taking time for nature was his antidote for the occasional black depression that would settle on him with the crushing suddenness of a cow lying down on a patch of bluebonnets. When an attack hit him, he got out and walked, prowling wherever he was, wishing he was "in Honolulu, Lima or Calcutta, or somewhere."[18] When he was in Corpus Christi, he walked downtown, watching the people—the rough shrimpers, the old Mexican fishing for crabs, the blonde on the beach, the checker players in the park. Such a walk usually ended up in one of his columns.

On the road between stories, Gipson's mind would roam where his body could not. Heading toward the Big Bend, he watched a huge orange moon coming up over the desert and got to thinking about life again. So many times, he mused to himself, his life had looked all silver and radiant, just like the moonlight-bathed landscape before him. How many times had that mixture of all his ambitions faded before him? He was thirty now, and where was he?

The blast of a trucker's horn snapped him back to reality.[19] He was on his way to the Big Bend and realized he had better quit worrying about the future, or he would never make it to the Chisos Mountains and the Civilian Conservation Corps camp there, where the government was working on a National Park site and J. Frank Dobie was working on a book. But he had a couple of other stories to do before he interviewed Dobie.

A few days later when Gipson stopped his car in front of a tarpaper-covered shack, Dobie—the man who back at the University had encouraged Gipson to do something else other than writing—was at the door.

"Come into this house," he said, taking Gipson's hand in both of his. Inside, the air was thick with Dobie's pipe smoke.

"How's the Texas longhorn book coming?" Gipson asked. He saw paper in a typewriter on a small table and a clutter of notes on a bigger table nearby.

"I'm just this minute chasing a longhorn bull over a ridge," Dobie said. "But sit down and tell me about yourself. I don't think that bull will get away for a little bit."

They rolled cigarettes and talked. After the smokes, Dobie led Gipson outside to show him the magnificent peaks circling the Chisos basin. On their way back to the tarpaper shack, Dobie stopped at the woodpile. "Like to chop wood," he said, "nearly as well as I like to ride a horse. When my mind doesn't work good, I come out and chop wood . . . . See, here's a piece of mountain ebony."

Dobie got a good fire burning in the wood heater. Gipson hauled in his portable typewriter, and both men hit the keys as night came. When Gipson finished a column, fine snow was falling. Dobie had already quit for the day and had gone down to park caretaker Lloyd Wade's cabin to see about dinner. As Gipson drove to the cabin, the headlights of his car stopped a mountain lion slinking in a nearby arroyo. The cat looked at the car for a minute, then ambled off into the darkness.

Dobie, Gipson, Wade, and Tom Mercer, a Railroad Commission inspector from San Angelo, sat on rough benches to a dinner of frijoles, chili con carne, and fried potatoes. After dinner, as the wind howled around the peaks and the snowflakes got bigger, the men talked of cattle and cowboys. It was nearly midnight before they got the last old longhorn rounded up.[20]

Back in San Angelo, *Standard-Times* managing editor Grady Hill was drinking coffee in the Angelus Hotel coffee shop, the "headquarters" of San Angelo. Everyone drank coffee there. A big local wool buyer was complaining about Gipson. "You ought to fire him, he's not worth a durn," the man told Hill.

Another man, a pioneer rancher from Knickerbocker, was listening to the conversation. "Jack, you're just all wet," he told the wool buyer. "That Fred Gipson is a good writer. He has that human touch. He's a humanitarian."

"Well, by golly, to each his own," the wool man said, slapping down his nickel for the coffee and storming out.[21]

Coincidentally, Hill had recently been talking with *Caller-Times* editor Bob Jackson about Gipson. Hill told Jackson he believed Gipson was the best writer in the chain but not the best reporter. He would go out on assignment to get a "spot" news story, get all strung out with the people involved, and come in with material for two or three columns. The basic news story usually went begging.

Gipson was growing dissatisfied, too. Kinsolving, when he hired him, had said he liked his colorful, personal writing. But Kinsolving was dead now. Gipson had the feeling his editors just put up with him, looking on him as some sort of newspaper freak because he could not or would not conform to standard style in his stories. Their attitude seemed condescending.

He stewed over these things but was still trapped in his constant dilemma: That $42 a week he was now making as a newspaperman was how he ate. Of course, to his mother back on the farm in Mason, that regular salary seemed good. What bothered her was that her son had never married and showed no signs of settling down.

Gipson devoted several columns to the issue. "No, from the looks of things, I think a man had better hold off on this marrying proposition just as long as he can. Believe it's a lot safer in the long run to talk about blondes than to marry them . . . ."[22]

Another time, he discussed marriage in more detailed terms: "In its early stages, marriage usually has a sort of stimulating effect, and apparently causes the patient to experience delightful and indescribable emotions, and it's not until a year or so later that the effect of its ravages begin to show up."[23]

Once he went to a fortune-teller to do a story. "You fear women," she told him. "She'll never know how much," he wrote. Another fortune-teller predicted he would never marry. This ". . . confirmed an idea I was beginning to get myself and left me feeling mighty sad and disillusioned . . . ." A third seer told Gipson he would marry a brunette with a tinge of red and have two children. Gipson was both anxious to find out she was wrong and hoping she was right.[24]

In another column, he mused about women's hats and how silly they were. It netted him a letter from an indignant San Angelo high school girl, Tommie Wynn, an avid fan of Gipson's column and an aspiring writer. His response was to call the seventeen-year-old high school senior and invite her to dinner. Tommie accepted, trying to put on a calm front, though inwardly petrified at the idea of going to dinner with an older, more worldly newspaperman.

They went to the Cactus Hotel, which had San Angelo's most elegant dining room. Tommie, frightened she might pick up a fork with the wrong hand or commit some other breach of etiquette, ordered a sandwich. She did not realize she was eating dinner with someone who did not know the difference and would not care if he did. They flipped a coin for the movie they would see. Tommie lost, but they still went to the film she preferred.

The shoes she was wearing had been bought at a sale and did not fit well. Inside the movie in the dark, Tommie quietly slipped them off. When the curtain dropped and she and Gipson walked outside, she was mortified to see the wrong shoe on the wrong foot. She was too embarrassed to switch them, but if her date noticed, he did not say anything.

The evening had not gone well. Tommie was ill at ease around such an older man, and she thought she would never see him again. But one day in church, she looked up and there he was, sitting with Homer Jordan, Jr. After the services, Jordan and his girl friend

Georgia Stewart asked Gipson and Tommie to join them on a picnic. Tommie agreed and Gipson went to get a watermelon. By the time he returned, Georgia, a nurse, had got an emergency call and had to go to work. So Tommie and Gipson went to Foster Park alone.

By the time he took her home that night, Tommie knew they were in love. But it would be weeks before she saw him again. That night Gipson had to leave for Corpus Christi, where he would have to stay for about a month.[25]

Tommie got her first letter from him a few days later. Her infatuation with him was certainly not one-sided. He was already calling her his "little queen." He felt that way, he continued, because ". . . she's the sort of a girl that would like to drift down a river in a boat or not be bothered a lot when the water in the swimming hole turns out to be not too clean and apparently gets as much fun out of eating a watermelon on a park table as dining among a clutter of silverware."[26]

By that September, they had decided to get married—eventually. Gipson had put in for a higher-paying job on the *Caller-Times* staff, but the management said they preferred his work as a roving reporter. He explained that to Tommie, then added, "It's beginning to look like you're going to have to live in a suitcase, honey. Reckon you can stand it for a while?"[27] In another letter, Gipson even offered an illustration of "us travelling about in a suitcase." The stick figure cartoon showed Tommie actually in a suitcase, carried by Gipson. A frying pan hung from the side of the luggage.[28]

With each letter, Gipson seemed to be getting more impatient about getting married but, at the same time, worried about the life he had to offer the lady he had begun to call his duchess.

> Do you suppose, honey, you could sometime get a big stick and threaten me with it to the point where I'd get down to trying to write fiction again? That's what I'd like, most of all. Then we could be fairly free to go and live where we liked, instead of having to stay where maybe we don't want. And I think that about all I need to do it is somebody to make me start writing. I'm afraid you're getting a terribly lazy man. He just sort of works when he has to.

His weakness in fiction, he went on to explain, was in plotting:

> I can write a story, when I can get a plot. But they seem so elusive. Can't seem to capture one. Frank King, head of the Associated Press at Dallas, jumped on me the other day for not

putting my material into fiction where it would bring some money. And yet, I just don't seem to get the hang of it, somehow. Can you do anything about it?[29]

On November 8, Gipson went to Beeville on assignment and checked into the Hotel Kohler. Once he was in his room, he opened his suitcase and pulled out a picture of Tommie. The picture perked him up and gave him a feeling of hope for the future. He looked through the desk drawer for some hotel stationery and started a letter that summed up his feelings:

> Do you know little lady that you are about the only thing in this world I really believe in? The only thing I have any faith in. Please—don't ever let me down.
>
> I am sure that by now you realize that you are about to take on a lifetime job of living with a screwball man, one who's always longing for something, seldom even knowing what it is he wants.
>
> Such a man, honey, can give you some happiness and a terrible lot of heartache and trouble. I only hope that you'll find the happiness worth the rest.

He ended the letter with what had become a standard warning: "If you were here tonight you would not be at all safe. I love you."

A written intimacy was developing between the young San Angelo woman and the roving newspaperman. With each letter to Tommie, Gipson revealed more of his need for her:

> Men are such pitiable, pitiful creatures . . . so full of bluff, so full of fear, fear that they won't be the men physically that will keep a woman happy and satisfied, that they won't be successful enough financially to keep her from want, that they'll lose face with the woman they love, lose the faith of the woman, that they'll even lose the little weak faith they have in themselves.
>
> Lack of courage drives more people to unhappiness than any one thing, I believe. And sometimes it seems like I just don't have a bit, that I just go on facing things because there's nothing else that can be done. There's not much fun, living that way.
>
> Now, do you have the courage to go on and marry such a craven creature . . . .[30]

They planned to be married on January 24, 1940. The wedding was to be a small one. But on the day before the intended date, a snowstorm blew into San Angelo. Since the suitcases were already packed and the wedding cake baked, Tommie and Fred impulsively called the preacher and the handful of invited guests and announced they wanted to get married a day earlier.

Attending were Tommie's parents, Mozelle Owens, a friend of Tommie's, and Joe and Zelma Howard, friends of the family. Charles would have been his brother's best man, but because of the bitter norther, Gipson called him and told him to stay in Mason.

After the wedding, they drove on ice to Mason, where they stopped long enough for Gipson to call his mother and tell her he was a married man—finally. Then they left for San Antonio and their first night together as man and wife.

Two months to the day earlier, in one of his love letters, Gipson had philosophized that ". . . on the day we get married there will be three or four hundred other couples in these United States getting married, too. Some will have $40,000 weddings, others will have to borrow to pay the preacher, and some will be happy and some won't . . . . We want to be on the happy list, just that, and nothing more."

Fred on his honeymoon in Mexico. (Courtesy Beck Gipson.)

7

Bill Manning:
Literary Agent of the Southwest

The winter storm that had blustered through West Texas the day
Fred and Tommie got married had followed them on their honeymoon all the way to Mexico. They had driven from San Antonio to
Del Rio and from there to Monterrey, a city where cold weather was
rare. Their hotel, the Gran Hotel Ancira, was not well heated, and
since their room was not much warmer than outside, they decided to
go exploring.

The honeymooners weaved their way across the dry, boulder-
strewn Rio Santa Catarina to the real Monterrey that most of the
touristas overlooked: the old bird vendor with his merchandise flutter-
ing in a straw cage, the *ninos* of the street begging for nickels, the
babies playing with hogs in front of their families' *jacales*. They
walked to the foothills, past a saloon where a beer-drinking hombre
strummed his guitar, past a monument to Hidalgo and finally to a
park, the only clean area in sight. They sat on a bench and ate lunch
before an audience of beggars and a hungry dog, aware of the good
and the bad smells around them—roses, violets, and wild orange trees
mixed with the stench of fly-coated, unrefrigerated meat hanging in a
nearby butcher shop, human and animal refuse in the street, and
other trash scattered everywhere.[1]

The next night they decided to leave the hotel for dinner at a
fancy nightclub and a carriage ride around the city. The newly married man preferred his cowboy boots and blue striped shirt to shoes

and more formal evening attire, but worried he would clash with his young wife who was dressed in her fanciest clothes.

"Who cares?" Tommie asked. "We know nobody. Nobody knows us."

So they went to dinner, Gipson looking like a cowboy; Tommie looking like a duchess, which is what he had started calling her in his column. They may not have known anyone, but they still got stares in the restaurant-club where they ate. Gipson was glad when the meal was over. Outside they found a carriage driver looking for business.

Gipson carried a blanket along as protection against the unseasonable cold. They climbed into the back of the carriage, and the driver clicked his horse into a walk. They rode along the *zocola*, the ancient downtown plaza. This was the night of the serenata, the traditional promenade, where the eligible young women of the town walk around the square in one direction, the young men in the other. One by one, they would pair off, and romances would begin. Tommie snuggled close to Fred under the blanket as the driver stopped so a mariachi band could make money off the Americanos. The music was good—romantic for one song, fast-paced for the next. Worth the price even at five pesos.

After the ride, the couple returned to the hotel. Their serenata was over. "Any time now," Tommie said, "I'm ready for us to go back home and settle down with our future."[2]

Their immediate future was not pleasant. The Harte-Hanks management had decided without consulting Gipson to station him in Corpus Christi permanently, a decision he found irritating. He did not dislike Corpus Christi, but he did enjoy traveling the state in search of interesting stories. What made him even madder was the pay cut: His weekly salary was dropped to $37.50.

Still fuming over the pay cut, Gipson rented a small, three-room apartment which ate up one-fourth of his now reduced monthly income. Most of his savings had been spent on a new car and the wedding trip. Despite the blow to his pride and self-esteem, he could not risk quitting in anger without a better nest-egg in the bank.

His job had done more than hurt his ego. Since fall, his stomach had tormented him. He had not been able to find a doctor who could come up with any physical reason for the pain. "They look at me," he had told Tommie in a letter shortly before they were married, "see that I'm carrying plenty of weight and tell me to get hold of myself, that I'm perfectly all right. Then I ask them what makes me jittery and despondent and they seem to get the idea that I want to take some pills, so they give me some pills, when it's not pills I want, just rest and peace . . . only I can't seem to get it anywhere."[3]

Since returning from Mexico, his stomach had been bothering him again, but so had Tommie's. He assumed it was part of the flu they had come down with on their return trip. Tommie thought the same thing but her trouble continued, especially in the mornings. By the time she was just about over the flu, she discovered she was pregnant.

When she was five and three-fourths months pregnant, Tommie was taken aback by her husband telling her, "Now, Tommie, don't expect me to care anything about the baby. I've never been interested in babies. I'll begin to care about him when he's three or four years old and able to talk and go places with me."[4]

In June, Gipson made a stand for more money, explaining that his weekly salary equaled his month's rent, giving him only three weeks salary a month to live on. That was all it took. Kunkel fired him.

Gipson went home to tell Tommie the news. She knew something was wrong when he walked in. His face was colorless. He was both angry and scared. "I guess I'm going to have to take you back to Mama," he said.[5] For several frightening hours, Tommie thought he intended to take her—pregnant for six months of her six-month-and-one-week marriage—back to her mother in San Angelo. She began to cry and did not stop until she learned her husband intended to take her with him back to Mason and his mama.

During their courtship by correspondence, Tommie had assured her husband-to-be that whatever he tried to do in life would be all right with her. That had been her answer to a question Gipson posed in a letter the previous November: "Do you think you could live with a man trying to write and sell free-lance fiction? I mean starve with him . . . . Well, no, it won't be that bad. I mean, I can always manage for food."[6]

In another letter, Gipson had predicted the reaction of family and friends to his quitting his job and gambling on free-lance sales as howling and "shaking of heads." "When I go down to the book stores and see the thousands of books for sale, some so much better written than I can write, I get disheartened. Then, I see stuff come out not as well written as I can do it and know that it's selling, and I think I'm foolish for not getting to work on it."[7]

After the Gipsons had moved back to Mason, it seemed the time had come for him to get to work on free-lance fiction. He spent a week or two looking for a job with a weekly newspaper in the area but found the best salary he could make was $15 a week. The choice was to take a job, earning less than he had in Corpus Christi, or to take a chance on himself. Tommie said it was time he took that chance. Gipson agreed.

He wrote Joe Small, who was now publishing his own magazine, *The Southern Sportsman*. The Steck Company had seventy percent interest in the magazine, leaving Small thirty percent ownership, a regular salary, and an office. In a letter back to Gipson, Small offered to pay him $5 a story. That would be helpful, but what Gipson had his eye on was the pulp western fiction market. Using the same portable typewriter he had had for years, he started writing western adventure stories. They were rejected so fast it seemed he got them back the same day he mailed them.

Despite the continual bouncing of his fiction pieces, Gipson was sticking to his promise to Tommie that they would not die of starvation. Mrs. Gipson provided their food, and Charles sent his older brother money to build fences on land he had managed to buy with his oil company earnings. Also, Gipson drove to Llano every other week to collect unemployment until it ran out after three months.

Though austere, their life was not without some pleasures. The Gipsons went to every movie that came to town. When *Gone With the Wind* finally reached the community, they took Mrs. Gipson to see the blockbuster color movie based on Margaret Mitchell's novel. But they did not see it all. Mrs. Gipson, whose father had been wounded in the Civil War, was still fighting it—she could not take the realism in the picture and demanded to be taken home.

In September, as Tommie neared the end of her pregnancy, she went to San Angelo to stay with her parents until the baby was born. The expectant father stayed behind, still trying to write saleable fiction. When Tommie went into labor on October 29, her mother summoned Gipson. Before he could get to the hospital, Tommie had given birth to a son. She was sleeping off the anesthesia when Gipson walked into the room. For a stunning instant, he thought she was dead; then he noticed Tommie's elated parents and relaxed. The baby boy looked exactly like his father—he had a long upper lip, the same face, and hair the color of sassafras tea. They named him Phillip Michael, but from then on, he was Mike.

In that first year of free-lance writing, Gipson had earned $150. Tommie's and Mike's hospital expenses wiped out all the profit and dug one dollar deeper into savings. The bill was for $151.

Despite his claims to Tommie that he would not care for his child until he was older, Gipson was a proud father. But he was not proud of his efforts at free-lance writing. He had dreamed for years of the independence it would bring; now he bore heavier shackles than ever. Unless he could start selling, he might be better off going back to newspaper work.

When he and Tommie went to Austin to show their baby to the Smalls, he talked it over with his friend. Small read most of Gipson's rejected efforts. His characterization, Small said, was excellent. But the plot, as Gipson was the first to admit, was the weak link.

Small offered an idea: "All right, I'll tell you what. You go down to that second-hand magazine store on Congress Avenue and get you a bunch of magazines. Go back home and read those plots, and then write them. Just write out a bare plot like a skeleton or a frame for a house. You put the meat on it."

"Well, that might work," Gipson grinned for the first time during the whole conversation.

"And then I'll sell those stories for you," Small said.

"You always were full of bull. You just might be able to do it. Okay, we'll give it a try."[8]

Gipson returned to Mason, his car full of pulp western magazines. Meanwhile, Small had some stationery printed with a two-color letterhead proclaiming: "Bill Manning. Literary Agent of the Southwest."

Back in Mason, Gipson started studying the magazines. He had been reading western stories for years, but until Small suggested it, he had never really thought about their structure. As he looked, he found that just as Small had told him, there was a skeleton beneath the colorful words, the blazing guns, and the ranchers' pretty daughters.

Before long, Small got Gipson's first effort. In his mind, it was beautiful writing, with a fair plot. Small twirled a piece of the fancy stationery into his typewriter. He addressed it to Rogers Terrell of Popular Publications, a company which put out six western magazines, including *Dime Western* and *10-Story Western*.

"I want to present a new writer to you, and I want you to really watch as you go through this story, how beautifully he handles characters. When his cowboys say something, it's like a cowboy would say it, not the drug store cowboy type," Small wrote.[9]

For a 5,000-word romantic horse opera in print, the pulps paid a half cent a word, which is what Gipson got for that first story Small handled. Encouraged by the $25 check, Gipson started turning out westerns at the rate of one a week, occasionally two, no small feat for a slow writer who had done very little deadline writing during his newspaper days.

Gipson was able to add a touch of authenticity to his western writing that others were not. And he could do so without much research because he already knew many stories about Texas frontier history. One of the bloodiest, most vicious episodes had unfolded right in Mason County, back in the 1870's. Gipson had pestered old-timers to tell him about the feud that had been triggered when a lynch mob hanged several men thought to have been cattle rustlers. Soon, so many dead bodies were being found that the most commonly asked question in the county became "Who done it?" People started calling the fracas the Hoo-Doo War. Texas Rangers finally restored order to the county, but hard feelings among survivors had lasted well into the twentieth century.

At first, Tommie's role in Gipson's writing was simply that of typist. But as she typed her husband's stories, she noticed things that could be changed—passive voice could be made active, snarled sentences could be simplified. She asked if he would mind her making some changes in one story that had been rejected.

"No, and if it sells, you can have the money," he replied.

The story did sell, and Gipson kept his promise. Tommie bought him a desk with the $45 the story netted, thinking that a comfortable place to write would further his creative efforts. But it was an imposing piece of furniture, not a typing table, and Gipson was furious that she had not spent the money on something essential. A card table—even a sawhorse—was all he said he needed for his typewriter.[10]

Gradually, Gipson's pay went up to three-quarters of a cent a word and finally to a penny a word—top pay for the pulps. Each month he sold about four stories, bringing in around $200, which was more than he could make working for a newspaper.

With Gipson finally beginning to make some money, the couple and their baby moved in July 1941 to a one-room apartment in the old Seaquist place in Mason. Their room was warmed by an old-fashioned wood-burning heater, but they did have an electric cooking stove. There was no sink, only a wash basin, and the bathroom was upstairs. Once a week, Mrs. Gipson drove into town bringing them milk, butter, eggs, and vegetables.

Although their financial situation had improved somewhat, Gipson told Tommie to avoid making friends. Accepting hospitality would mean returning hospitality, and they could not afford to do that. But family was different. Charles and his wife, Mildred, and their son, Don, who was only a few months younger than Mike, had moved back to Mason and built a house. The Gipsons were frequent visitors. And the whole Gipson family usually met every two or three weeks for covered-dish suppers and "42" games.

Small and his wife, Elizabeth, came to Mason that summer so "Bill Manning" and his client could discuss future plans. They arrived with a big bottle of cheap red port Small had bought in Fredericksburg. After the glasses were filled, it did not take many swallows of the stout stuff before the world began to look a little brighter to the young magazine publisher and his friend, despite the looming war and the constant grind of trying to make a living.

The two couples camped on the Llano one night. When the trotlines were baited for catfish and Gipson and Small were full of the bust-head wine, they hatched story ideas and schemes calculated to make them millionaires while their wives visited and watched the children. Small dreamed of taking over full control of his *Southern Sportsman*, and they worked out the details for Gipson to write a syndicated column for country newspapers.

They decided to call the column "Around Our Place" and to peddle it that summer. Gipson wrote two or three columns at a time. Small handled getting them set in type, matted, and distributed. Tommie typed countless sales letters.

"Around Our Place" was like a weekly letter from home, sprinkled with anecdotes, philosophy, and sometimes even a plug for one of Gipson's pulp stories:

> "Gunsmoke in the Moonlight" is another of our brain children scheduled to appear in the November issue of Ace-High Western. It is a gun-slamming, powder-burnt child that had me ducking all around my typewriter as I produced it, trying to dodge whining and promiscuous lead.[11]

Other columns were filled with the happenings of the Hill Country people Gipson knew: the man who paid a $6 long-distance bill because his watch broke while he was trying to make his call inside three minutes; the neighborhood chicken dinner brought about by the host's accident with a shotgun in the henhouse; and the old cowman who decided to retire and raise chickens but worried how the little chicks would ever be tall enough to suck.

Gipson called one of his philosophers The Grazer. "It's funny," mused The Grazer, "how many people chase around till their tongues

71

hang out looking for a good time. Me—I can just crawl up on a pole pen and listen to fattening hogs popping dry corn and have the best time on earth.''[12]

Then there was the subject of Mike Gipson. Besides the happiness he brought his parents, the boy provided continual stories for his father's columns. His ''child of the flesh, Mike the Mighty and Dirty,'' was as ''wild as a corn-crib rat. He's rowdy as a bull calf when the grass greens in the spring. He's tougher than a bootheel and pesky as a heelfly . . . . But once he's fed, clothed and showing off before company, he's the greatest boy ever born . . . .''[13]

The week before Mike turned one year old Gipson recalled some of the things that had happened to the toddler in his first twelve months of existence: Just on one day, Gipson had had to pull the boy out of the stock tank three times and had dragged him twice from a red ant bed covered with the stinging insects; had dug a mouthful of smoking tobacco from his mouth; collected the confetti he turned unread magazines into; and had endured countless diaper changes, diaper washing sessions, wild shrieks, and the scratch of tiny fingernails on screen doors.

Thinking about all that made Gipson remember something his father had told him years before: ''Son, you'll never pay for your raising until you've raised a youngun of your own!''[14]

Mike could barely walk when his father took him for his first romp in the woods. Before long, the one-year-old got as much satisfaction out of the treks as his father. ''There's no ailment Mike's ever contacted . . . that a tramp thru the woods won't cure . . . . He's his papa's son to the core. His first spoken word was 'fish.' I expect his next to be 'coon' or 'hound dog.' ''[15]

Newspaper editors, already worried about the wartime scarcity of paper, apparently did not go for Gipson's mixture of folksy humor and occasional no-holds-barred political opinion. The column never really got a good start and by early 1942, Gipson and Small gave up on ''Around Our Place.''

By August 1942, the Gipsons had enough money saved to think about building a home out in the country. Gipson's mother deeded him a long, narrow eleven-acre tract that took in a little dry creek on one end. The wartime construction limit was $500, which was enough for a two-room house with a two-holer outhouse some yards away. Harve Land, the uncle of Charles' wife, Mildred, built the house with assistance from a carpenter's helper.

A year later, as more and more men were being drafted—even those with children—the Gipsons reluctantly moved to Austin so Tommie could get a job if Gipson was inducted. Gipson's mother would be able to keep an eye on their modest house until the world got sane again and they could resume their homesteading.

Tommie and Fred rented a house across the street from the Smalls. That way, if Fred did have to go fight, Tommie would have friends nearby. With the two families just across the street from each other, "Bill Manning" found it easier to handle Fred Gipson's literary career.

After the Gipsons settled in their new residence, Gipson produced a story that Small thought was too good for a pulp magazine. It read beautifully. So instead of sending it to a sure market, Small sent it to *The Saturday Evening Post*. Small was no amateur when it came to waiting on the mail or sweating the sale of a story. He had written dozens of short stories himself before he quit the university and started publishing magazines. He knew the feeling of leaving a manuscript in the mail box and finding it returned after what seemed only a day. The *Post* was fast. The story was soon back, but with a nice letter, which meant it had come real close. In fact, the letter-writer said as much.

Such a nice "no" must mean something, Small figured; so he put the story in a new envelope and got it off to *Collier's*. Small did not think Gipson would like what was going on, since the story would surely sell for $25 or $50 to one of the pulps used to his work. He decided not to tell him what he was doing.

Soon he received a letter from *Collier's*.

"Dear Bill Manning: We have your story by Fred Gipson. Where have you been hiding this author? Our check for $500 is forwarded. Will you send us some more material from this author?"

Joe and Elizabeth ran over to the Gipson house with Joe waving the $500 check, the mother lode. Gipson had been napping and was still a little foggy. Finally, he said, "Well, I'll be dog-goned. Now I wonder how many stories we can sell 'em a month?"

Elizabeth Small could not believe Gipson's casualness. "Fred Gipson, get excited! My Lord, you're standing there like nothing's happened at all. Don't you know this is a memorable time!"

So Gipson made a show of being excited, mostly for Elizabeth. Then he sat back on the bed smiling.

The occasion seemed like as good a reason as any for some drinking. The two couples went across the street to the Smalls' house. The celebration lasted until about midnight when Gipson announced, "I don't think I can make it back home. I'm tired."

"You're going to come home now if I have to drag you," Tommie said. "I want to go to bed."

"You can't drag me across the street," Gipson said, taking the challenge and hitting it back.

"I bet I can!"

Gipson lay down on the porch. To the amazement of everyone but Tommie, she tugged him feet first off the porch, down the steps, out into the yard, and over the curb.

Her husband was laughing and bending over to keep his head from bouncing on the pavement. When they reached the other side of the street, it looked like he had her after all. Somehow, she had to get him over the curb. And somehow, she rolled him over it.[16]

Fred and Tommie, c. 1946. (Courtesy Beck Gipson.)

8

"My Kind of Man"

Gipson was miserable. Tommie had found a job that paid $90 a month. He was busy writing, hoping for another sale to *Collier's*. There was the close, pleasant relationship with the Smalls. It should have meant stability, happiness—but those things somehow seemed to be eluding Gipson.

Mainly he missed Mason. His firing in Corpus Christi had at least freed him from having to live in a city. Now he was back in a place where he felt sardined against his next door neighbor, where only a hedge separated his yard from someone else's. At night, city sounds intruded on his privacy—a blaring radio, the screech of tires. Austin had grown into a city of 100,000, much larger than it had been when he was in the University. As far as he was concerned, Austin was just too big and too far from Mason.

Gipson decided he was going home; Tommie, on the other hand, was not having a bad time in Austin. Finding a job had taken her several months, and her work assured them a regular income while Gipson wrote. Older men were now being drafted, so the original reason for moving to Austin seemed more important than ever to Tommie.

Her husband did not see it that way. "Well, I'm going home whether you do or not, and I'm taking Mike," he finally told her. Tommie resented the "either-or" attitude, but she had no choice. They moved back to Mason and their two-room house in the country.[1]

The house they had built was small but surrounded by a lot of land, which gave a sense of openness. To Tommie, life there was like a picnic in the country. They did not have electricity, only a kerosene stove for cooking. Though it was 1944, the Gipsons were living essentially as Fred's parents had been when he was born. Only the younger couple, with no cotton or corn crop to rely upon, were perhaps poorer. Their income depended on the taste of pulp western magazine editors in New York.

Gipson hammered out the western yarns in the front room of the little house, which held the couple's double bed, four-year-old Mike's bed, and the desk Tommie had bought for her husband. He worked in the mornings while Tommie cleaned, cooked, washed, and watched after Mike—until he got stuck on a story. Then she dropped whatever she was doing and talked it over with him until he got moving again. Sometimes when Gipson's muse would be mired up to its figurative wheel hubs, Tommie would take over the typewriter and write that part of the story as she saw it. Occasionally, Gipson would accept her work, and it would end up running exactly as she had written it. But he would usually rewrite it, saying the same thing in his colorful way.

Although he was getting some writing done, Gipson could not stand to be at the typewriter for more than about half a day. In the afternoons while Tommie retyped what had been written earlier, he did physical work outside, went for walks, or went fishing, sometimes taking Mike along. The walks not only gave him time to think and a chance to wind down from the morning's work, but oftentimes carried him back to his boyhood days. Those days of his youth were hardly past before he had found himself craving the impossible—their return.

His mind drifted back now to the time several years earlier when he had accompanied his two young nephews, Dick and D. B. Polk, on a walk in the woods. The boys had just made slingshots using pieces of an inner tube. Gipson could not resist the urge and found a beautiful forked limb in a nearby bush, broke it off, whittled it down, and armed himself with the favorite childhood weapon. Time was, he could hit a scurrying lizard at twenty paces with a slingshot.

Squeeler, a hound pup, loped along beside them, sticking his nose in every clump of bushes and prickly pear he could find. The pup picked up a trail, announcing it with a howl. As Squeeler trotted ahead, Gipson and the boys loaded their slingshots. They did not have to wait long. Suddenly, a catclaw bush rustled and out shot a jack rabbit. Three rocks whistled in the direction of the fleeing rabbit. As Gipson stuck his throbbing thumb in his mouth, irritated that he had forgotten to drop it as he released the stretched rubber, he realized all three shots had missed. The rabbit was long gone.

By afternoon, they reached one of Gipson's favorite swimming holes. But now it was moss-covered and smelly, not the clean, elm-shaded pool he remembered. Still, it was a swimming hole, and the boys shed their clothes. When D. B. bent to get his feet out of his overalls, there she was—the Belle of Wichita smiling coyly from the seat of his flour-sack drawers. Her rosy cheeks were faded from repeated washings, but it was the same sweet smile Gipson remembered on the flour-sack underwear his mother used to sew for him. Now, he was embarrassed to admit, he wore striped, store-bought shorts. A true country boy, Gipson knew, would never wear store-bought underwear. But times had changed.

They wallowed in the water awhile and then rested in the sun. Gipson used to do that when he was young without anything to worry about. But now he was a man, and a man had more important things to do than lie in the sun next to a swimming hole and stare into the sky, pleasant as it was.

The yelling of one of his nephews interrupted Gipson's thoughts. Dick was chasing after a horned toad he had spotted near a red ant bed. The dirt-colored, pointy-headed fellow had been ambushing ants until Dick began poking a stick at it. It flattened out in fear and anger, but Gipson interceded in its behalf, explaining to the boys that a horned toad was a harmless, helpful creature that should be spared. Years earlier, Gipson's father had told him not to kill lizards since they ate the bugs that ate cotton.

The sun was getting low. Gipson reluctantly said they had better be heading home.[2] A man should not spend all his time traipsing around in the country—or should he? The more he thought about it, the more he wondered if maybe old Charlie Sanders had had the right idea about life.

The daylong walk with the boys had not been very long ago, but Dick and D. B. were already young men and soon would be facing the same question themselves.

For now, Gipson had no choice as to his answer. He went back to his wife and son. Tommie had probably finished typing what he had written that morning. After supper or after breakfast the next morning, they would go over it, edit it again, and she would probably type it another time. Within a month or so, maybe, they would get a check for $45.

77

Gipson loved company when he was between stories. When he invited John William Brown and Dub Harrison, two old friends, to stay for a weekend, Tommie busied herself cooking enough food for two days—roast, beans, and a chocolate cake. She and Gipson and Mike went into town for the mail, and when they returned, they found that the two friends had arrived and made themselves at home. Evidently they had been hungry. They had eaten all the food Tommie had prepared for their entire visit.

Another time, the Smalls came and spent the night on cots in the kitchen. But Joe could not sleep: the ticking of the Gipson family clock in the next room kept him awake all night. The next day, the two friends drank red wine and did what they always did—schemed ways to make a million dollars.

When the Smalls went back to Austin, Gipson returned to the drudgery of churning out the westerns. Most of the stories he sent to the pulps were selling. But despite his building experience, there still were rejections. The reason given was familiar—too thin a plot.

One often bounced story, not too loosely based on Charlie Sanders, was one Gipson called "My Kind of Man." Gipson liked the story and thought it was as good as any he had written; it irritated him worse than a grass burr in a boot that the story did not sell. Almost in desperation, he sent it to *Southwest Review*, which had published his story about old Sam, the tick inspector, eight years earlier. Maybe Donald Day, the new editor, would be interested in "My Kind of Man."

Mailing the story to *Southwest Review* proved to be a literary jackpot. Although the *Review* could only pay $25 for the story, the little magazine had a quality reputation. Day believed "My Kind of Man" had potential and sent the piece to *Reader's Digest*, the top-paying magazine in the nation. The *Digest* people agreed with Day that the story was good, so good they bought it for $1,600.

"My Kind of Man" appeared in the Fall 1944 issue of *Southwest Review*. A slightly condensed version ran in the November issue of *Reader's Digest*. Gipson's four-page story began on page 73 of the 128-page issue. There was no editor's note saying who Gipson was, just a subheading below the title that the article was a "story of hound dogs and a boar coon." Gipson had exercised some poetic license, but the central character was called Charlie. Charlie, Gipson wrote, "was my kind of man. He could tear off a piece of oak leaf, hold it against the roof of his mouth with his tongue, and blow on it to call a fat turkey within gun range at gobbling time."[3]

The $500 sale to *Collier's* had seemed like big money; the $1,600 from *Reader's Digest* was a fortune. Most of the sudden wealth went into the Gipson house. They added two rooms, along with an even more luxurious addition: an indoor bathroom. For the Gipsons, there was also an increased sense of accomplishment and hope for the future. Tommie was twenty-four; Fred, thirty-six. Tommie felt it was time for another child. Her husband was not so sure. One day Tommie was driving past some run-down houses in town and was amazed at all the children she saw running around the neighborhood. She went back to their place and told her husbnd what she had seen. ''The poor people do it,'' she said, emphasizing the word ''poor.'' ''We can, too.'' Gipson agreed. By September, Tommie was pregnant.[4]

The war was nearly over, but men were still being drafted. Despite Fred's age and Tommie's pregnancy, his induction looked inevitable. The draft notice arrived in April. Tommie went to see Bill Bode at the local draft board to ask if her husband's departure could be delayed until their baby was born. The older man, who had known the Gipson family for years, looked up at the ceiling, obviously embarrassed. He told Tommie that he had not heard she was ''in a family way'' and assured her that Gipson could stay until the baby came. But with the war winding down, Gipson never got a second notice.

Gipson knew there was more to be said about Sanders and coon hunting in Mason County. Excited by the success of ''My Kind of Man,'' he began work on a more ambitious project, a task that seemed harder than building a barbed wire fence across a quarter-mile chunk of granite. He had done that, but could he write a novel?

He began the project, sticking to the pace he had set in writing for the pulps—working in the morning, spending the afternoon in physical activity. If he did not go fishing or to town to visit with some old friend like Frank Polk, the bootmaker, there was always work to do around the home place.

But if he had a choice between working and fishing, he never had much trouble making up his mind. Since his childhood days, when he and Charles went fishing in the Llano with their father and Sanders, Gipson looked on fishing as almost a sacred rite. As far as he was concerned, there was nothing better for a man.

''Fishing makes a man feel like a boy again,'' he wrote when he worked for the *Caller-Times*. ''If old Ponce de Leon had just forgotten all about his 'fountain of youth' and come to Texas with a cane pole and a can of worms, he wouldn't have died all heartbroken and disappointed like he did.''[5]

Once on a fishing trip with Small to a hidden pond Gipson knew about on Mill Creek, he told his friend there were so many big bass in the pond that when the water got low, the fish had to swim in shifts. The two men tried every lure they had in their tackle boxes—tossing everything but their hats at the fish. But the fish were not impressed. Country bass did not understand fishing lures, Gipson guessed.

After much experimentation, Gipson and Small concluded what the fish were hungry for was frogs. They hunted frogs as hard as they had been fishing and came up with three river frogs. They got back to Gipson's place that night with three legal bass and enough ticks to keep them busy for weeks.[6]

What Gipson preferred to use as fish bait were helgramites—an opinion that guaranteed him an argument any time he wanted one. Most fishermen, he found, had not even heard of helgramites. When he was in the University, Gipson had written a column on helgramites, explaining that a "helgramite is a little animal that lives under rocks out in the stream until he sprouts wings and cracks his hide open and comes out an insect. Some say he's a dragon fly then. But that's beside the point."

The only important thing was that a helgramite was good fish bait:

As such, he's maybe three or four inches long, pretty tough and squirmy, and without any legs to speak of. In some ways he's like a crayfish. For one, he travels in reverse—when he travels, which isn't often. Then, too, he carries a pair of nippers calculated to make the laziest sort of fisherman yell and jump straight up 10 feet and out into the creek when he feels a pair of them clamp certain parts of his anatomy.[7]

Fishing, like walking, gave Gipson time to think. If the fish were not biting, he had plenty of time to block out the next day's scenes in his mind.

Work on the novel went smoothly for a while, as page after page of double-spaced manuscript piled up. Then two-thirds of the way through, it dropped dead. Gipson could not get it moving again.

His anguish over the stunted novel was interrupted by Day, who wrote that he would like to come to Mason to meet Gipson. Day drove from Dallas to Mason a few days later. He was practically speechless when he saw the Gipson homestead. To him, the couple were living in extreme poverty. Gipson took Day on a fishing trip to get acquainted.[8]

The Dallas editor, however, had more than fishing on his mind.

9

Fabulous Empire

The sign on the building in downtown Ponca City, Oklahoma,
read "101 Ranch Indian Traders." After studying the trading post
for a moment, Donald Day walked inside. A couple of Indians glanced
at him suspiciously, but it was the cold blue eyes of the old man in
the Stetson that made the visitor uneasy.

Day was beginning to wonder if the drive from Dallas had been
worth the trouble. Colonel Zack Miller, the man who had ramrodded
the famed 101 Wild West Show, looked at Day "belligerently, as if I
were another impatient creditor."[1]

When he was a boy, Day had seen Colonel Miller's extravagant
circus-rodeo which had been as popular as Buffalo Bill Cody's western
touring company. Cody had been dead since 1917, but now in 1944,
Miller was still very much alive. Day remembered seeing Miller ride
into the big show-tent to the sound of a trumpet, astride a jewel-
studded saddle on a high-stepping horse.

Miller's huge 101 Ranch had been broken up in 1937, and now
the old man spent most of his time at his trading post. Day had not
thought about the 101 Wild West Show in years, but the submission
of a free-lance manuscript on Miller to *Southwest Review* had jogged
his memory. He had driven to Ponca City to talk to the old showman
and check some of the facts in the story.

Day explained what he wanted, but the old man was cranky. The
magazine editor tried a little buttering up, telling Miller how much he

had admired the 101 Show as a youth. That gentled him. Day read the old man the article, and then Miller started talking—for nine hours. The *Southwest Review* editor recognized it was a story that needed to be told to everyone and the sooner the better. Even a man as storied and tough as Zack Miller could not survive forever. Before he left, Day got Miller to agree verbally to tell his story for a book if the right person could be found to take it down and write it as well as Miller talked it.

Now, in Mason, Day told Gipson he believed he was the man to do the job.[2] Day said he had given some thought to trying the project himself but did not think he was the right kind of writer. He felt he could get an advance or commission from *Reader's Digest* for a story on Miller. Gipson and Day and Tommie talked it over, and Tommie urged her husband to accept the offer. The novel, caught in the literary gun barrel, could wait.

Day returned to Dallas, got in touch with Miller, and set up a meeting between the old cowboy and the Mason County writer. In late November, Gipson and Tommie left Mike with relatives and drove to the Kerr County ranch of Mrs. Ethel M. Raigorodsky, a friend of Day's who had offered her home for the interview sessions. The rustic ranch house stood on a bluff with a view of the nearby Kerrville hills and a clear creek running below.

Miller was a grand storyteller and hated to slow down once he got started. Gipson used his typewriter to take down the Colonel's stories but found the interviews the most hectic he had ever handled. Miller would say he did something on a particular date and Gipson would grunt, making a note to find out what the actual date was. But when he checked later, Gipson found the old man was right. Miller had remembered exactly when he sold a cow or bought one, or broke a horse.

A welcome break to the interview sessions would be a meal prepared by Mrs. Raigorodsky. Gipson soon found, however, that Miller really told some of his best stories at the table, and Gipson would have to jump up and get the material on paper before it went stale.

Tommie knew shorthand but could not keep up with Miller's steady stream of anecdotes, so Gipson got what he could on the typewriter. Each page made a story, and when the interviews were completed in a month's time, Gipson had collected an overwhelming volume of information. The thousand pages of notes was 250,000 words, and considering wartime paper shortages, it was way too much material. The best stories would have to be tied together to develop the overall story of Miller. The rest would have to be culled and saved for future use.

A month after returning to Mason, Gipson was in the throes of another attack of writer's block. The idea of sorting through all the material had him cowed. He began talking about dropping the project, but before deciding anything drastic, he would go fishing. While he was gone, Tommie started going over the Miller notes, attempting to arrange the stories in chronological order.

Miller himself saved the project, simply because he was such a good storyteller. A review of the tales showed the old man apparently had given a great deal of thought to his story and had put it together pretty well. The writing job was fitting the pieces together, figuratively sandpapering the rough edges and checking the facts. Gipson went to work on the book.

In the spring of 1945, Gipson left for Ponca City with the completed manuscript to check with the old man on names and dates. By the time he got to Oklahoma, his stomach was in knots. He was afraid Miller would not like the book, but he had to check its accuracy. Nervously, Gipson began reading the manuscript to Miller. Miller would get excited and say, "That's just exactly the way it was," and then start telling the story all over again.[3]

When the Ponca Indians learned Gipson had written a book on Colonel Miller, the last remaining member of a family that had befriended them, they felt the old man had been done a great honor. To show their appreciation, the Poncas announced a great party in honor of the writer. Though Gipson was the distinguished guest, the party somehow cost him a side of beef and ten sacks of flour. But it was a party he never forgot: a gathering of drunk Indians, an old drunk cowboy, and before it was over, a drunk author.

When Gipson got back to Mason, Tommie started typing the final edited version of the manuscript. She finished all but the last few pages before June 17 when their second child, Thomas Beckton, was born.

Mike was tremendously excited about having a little brother. During the last few weeks, he had been allowed to feel the baby moving and had been fascinated by the miracle of life. The four-and-a-half year old had asked his mother what the new baby would be named.

"If it's a boy, we'll name him Thomas Beckton," she had replied. "If it's a girl, we'll name her Martha Wynn."

"But, Mother," Mike asked, all wide-eyed. "What if it's a puppy dog?"[4]

Meanwhile, Day sold Houghton Mifflin Publishers on the Miller book, which would be called *Fabulous Empire*. The profits would be split three ways, equal shares going to Gipson, Miller, and Day.

Fred with his second son, Beck, about 1946. (Courtesy Beck Gipson.)

Shortly after Beck's birth, Day took Gipson to New York to meet the people at *Reader's Digest*, Houghton Mifflin, and an agent, Maurice Crain.

Gipson felt right at home talking to Crain, a native of New Mexico, who had grown up at Canyon in the Texas Panhandle. He had graduated with honors from the University of Texas and then worked his way East as a newspaper man, finally getting a job with the New York *Daily News*. Crain had married a Texas girl, Annie Laurie Williams, who worked for the *Morning Telegraph*. Her ambition was to start a literary agency, and with Crain's newspaper salary to keep them going, she went in with Mavis McIntosh to form the McWilliams Literary Agency. Later, the agency was split into two corporations, McIntosh and Otis, Inc., and Annie Laurie Williams, Inc. The agency bearing her name handled stage and motion picture rights, while McIntosh and Otis handled literary matters. Crain, after serving in World War II, had started his own literary agency, which operated with his wife's business.[5]

In October, Gipson sent a V-Mail letter to one of his old University friends, Army Captain Alexander Louis, who was still overseas. He told Louis about his book, promised him a copy, and added, "We could even break out a bottle maybe and drink to its success." Gipson then brought his friend up-to-date:

> I'm still grinding out fiction most of the time now. Writing that book set me back awhile and I don't have much short stuff out right now. But *Reader's Digest* informs me they're making a cut of one, which comes close to meaning an acceptance, but you're never sure you've hit that magazine till the stuff comes out in print. I visited their outfit while I was in New York; they killed the fatted lamb for me. Hope I made a good impression. They had trouble understanding my Texan, but otherwise we seemed to have gotten along fine.[6]

Despite his success with "My Kind of Man," Gipson's stories that were long on character but short on formula plot were still not making it in the pulps. But Gipson was more interested in the stories that *Reader's Digest* might buy through *Southwest Review*.

Day bought "The Melon-Patch Killing," a colorful tale of watermelon thievery, and ran it in the Spring 1945 issue of the *Review*.

The story was based on a true-life happening in Mason County that had been related to Gipson by J. Marvin Hunter, whose father established the Mason *Herald* in 1892.

Stealing watermelons was part of boyhood in Mason County. Hunter had told the story in a fairly amusing style, but he was a chronicler. Gipson took the story, presented it from the viewpoint of an eleven-year-old printer's devil (Hunter), and made it come alive, since he had a passing familiarity with Mason County watermelons and their theft. He had had a county-wide reputation as a purloiner of watermelons when he was a boy. Sometimes he got away with it—sometimes he did not.

One time when he was accused, he was actually innocent. Gipson's father had warned Fred and Charles not to eat any of the melons ripening in their patch. They abided by that—the sweetest melons were those found glowing in the moonlight in someone else's patch anyway. But when the Gipson boys found a watermelon that had already been chewed on by a skunk (there was still plenty of the melon left), they could not resist.

When Beck Gipson saw the dried juice on the boys' faces, he accused them of breaking open a melon. They denied it and got a whipping for lying. Then they tried the truth, explaining that a skunk had started the job and they just finished it. That netted them a second whipping. Since they had lied the first time, Mr. Gipson had no reason to believe the true story.[7]

Appearing in the same issue with "The Melon-Patch Killing" was "Blizzard Trail" by Jeff Morgan, as told to Fred Gipson. The brief story was about how Morgan, an old-time cowboy, endured a fierce winter storm on a trail drive in 1896. In the watermelon story, Gipson described watermelons so well that the pages were practically sticky. In "Blizzard Trail," a reader got the idea of what it was like to be caught in a Panhandle snowstorm:

[T]he horse wrangler set out to light a fire. He couldn't make it. His fingers was too stiff; he kept breaking the heads off his matches. By the time he got one lit, that squalling wind had scattered his kindling to hell and gone. His match blowed out. He called it off as a bad job and come to stand beside us at the calf wagon. Both his ears was white and I knowed they was froze. His hands was as blue as the hide of a catfish.[8]

As Gipson fought to pound out copy that Day might be able to sell to *Reader's Digest*, Day was involved in his own battle in Dallas. He had been editor of the *Review* since 1942, when he got the job on the strong recommendation of J. Frank Dobie. Day believed the *Review* should strive for a wider audience and become something like a *Reader's Digest* of the Southwest. Other forces at SMU wanted to keep the *Review* as a small but quality literary publication.

In the Fall 1945 issue of the *Review*, Day resigned in print in an editorial labeled "And the Tubes Are Twisted and Dried." He wrote that some "prophesied that the *Southwest Review* was well on its way to the comic book level." He retorted that the last year's issues of the *Review* should "give their own testimony." The *Review*, he continued, had "opened its pages to new and vigorous contributors, creative writers; the vanguard of those who will one day do for this region what the great sensitive minds have done for the world."[9]

In the last issue under his editorial control, Day used every piece on hand by his friend Gipson. To anyone who did not know what was going on, the Fall 1945 issue of *Southwest Review* looked like the whole Gipson family had taken up writing. There was "Throwback," by Tommie Gipson; "Hound-Dog Men Are Born," by Fred Gipson; and "Long Tom: The Wild Gobbler," by Mike Beck, a pen name based on the first name of Gipson's two boys. All the stories, of course, were by Gipson.

By April 1946, Gipson was worrying about promoting *Fabulous Empire*. Saddled with getting only one-third of ten percent of the profits, he started making plans. On April 20, he wrote the new editor of *Southwest Review*, Allen Maxwell, submitting a story, "Dinner Bucket," and asking that the *Review* give him a few inches of advertising space to promote *Fabulous Empire*.

In early May, Maxwell wrote Gipson that he had enjoyed "The Dinner Bucket" but did not feel it measured up to his previous *Southwest Review* stories. He suggested Gipson rework the story "by a tightening of the line of action and more concentration on the dinner bucket as a symbol."[10]

Fighting an urge to wad up the letter and hurl it against the wall, Gipson found the last paragraph on the first page of Maxwell's letter had better news—a counterproposition to his request for ad space. Maxwell agreed to run a quarter- or half-page ad touting *Fabulous Empire* "on account," with the hope of seeing another Gipson story "in the near future."

Gipson quickly accepted Maxwell's offer, defended his story but agreed to work it over when he got a chance, and said there was no use in trying to get an ad in the upcoming summer issue of the *Review* because ''. . . the publishers have never decided yet just what the sales price of my *Fabulous Empire* is to be. Nor are they for certain yet just when it will come out, other than 'sometime this summer or fall.' ''[11]

The delays on the book were disheartening; the rejection of "Dinner Bucket," irritating. But both developments were minor compared to what was happening at home: Tommie had had a miscarriage and was in the hospital at Brady, the closest medical facility. For a while she had been near death.

The money from his *Reader's Digest* story had long since played out, and the hospital bill was growing daily. Gipson had paid a good portion of the bill and planned to try to pay the rest in installments. Various friends, including Louis, offered to loan him money. But in a letter to Louis on May 10, Gipson thanked him and said he did not need help, yet.

Tommie finally improved, and after she was dismissed from the hospital, Gipson took her to San Angelo to stay with her mother.[12] Her doctor had ordered her to recuperate at least six weeks before trying again to keep up with Mike and Beck, who by now was walking. When Tommie got back from San Angelo, she was still too weak to handle the children. Gipson hired a local woman to take care of Mike and Beck at their place; he rented a room at the Fort Mason Hotel across from the courthouse for use as an office. With Tommie's help, he went back to work on his novel.

Tommie's recovery was the most important thing to Gipson, but the money situation was getting worse. He borrowed money from the Smalls, from Tommie's mother, and from John William Brown, his old college friend. Then he wrote Louis that he would take him up on his offer of a loan if he could still afford it.

In July, there was good news. Crain had managed to sell the editors of the new *Holiday* magazine on the idea of serializing part of *Fabulous Empire*. Just what the pay would be he did not know, but the deal was sweet for two reasons: The money was badly needed, and magazine serialization would be good advertisement for the whole book, assuming it ever appeared.

Gipson had more good news that he wrote about to Louis. "Sad Sam," Gipson's story of a rodeo horse that lived to be twenty-three, was to appear in the October 1946 issue of the *Reader's Digest*.[13] That would mean good money. The story had actually been sold to the *Digest* first through Day, and then "planted" with the *Review*. When it appeared in the *Digest*, however, it would say, in small type, "Condensed from *Southwest Review*."

Fabulous Empire finally hit the bookstores in September.[14] The reviews were more satisfying than a good coon hunt, except maybe the review that appeared in the October 12 issue of *Texas Week*. At first glance, it looked good. The reviewer called Gipson a "triple threat" writing man, a fellow who could turn out pulp fiction, "earthy regional pieces" and "yarns for slicks like *Liberty* and *Collier's*." In *Fabulous Empire*, the reviewer said, he had combined all three styles.

After recounting the Miller story, the reviewer said it was a shame Gipson "did not come nearer being a contemporary of Zack's. Literally, there always seems to exist a . . . mental hazard when an intellectually honest young writer sets forth to record from the source, the life and times of a once colorful figure, several generations removed." Nevertheless, the reviewer continued, Gipson was a good reporter. His "shortcomings as a biographer do not deprive the book of its intrinsic merit, nor its swashbuckling central character of his picturesque virility."[15]

The opinions of the unnamed *Texas Week* reviewer aside, the reading public liked the book. It made the bestseller lists—not to the top of the list, but just being on the list said a lot for a first book. Already, 8,500 copies had been sold, and Houghton Mifflin was bringing out a second edition.[16]

Tommie and Fred drove to San Antonio for an autograph party. Anticipating good income from the book, they bought Gipson two new suits, a navy and a soft brown plaid, to wear during the rest of his publicity tour. As they headed out of town, Gipson took a last drag on a cigarette and tossed it out the car window. They drove on a few more miles before they began to smell burning fabric. The cigarette had landed in the back seat and burned a hole in each pants leg—eight holes in all. Tommie was able to mend the blue pair, but the plaid pants had to be rewoven, which took a couple of weeks.

By October, Gipson had copies of almost fifty reviews of the book. Only two were less than favorable—the one in *Texas Week* and a review by Stanley Walker, former city editor of the *New York Herald Tribune* and a native of the Lampassas area.

"Very likely the *Texas Week* boys hit at the greatest weakness in the book, its lack of projected theme," Gipson wrote Maxwell. "Stanley Walker's criticism seemed a bit foolish to me."[17]

Ed Cole reviewed the book in the San Angelo *Standard-Times* on September 1, 1946. Though long, the review did not come right out and say *Fabulous Empire* was good, but it gave that general impression. It ended with this: "*Fabulous Empire* is Fred Gipson's first book. It won't be his last."

The casual reader of Cole's review would probably think Gipson was even then hunched over his typewriter, whipping out another book. In truth, he was out peddling *Fabulous Empire* like a sack of potatoes.[18]

Col. Zack Miller, the subject of Fred's first book, *Fabulous Empire*. (Courtesy Zack Miller, Jr.)

10

$25,000!

Charlie Sanders was getting old, but his long legs still carried him around. Every now and then, he would drop by the Gipson house, just like he had been doing since Gipson was a boy. The visits were as exciting for Mike and Beck as they had been for their father years before. Sanders still liked to walk around with a fox or some other animal tucked under his arm. It fascinated the boys and Tommie, but Gipson was used to it.

If Gipson was not home when Sanders happened by, he would settle his lanky form in the front door to wait. To pass the time, he liked to count the pennies in a pint jar saved for Mike. If Gipson still had not shown up by the time he had made his count, he would spill the coins and start over again.

The summer visits were the best because the animal smell on Sanders would not be too bad. In the winter when he had been running his traps, if he sat too near the fire, the odor was potent. When it was cold, Sanders wore layers of clothing, and each layer exuded a different animal odor. The most common odor was also the strongest—skunk. He would have on two or three pairs of pants, an undershirt, a cotton shirt, a flannel shirt, and, if it was really cold, a jacket. The Gipsons finally learned to bank the fire when Sanders came around for a winter visit.

The visits were not exactly as they had been when Gipson was a child, however. Sanders did not appear at mealtime as often, and he never seemed quite comfortable around Tommie, whom he considered a city woman. He and Tommie liked each other but had a hard time finding common ground for conversation. He did, however, appreciate her looks. He often told Gipson that Tommie was "pretty as a picture" and ought not to have to work.[1]

The summer before *Fabulous Empire*'s publication, Gipson had not done much work himself, but not out of laziness. Tommie's illness had taken a lot out of him, and the summer heat seemed to suck the spirit from a man right along with the sweat.

By fall, Gipson's favorite time of the year, his energy began to pick up. He was ready to begin another book, but was still casting around for an idea. In the meantime, he was able to knock out short stories based on people he knew or on old tales he had heard. He had several stories accepted by *Progressive Farmer*, including "Black Cat Bachelor," which was inspired by a story he had heard from his father about Sanders.

In an editor's note accompanying the story, Gipson was quoted as saying, "It's so near a true story that I might have to go on the dodge after it's published, except for the fact that the hero is unable to read or write. Maybe nobody will read it to him when it comes out . . . ."[2]

With the publicity work on *Fabulous Empire* out of the way, Gipson drifted back to the novel he had been working on, which was about two men he knew pretty well—himself and Sanders. Gipson was twelve-year-old Cotton; Sanders had evolved from "Charlie" to "Uncle Dewey" to Blackie Scantling.[3] Cotton wanted to be free to roam like Blackie, but his mama, like Mrs. Gipson, wanted her son to amount to something.

The previously written part of the novel dealt with the adventures Cotton had with Blackie. When Gipson turned to the project again, it seemed apparent that Cotton needed more initiation into life. Something had to be done to elevate the novel above a mere collection of episodes, no matter how colorful they were.

Tommie suggested that Cotton's initiation could involve a change that Blackie would have to undergo. Marriage, which never happened to the real Blackie, seemed to be the answer. What better way to settle a man down, Tommie said. Even a hound-dog man could be tamed by matrimony.

Book writing, Gipson began to discover, was a lot easier when the writer knew where he was going. Still, he resisted planning too much. At the University, he had been taught to make proper outlines for stories. But just as he could not stand the confines of city living, he found being pinned to an outline was too restricting.[4] He preferred the wide open spaces of both land and thought. Though the general idea existed, the words and paragraphs and chapters were fitted together in pieces. Building a novel as painstakingly as the old German settlers around Mason had stacked their stone fences was artistic, but not immediately profitable.

In November, Gipson went to Dallas for the annual meeting of the Texas Institute of Letters to, as he wrote Allen Maxwell, "see whether or not my *Fabulous Empire* takes a beating in the literary contest sponsored by Carr Collins." Gipson had never met Maxwell and promised to look him up while in Dallas.[5]

The awards dinner was at the Venus Restaurant, and even though he did not win the $1,000 award for the best non-fiction book, Gipson had a good time. He enjoyed talking with more experienced authors and listening to John Selby, editor of Rinehart and Company, who said he was looking for good biographers from Texas.

While in Dallas, Gipson discussed future story possibilities for *Southwest Review* with Maxwell. He clarified his feelings in a letter to Maxwell after returning home:

> I appreciate your position as editor in wanting the best material you can get for the *Review*. At the same time, you'll have to appreciate my position as a free-lance writer who must first make a living before contributing much to low-rate publications. That's why I've turned in so little copy to you.
>
> I'm a slow writer and my stuff must bring a good rate for me to exist. Therefore I have to shoot fire at the high-paying markets. And if the stories stick there, then of course all [that] leaves for the *Review* is the cut-backs.
>
> I'm sorry it has to be this way, because I know you're not in position to pay top rates. But until something I write pays off pretty good, I'm afraid the situation will continue.[6]

Gipson soon had a shot at another prize: His publisher, Houghton Mifflin, was offering a $1,000 prize for a novel by someone who had contributed to the *Southwest Review*.[7] The prize money would be in addition to whatever advance and royalty was paid.

When Gipson finished his book, which he called *Clipped Wings*, he sent it to Maxwell at the *Review*. Maxwell thought it was so excellent that he wanted to change SMU's long-standing policy of not publishing fiction. But Gipson was obligated by his *Fabulous Empire* contract to offer Houghton Mifflin first chance at his next work. Maxwell attached a glowing and sincere letter of recommendation and forwarded the manuscript to the publisher.

Gipson decided to let Crain handle the book, though he believed as Maxwell did, that it had a good chance of being accepted by Houghton Mifflin and also winning the $1,000 prize.

When Crain got the manuscript, he and his wife, Annie Laurie, stayed up late reading it. The book, the agent wrote, had given him "... more belly laughs than I have enjoyed since Tige was a pup." It would sell to Houghton Mifflin, Crain opined, unless some Bostonian was "too thick to see the point of Texas humor."[8]

Donald Day's reaction was the same after he read the manuscript. "It nearly re-tore this pore old belly of mine open from laughing and nearly tore my old wore out heart apart from crying. It's a good book in my league," he wrote.[9]

A complication neither Gipson nor Crain expected was interoffice politics at the venerable publishing house of Houghton Mifflin. The novel had gone to the firm's New York office, which at that time was not getting along well with the original office in Boston. The manuscript was tied up at the New York office for nine months. Finally, the juvenile section of the company wrote Gipson and said they liked parts of the book but not all of it. If he would make certain changes, they might be interested.

Gipson was undecided, but Tommie persuaded him to take a chance on the manuscript as it was. Crain began circulating the manuscript to other New York publishers. Several said they were interested, but not to the point of buying it unless there was a substantial revision. Reports of continued rejection, despite Crain's attempts to keep his client's hopes up, had Gipson depressed. The decision not to make revisions appeared to have cost him a book.

Day suggested that Gipson get back into newspaper feature writing, but not just for any newspaper. He had in mind the Denver *Post*, the legendary paper revitalized by Frederick G. Bonfils and Harry H. Tammen, that had been a training ground for men like movie writer Gene Fowler and successful humor novelist H. Allen Smith. Through Day's connections, it was arranged for Gipson to work in Texas as a roving feature writer for the *Post* and its Sunday magazine, the *Rocky Mountain Empire*.

Gipson started doing feature stories about people and places in Texas, but the *Post*—and Day—thought he should move to Colorado and work for the paper full-time. Day wrote, "You could live away from here [Denver]—out in the mountains, perhaps in a smaller town—where you could get to the people and find good fishing places for Palmer [Palmer Hoyt, editor of the *Post*] and me. You could still do your outside writing." Day told Gipson to send him an air-mail letter on what kind of salary he would need so he could relay the information to Hoyt. If Hoyt felt he could pay the amount, Day said, "then you can come up, expenses paid, for an interview."[10]

Gipson got the job and began making arrangements by mail with Elvon Howe, editor of the Sunday magazine. The first step Gipson took was to explain candidly the way he felt about his planned move:

> I look upon the job as a meal ticket and second as a chance to travel some and gather material for possible future books, short stories and *Reader's Digest* articles. So long as the job gives me that opportunity, without tying me down too completely—and so long as the editors feel that I am giving them satisfaction for that money—then I'm definitely interested in holding it.[11]

With the novel *Clipped Wings* in limbo, the Gipsons packed for the move to Colorado. They would keep their land, of course, and rent their house to some young couple. Gipson did not intend to leave Mason forever, despite what he might have had to promise in order to get the job.

In February 1948, after a farewell visit with the Smalls, their families and other friends, the couple loaded their luggage and two kids into a secondhand red Packard and drove to Durango, Colorado. The post-war building boom had not yet come to Durango, and the Gipsons had trouble finding a place to live. Finally, the *Post* used its influence to get them into an apartment over a grocery store about a block from the Italian section of the old mining town.

Gipson's job would be to roam the territory, much as he had done for the Harte-Hanks papers in Texas, and to write interesting features. He left on his first assignment before they had everything unpacked.

The rough winter weather in Colorado often made traveling unpleasant, and hazardous. Toward the end of one feature-story trip, Gipson was heading back to Durango from Ouray when the sun went down and the road started icing. Under the best of circumstances, the steep and winding road was regarded as one of the most treacherous in Colorado. At night when it was icy, even the native did not risk driving it.

But Gipson wanted to get home and, after studying the map, concluded he could make the final sixty miles to Durango without much problem. At practically every turn, however, the car went into a skid. Each time, Gipson fought the car and kept it from going off the road—and straight down. After several close calls, he stopped and put chains on the wheels. During that operation, his coat froze to the road. He had to crawl out of it before he could get up and then tear it off the pavement. When he finally got to the small apartment that was their home, his nerves were worn ragged. He was crying and shaking when Tommie met him at the door.

Tommie had not been having an easy time of it, either. There were seven saloons in their block alone, and a lot of drunks. One night, awakened by someone knocking on the door, she thought it was Gipson getting home late again and that he could not find his key. Still practically asleep, she had opened the door and stepped outside before she saw that the man was not her husband but an Indian—a drunk Indian. Tommie recalled the horror stories she had heard.

"You have the wrong place," she said firmly. "The hotel is next door." But the Indian did not seem to understand. Finally, she had to walk across the porch—in her nightgown—unlatch the gate at the top of the stairs and help the reeling Indian down the steps. It did not occur to her until later that that had been pretty risky.[12]

Although Gipson managed to find some interesting stories and had a by-lined spread in each week's *Rocky Mountain Empire*, it was not a happy time for him and Tommie. The novel still had not sold, and he did not seem to have much time for his free-lance writing.

By summer, Gipson had had enough. "We're going home. I can't take any more of this nonsense," he told Tommie, even though he had no other job prospects.[13]

Clipped Wings, meanwhile, had been making about as many rounds in New York as its author had in Colorado. Finally, Crain took the manuscript to John Fischer, editor-in-chief of Harpers, who liked it but felt that he had already accepted too many manuscripts with a rural Texan backdrop. Because he was a Texan and worried that he was becoming biased in favor of books from his native state, Fischer passed the manuscript on to one of his young editors, Evan Thomas, son of Socialist presidential candidate Norman Thomas.

Thomas read *Clipped Wings* with growing delight and enthusiasm. When he went to Fischer to announce he had discovered something, Fischer decided that Thomas' reaction was proof enough of the manuscript's potential.[14]

Harpers accepted the book and Crain wired the good news to the Gipsons, who were packing for their return to Texas. Even though Gipson had already made up his mind to come home, the telegram made him feel a lot more comfortable with his decision. A man did not have to work at something he did not like, Gipson believed, but he did have an obligation to feed his family.

"Your poor little orphan manuscript that nobody wanted—your own phrase, quoted out of a letter some months back—is now a literary discovery," Crain wrote. "The enthusiasm at Harpers is general and genuine." About the only part of the book Harpers did not like was the title, which Thomas suggested be changed to *Hound-Dog Man*.[15]

The happy news soon became even sweeter—stunningly so. Gipson's book was accepted by the Book-of-the-Month Club as a dual selection with *Cheaper by the Dozen*. With the book club contract came a guarantee of $25,000.[16] An enthusiastic Gipson dashed off a letter to Small back in Austin:

> Dear $25,000—I mean Hosstail Joe!
> I ain't rattled, see. Just $25,000 nervous! You see it's like this—$25,000! . . . Twenty-five thousand pesos. TWENTY-FIVE THOUSAND! (Read it again!)
> Just got the telegram from Crain last night. Taking it all very calm. You know Gipson. Takes everything in stride. $25,000! Never gets upset! $25,000! Never gets thrown for a loop! $25,000! Twenty-five thousand!
> Love and twenty-five thousand kisses!
> Sincerely and calmly,
> $25,000 (I mean TWENTY-FIVE THOUSAND!)[17]

The $1,600 check from *Reader's Digest* had seemed like all the money a man could hope for at one time. But $25,000! If a man had a $5,000-a-year job, it was considered good money. Five times that was incredible wealth.

Crain was just as excited as Gipson:

> Dear Fred: Ain't it a wonderful world! I lay awake last night, as I expect you did, thinking how the book club acceptance will affect the course of future events and everywhere I look the land is bright . . . . [It] is going to make whatever you write hereafter so easy to sell that our main care must be to make very sure that you select the most appropriate subjects and offer nothing that will not advance the career now so auspiciously launched . . . . Anyhow, you won't be pressed for money and can write what you like . . . . Boy, I'm so happy for both you and Tommie that I could weep.[18]

The sale meant more to Crain than the ten percent commission it would net him. As the manuscript went from publisher to publisher, Crain had grown increasingly uncomfortable. He felt that if he was wrong about *Hound-Dog Man*, he did not have much hope as a literary agent.

A short time after returning to Mason from Colorado, Gipson decided to accept Crain's suggestion that he, Tommie, and the boys come to New York for a visit with Crain and his wife, Annie Laurie, and the people at Harpers. Gipson did not want to make the trip in the old Packard so he went to the bank in Mason to borrow money to buy a new Ford. The bank was not impressed with Gipson's guarantee of at least $25,000 on the novel from the book club. They would not loan him the money. The Mason bank knew cattle, goats, pecans and land. A guarantee from some New York company did not seem like concrete collateral to them. Furious with the bank, Gipson loaded the Packard and headed for the East Coast.

Crain believed there was an excellent chance that *Hound-Dog Man* would be made into a movie. Annie Laurie, who had sold Kathleen Winsor's *Forever Amber* and Margaret Mitchell's *Gone with the Wind*, felt so, too. Gipson had met Crain's wife on his first visit to New York and told Tommie about her. Tommie had formed a mental picture of a typical, tough New York businesswoman. When Tommie first saw Annie Laurie, however, her jaw unhinged. Before her was an ungirdled woman in her mid-sixties, draped by a flowered chiffon dress. Her bright blonde hair, in Shirley Temple curls, was topped by a Salvation Army-like hat, which was tied under her chin. Tommie tried, but could not cover her surprise and amusement. Annie Laurie read her expression. Fortunately, she read it wrong: "Surprised, aren't you? No one thinks a cute little blonde can be a brilliant businesswoman, too."[19]

After a week's visit with Crain and Annie Laurie at their Connecticut farm, the Gipsons went to New York. Crain introduced them to Fischer and Thomas at Harpers. Annie Laurie escorted them on a strained visit to John Steinbeck, a client of hers, whose wife had recently left him, taking his two children. Annie Laurie marched the Gipsons through Steinbeck's studio as if they were on a sightseeing tour. Steinbeck made an effort to be cordial, but Tommie could tell by the way he looked that he was barely able to manage a friendly facade.

Suddenly, Gipson was being looked on as a literary "property." In New York, it had been suggested he move there, where he would be closer to his agent and publisher. But, he had no desire to live any place except Mason. He pledged his determination to stay at home in a letter to Elizabeth Stover, also on the *Southwest Review* staff. Maxwell read the letter and reacted to it in his next letter to Gipson: "Delighted you have determined to stay on at Mason rather than pull up stakes and settle elsewhere. One of the big troubles with Texas is that so many people who ought to stay light out for those northern flesh pots.''[20]

By early fall, despite the acceptance of *Hound-Dog Man*, Gipson was growing uncomfortable. He was having trouble deciding where to go in his next novel. Gipson's insecurity and fear of failure were never far below the surface. Others, namely Tommie, his agent, and the editors at Harpers, seemed to have more confidence in him than he had. Gipson felt better when his former writing professor at the University of Texas, DeWitt Reddick, wrote asking permission to include ''My Kind of Man'' in a writing textbook of his that Harpers was publishing. Gipson quickly granted the permission, honored at Reddick's decision to use his story as an example of good writing. ''He's the most inspiration[al] instructor of writing classes that I ever had the good fortune to encounter,'' Gipson wrote.[21]

On November 1, Gipson wrote Maxwell, bringing the *Review* editor up to date on *Hound-Dog Man*. It would be out by January 5, 1949, he said, adding that Harper's was ''labeling it as their 'Fiction Find' for the year and have given it a double-page spread in their winter catalogue. Sure hope the sales will come up to expectations.''[22]

An English publisher, meanwhile, had bought the rights for an overseas edition of *Hound-Dog Man*—only the book would not be called that in England. As Crain informed Gipson, ''Their nomination [for a title] is 'Cotton Kinney,' which they say fits in with the Tom Sawyer, Huckleberry Finn titles in the same tradition.'' He added, ''I am impressed by the fact that the English publisher has independently perceived the kinship between Fred Gipson and the early Mark Twain.''[23]

In December, the *Book-of-the-Month Club News* devoted three pages to *Hound-Dog Man*:

> There appears occasionally a book with fresh winds blowing through its pages. It seems to create new physical sensations of taste and sound and smell. It seems to introduce us to a world in which language and emotion are rejuvenated and alive with new experience. Mr. Gipson's unassuming and exquisite story of a backwoods community in Texas has that quality.[24]

The last of the three pages, headed ''Fred Gipson *wanted to tell his own story*,'' was written by Donald Day, who traced Gipson's background and the long search for a publisher. ''When half the publishers in the country wanted him to rewrite [the novel], he stubbornly refused, insisting that it was right. Frequently, there wasn't even grocery money. Fred almost gave in when fair-sized advances were dangled before his eyes if he would do this or that to it.'' But Tommie, Day continued, would not have it. Neither would Crain. The result, he said, was a ''real'' hound-dog man, not a ''New Yorkerized'' version.

Gipson, he continued, wrote ''erratically and with great labor. He never has 'just quite the right word' to say what he wants to say. But when the writing is done, the result is dancing poetry of pure Anglo-Saxon words which prove that lusty vitality does not need sophistication to say things beautifully.''[25]

Fischer sent a letter touting the book to various bookstores across the country. Harpers, he wrote, had had trouble getting the manuscript into type: ''First of all, the manuscript kept disappearing; some copy reader or editor, or stenographer was always carrying it off . . . . One bunch of proofs turned up in the basement, where it was being read by a messenger boy who had never before been known to look inside a Harpers book.''

Blackie Scantling, the book's central character, ''may well become a legendary American character, along with Huckleberry Finn and Jesse James and Casey Jones.'' Harpers, Fischer concluded, thought the book was ''right in the middle of the oldest and finest tradition of American storytelling.''[26]

The book was released in Dallas, and a short time later, it was obvious the gamble had been a good bet. John Woodburn reviewed the book for the *Saturday Review of Literature*. He suggested Gipson was well aware of the old publishing axiom that no book about a dog had ever been a failure. The story, he said, ''is told in a pleasant, homespun Texas drawl . . . . There are some unaffectedly lyrical passages . . . .''[27]

Orville Prescott of the *New York Times*, whom Crain said was hard to please, ''just plain loved the book.''[28] The San Antonio *Express*'s Sunday magazine ran a story on Gipson, calling him a ''tall friendly Texan who is pleased but not impressed at having hit the literary jackpot.''[29]

Gipson's old friend Bill Barnard, who had been on the *Caller-Times* staff in Corpus Christi and was now working for the Associated Press, did a story on him which got good play, especially in southwestern newspapers. Bernard called *Hound-Dog Man* ''a fine work of fiction and a triumph of reporting.'' The book was selling ''great guns,'' he said, and Gipson had already been able to afford a new refrigerator.[30]

In Dallas, Miss Elizabeth Anne McMurray of McMurray Bookshop, threw an autograph party for Gipson. ''This isn't any ordinary autographing party, though Fred will enjoy signing copies of the book for you if you want him to. Mostly it's the only way we know for a lot of old

Fred with some of his hound dogs in the early 1950's.
(Photographer unknown.)

friends and new friends and coon hunters to meet and get to know Fred Gipson,'' the invitation said.

At forty, Fred Gipson had ''arrived.'' His first novel was an overwhelming success. For the first time in his life he had some money and he was back in Mason where he could spend his free time fishing and romping with his two young sons. And there was Tommie, to whom he dedicated the book:

> The real Blackie said of her: ''She's too pretty to work. A little old girl like that, a man ought to put in a picture frame and set on his mantleboard, just to look at!''

Gipson had all a man could ask for. Or so it seemed.[31]

11

"We'll Just Have To Grow the Grass Back"

A wagonwheel-sized full moon hanging over Mason County that night would have helped. But the sky was black except for the stars. The single flashlight beam playing through the early morning darkness was of little use. Fortunately, all three men had had so much bust-head wine it did not hurt too bad when any of them tripped and fell. The woods were full of sounds, and if there had been a mist falling, it would have been a good night for a coon hunt. Occasionally, the light caught a pair of startled eyes that quickly disappeared as the men approached.

Gipson led the way through the woods along the creek. Behind him were Joe Small and a friend who was a doctor at the Veterans Administration Hospital in Kerrville. The doctor had been bothering Small for some time to take him to meet Gipson. He had read *Hound-Dog Man* like thousands of others and was anxious to meet its author. More than that, however, he wanted to meet "the real Blackie Scantling."

Gipson had graciously invited Small and the doctor to Mason, but was less than enthusiastic about disturbing the cantankerous Charlie Sanders. The trip through the woods was a direct result of the doctor's accusation that there was no real Blackie, which he said was why Gipson was stalling.

"I could take you right over here, a half mile through the woods . . . and you could meet 'Blackie' in the flesh, but he's asleep now. Been asleep since sundown," Gipson told the doctor.

The doctor persisted as the wine level in the bottle continued to drop. Finally, Gipson gave in. The stumble-walk through the woods ended at a small cabin that looked about like Gipson had described in the book. Gipson began pounding on the door. He had been right—Sanders was asleep. Eventually, Sanders came to the door, his pupils no bigger than BB shot. When he saw it was Gipson, he told them to come in.

Before they went inside, Gipson whispered a warning to his two companions: "Now, take it easy with him. Even in the early mornings, he's not in a very good mood—this time of night, he'll be in a pretty bad mood."

There were two beds inside the cabin. One was where Sanders had been sleeping; the other was for his dogs. The doctor soaked in the scene, clearly impressed. Then he rushed over to Sanders and began laughing and pounding him on his thin shoulders.

"I'm sure glad to meet you . . . . I've read so much about you . . . . I bet ol' Fred there wasn't any such person as you . . . ."

Sanders' blue eyes glared at the doctor.

Small, realizing there could be trouble any second, stepped up with the jug: "Wouldn't you like to have a little swig on this?"

"Don't mind if I do," Sanders replied, reaching for the wine. But he took more than a swig, holding the bottle to his mouth until Small and Gipson thought he might be in danger of drowning. When he finally dropped the bottle and wiped his mouth, he said, "You know, that's pretty good stuff."

The doctor resumed the barrage of compliments and then started asking questions. Sanders continued to frown and Gipson was getting uneasy. Sanders was an old family friend, but a man could be pushed too far, especially a man turned out of bed in the middle of the night by three semidrunks.

Small handed the old man the bottle for another hit. "Don't mind if I do," he said as he took another hard drink of the spiked wine. Shortly after that drag, Sanders' eyes began to open a little wider and a weak grin eased out on his face. He was waking up.

The real-life hound-dog man studied the doctor intently.

"Are you married?" Sanders asked the doctor.

"Oh, hell, yes," he slurred.

"You know, your wife sure must have wanted to go to a wedding!" Sanders blurted, springing the trap.

But by this time, the doctor had had so much of his own medicine the insult was lost on him. Gipson and Small had paced themselves and were able to help the dizzy, groaning doctor back to Gipson's house.[1]

104

In the months following publication of the novel that would not have been written had it not been for Sanders, Gipson traveled the state making promotional appearances. When he did have time to be home, he was busy with repairs and improvements funded by the income from the book. Still, he continued to peddle stories, though the payment was insignificant compared to the money *Hound-Dog Man* brought him. In February, he got a small check from *Southwest Review* for "Town of Beer and Sorrow," a story set in Ojinaga, a tiny Mexican town across from Presidio in the Big Bend of Texas.

". . . I know of no other place on earth quite so fitting for solitary beer-drinking," he had written. A man sitting in an Ojinaga cantina nursing a cold beer and staring out at the distant Chinati Mountains had a lot to think about. What had happened in those mountains over the centuries? Who had died there? Who had been born in their midst? Who had hunted on their slopes?

"Answers to such questions one does not find, even in a beer bottle. But it was over bottles of beer that I became acquainted with one Juan Hernandez Jesus Enrique Morales, who explained to me why this is now all desert country."

Morales told how the Devil brought drought, disease and misery to the people who lived on the Rio Grande. The Devil, disguised as a great owl, had even taken Morales' beloved fighting cock.

"I . . . thought of Juan and his tragic loss of a rooster—and sorrowfully turned and ordered more beer," Gipson wrote.[2]

The somber tone of the three-page story in the *Review* reflected another downturn in its author's outlook on life. *Hound-Dog Man* had been successful beyond his expectation, but now Gipson was desperately trying to come up with another book. A second novel was stillborn, though he had worked on it six months.

On September 12, Elizabeth Stover wrote Gipson that two *Southwest Review* readers had taken time to call and say "Town of Beer and Sorrow" had been the best story in the last issue: "[They] and others demand more Gipson." The letter also contained $25 for reprint rights on "My Kind of Man," which had been used in Dr. Reddick's feature-writing book. Gipson thanked her for forwarding the check, saying they always looked good to him. But the tone of his letter was as downbeat as his *Southwest Review* piece:

> Please let me get my head up again before demanding more stories. I'm within about two weeks time of finishing

another novel—I hope. Worked six months on one that wouldn't go, then had to start over and do another. And have been in rather poor health all year. So I'm pretty short right now. Doubt if anything I'd write would be worthy of appearing in the *Southwest Review*.[3]

Some writers never feel better than when their writing is going well, like a mother expecting her next child. For Gipson, though, it was always a rough "pregnancy." The danger of a literary miscarriage always haunted him, or failure of the effort if he did finish it.

The attention he was getting because of *Hound-Dog Man* was not easing the pressure, but it did sell books. *Life* magazine wanted to do a story on a backwoods writer who had suddenly hit the big time, showing Gipson on a coon hunt. Gipson agreed and promised Mike he could go along.

Gipson's nephew, D. B. Polk, who owned two coon dogs, ran two coons up an old tree that had a hollow near its top and one near the bottom. He climbed the tree and put a chunk of wood in the top hole; then, as the dogs kept the coons inside, Polk blocked the lower hole with a pointed rock.

The *Life* writer and photographer got to Mason clearly bored by the assignment and personally repulsed by the idea of two brutal dogs ripping up a poor, defenseless coon. Shortly before sundown, Polk led everyone to the tree, where the coons had been trapped for twenty-four hours and were beginning to tire of it. Tom McAvoy, the photographer, immediately began setting up his lights and camera. Gipson watched for a moment, then politely suggested that he did not think McAvoy was arranging his equipment right for this particular circumstance. But McAvoy cut him short; he had taken pictures in Russia and all over the rest of the world and knew what he was doing, he said.

Gipson shrugged and let him finish his work. Then, at McAvoy's instruction, Polk and Gipson uncovered the holes in the tree. The cameraman said he was ready, as Polk's dogs yelped for the action to begin. Quickly, Gipson yanked out one of the coons, who squalled like a mountain lion. It fought so viciously that Gipson had to flip it away in a hurry. The angry coon landed right between the *Life* staffers and tried to climb the startled McAvoy.

The photographer headed one way, and all the lighting equipment seemed to go the other way. The old boar coon whipped both dogs, bit Mike above his high-top shoes, and then turned on the photographer again.

When it was all over, photographic equipment was scattered all around the tree, the two *Life* men were off in the brush, and Gipson was doubled over in laughter. Fortunately, the second coon had stayed in the tree and was less ferocious when it emerged, so the shaken photographer was able to get some pictures.

When Mrs. Stover wrote again, on October 24, she enclosed a clipping of a Hollywood column by Sheila Graham that said *Hound-Dog Man* would likely be made into a movie. "Like you," Gipson wrote back, "I hope the squib from Sheila Graham's . . . column means what it says. However, if it does, nobody's got around to informing me of a movie sale . . . as of the present." But, he added, negotiations were under way.[4]

Crain wrote that Annie Laurie was confident a movie deal would go through and informed him $17,476.52 was in Gipson's royalty account at Harpers. He was looking forward to Gipson's next manuscript, he said, as were a lot of other people. "You have quite a few rooters scattered around."[5]

Gipson decided to call the next book *The Devil to Pay*. He was having trouble, however, shaking the idea that his second novel was not as good as *Hound-Dog Man*. But maybe it was just his long-nurtured sense of insecurity. His lack of confidence was not bolstered by the letter he got from Crain the third week in October. Crain said he and Harpers both felt *The Devil to Pay* was not a good book to follow *Hound-Dog Man*.

Harpers would probably publish it, Crain told him candidly, but it would not be smart to do so. "If you were an old man and this were your last book, no doubt they would go ahead and bring it out," he wrote. But since Gipson was not an old man and since he had money in the bank, shelving *The Devil to Pay* was Crain's recommendation. Still, Crain continued, Gipson had not produced a bad manuscript. Basically, though, it was just a long short-story, "not another square-cornered, fine grained building stone without flaw or blemish to lay on top of [*Hound-Dog Man*]."[6]

The same day that Crain wrote his reaction to Gipson's latest effort, Evan Thomas mailed what amounted to a concurring opinion: "I know you can and should be represented by a better novel as a successor to *Hound-Dog Man*." He added, however, that it "again proves your capabilities as a writer. It adds to our confidence in you and it should and MUST not lessen your confidence in yourself . . . ."[7]

Harpers did not want to scare Gipson away. The day after Thomas wrote his letter, executive editor John Fischer wrote Gipson.

He suggested laying the novel aside and proposed an idea: A book centering on the relationship of a boy and his father.[8] This idea set well with Gipson. He and his father, especially as Gipson came to be a man, had enjoyed a special kinship in their hunting and prowling and talking together. And now, with two boys of his own trailing him around, Gipson knew what his father must have felt when he and Charles were growing up.

By November, Thomas was planning a trip to Mason to discuss the plot line with Gipson. He arrived in January 1950, and was treated to a first class introduction to Texas—its people, its country and its cooking. Gipson gave him a tour of the Mason area, and when Thomas, Fred, and Tommie were not playing canasta, they were sitting around the fireplace, drinking Scotch, talking books, and sharing stories. When Thomas left, Gipson had his next novel mapped in his mind and was ready to knock it out. He had some things he wanted to say.[9]

In March, Crain forwarded $10,000 in royalties on *Hound-Dog Man* from Harpers, less his ten percent, along with word that Gipson had another fan. According to news reports, when President Truman went to Florida for a two-week vacation, he took two books to read: Gipson's *Hound-Dog Man* and Arthur Schlesinger's *The Age of Jackson*. "Afterward he told the reporters that he had thoroughly enjoyed both books," Crain wrote.[10]

Hound-Dog Man had also been read by a Texas Institute of Letters committee, which picked the novel as the 1949 winner of the McMurray Bookshop Award. With the honor came a $250 prize. But Gipson's satisfaction with the prize and the continued acclaim for *Hound-Dog Man* was watered down by his lack of progress on the book suggested by Fischer. Gipson knew what he wanted to say, but he was having a hard time getting started.

Nothing made him want to go fishing worse than sitting and looking hopelessly at the typewriter on its metal table in the southeast corner of the living room of the ranch house. As he sat and stared, he thought of all the things that needed doing. Then he would go do them. He hauled in sand for the boys' sandpile, watered the lawn, and hoed the vegetable garden. Nails that had worked out of the wood-door facing needed hammering back in, and he did that.

Next to the typewriter stand was a card table and adjacent to that was a large cardboard box, which soon would be full of paper balls—each ball representing a beginning he was not happy with. Finally, when the words did start coming right, the card table was where he put each good page. Later, Tommie used the same typewriter and began the editing and retyping process.

By early April, when the bluebonnets were in full, perfumy bloom, the assembly line had manufactured a book, *The Home Place*. A short time later, Gipson mailed Crain the first installment of the book. "I am delighted with the first chunk of book," he replied, adding, "it tastes like more."[11] Less than two weeks later, he had more. "Allowing for polishing to come . . . I am pretty well satisfied. [It] is brimming over with the special kind of charm that we Gipson fans have learned to cherish—the small boy stuff, the father and son stuff, the half-humorous, half-sentimental, salty-old-character stuff, the love of nature and of the land."[12]

When Thomas got the manuscript from Crain, the editor's comment was succinct: "I've read *The Home Place* and I like it."[13]

Thomas and Crain both realized *The Home Place* was a radical departure from *Hound-Dog Man*. Where Gipson's first novel had been something a little different—which probably entered into its difficulty in being sold—*The Home Place* was much more conventional. In no way was it a sequel.[14]

The new novel was about recently widowed Sam Crockett of Kansas City, who decided to quit his good job and take his three sons and grandfather back to the old home place in the Texas Hill Country. It had been easy for Gipson to write about coming home. The satisfaction of returning to Mason from Colorado was still fresh on his mind. Also, now that he had some money thanks to *Hound-Dog Man*, Gipson was doing in real life what he had Crockett doing in fiction: improving the land on which he had been raised.

Gipson had always been galled by man's abuse of the land. As a newspaperman, he had written columns advocating soil conservation and complaining about the messiness of oil field operations long before it was a generally accepted cause.[15] Now, he felt, there was something he could do. For one thing, Crockett could be a not-so-subtle spokesman for Gipson's philosophy: Man was taking more from the land than he was putting back. Such an arrangement would not work forever, Gipson believed, and he used Crockett to say so: "Sam could see a time coming when everybody—not just the farmers—would be paying for that robbery. Paying in droughts, in floods, in hunger and in wars."[16]

The novel spanned a one-year period and contained rich descriptions of how the land had changed during that time, as Crockett struggled to make a living off the old family farm. To keep the book from being nothing more than a fictionalized agricultural journal, Gipson worked in a romance between Crockett and the daughter of a rich adjoining landowner, with another subplot dealing with Crockett's father, Grandpa Firth.

The only delay in wrapping up the manuscript had been a bout Gipson had with the flu. When Crain had the last installment of the book, he wrote Gipson that while he was still pleased with it, it did not have "the easy flow of *Hound-Dog Man*." The important thing, Crain said, was that writing the book doubtless had added to Gipson's skill as a writer. Book writing was something that improved with experience, just like any other endeavor, he believed.[17]

On April 24, Crain wrote that Harpers was satisfied with the last installment of *The Home Place* and did not see the need for any revision of the manuscript. Book number three was behind Gipson.

Crain, meanwhile, was busy trying to sell serial rights, and Annie Laurie was still shopping for a good movie deal on *Hound-Dog Man*. She had received a $5,000 offer but had turned it down.[18] Gipson had a hard time understanding why his agent rejected a $5,000 sale. That still seemed like a lot of money to him. But Annie Laurie felt the book would eventually sell for much more and wanted to hold out for a percent of the movie's gross as well.

By June, although the *Saturday Evening Post* and *Country Gentleman* had turned down *The Home Place* for serialization, Crain remained optimistic. And he was already discussing a new book possibility: a picture book on Texas, with Gipson writing the captions to someone else's pictures.[19] Gipson, however, was not too taken with the idea.

In fact, he was not very interested in anything having to do with writing. The fast pace on *The Home Place* had exhausted him. Just looking at his typewriter made him want to cry. So he decided to give up writing for a while, at least for the summer. The family was not suffering for money for once, and there were more things he wanted to get done around his own home place.

For one thing, he wanted to add a rock-veneer back room to the house, which he only part jokingly called "The Gipson Shanty." He bought the material in Mason, and he and his brother did everything from the carpentry work to the plumbing. It felt good to do some work that did not involve sitting all day, wearing himself out trying to put good words on blank pieces of paper.[20]

When Gipson heard in July that the People's Book Club had accepted *The Home Place* for its December selection, he was excited and relieved, knowing it meant he could lay off writing awhile longer.[21] A few days later, he got a letter from Crain, filling him in on the book club deal. The club would print 100,000 copies of the book, which Crain estimated would be worth $5,000 to $6,000 to Gipson, in addition to the royalties from Harpers. An even more important aspect of the book club sale, Crain said, was the public relations value, which would increase the chances of a movie sale.[22]

By August, Gipson was nearly through with the new addition to the house and had begun kicking around another novel idea. He outlined it briefly to Crain, who sounded out Thomas on it. Neither was too interested, however. Crain wrote Gipson that he had plenty of time and should continue to meditate on the next book. Meanwhile, he added, the publication date for *The Home Place* had been set for September 27, 1950.[23]

Dean Chenoweth, editor of the San Angelo *Standard-Times*, drove to Mason to visit Gipson on September 16. Despite a not-too-amiable parting with the Harte-Hanks papers almost a decade earlier, Gipson still had a lot of friends in the chain, including Chenoweth, whose paper covered a vast hunk of West Texas and wielded considerable influence. When Chenoweth arrived, Gipson, wearing khaki pants and a white T-shirt, was doing mortar work on the rock wall of the back room he had been working on all summer. He posed for a picture with his trowel in hand and then took Chenoweth outside to show him what he planned to do with his land now that he had some money to spend on it.

There, under some brush in the front yard, was a scraggly piece of bluestem grass. When he was a boy on this same land, Gipson explained, that kind of grass used to grow so high he would sometimes have to climb a tree to spot the cows. Now that grass, and most other native varieties of West Texas, was almost extinct. Bringing back the grass was going to become his personal cause, he said.[24]

Actually, Gipson's fictional Sam Crockett had a head start on him: "Grandpa Firth shook his head . . . . 'Why, I can recollect when it [the grass] stood belly-button high, all over them hills.' 'So can I,' Sam said shortly. 'But it's gone now. Like everywhere. We'll just have to grow the grass back.' "[25]

It would be a while yet before Gipson could devote his full energies to his grass project. In the meantime, he would be content with the greening of his bank account: 20th Century Fox had bought the movie rights to *The Home Place*, and favorable reviews of the book soon were pouring in.[26] Gipson had done it again.

As part of the book's promotion, Harpers arranged a two-week autographing tour of Texas, which Gipson viewed with mixed feelings. He hated spending two weeks living out of a suitcase and eating hotel food, but then again, he enjoyed meeting people who liked his books.

The only real worry he had was the letter from Donald and Beth Day, a joint ''review'' of *The Home Place*:

> Generally speaking, you've grown up in this book. This ''Fred Gipson'' we see here is even so much more of a person and a writer that we have both taken a new lease of ''love'' on you . . . . But this book imposes (as does any good job) a terrible burden on you. Where do you go from here? You show to us a capacity for going, and by God, you've got to go.[27]

A haunting question. ''Where do you go from here?'' Gipson was not exactly sure.

that idea. When Crain got back to New York, he talked with Thomas and then reported to Gipson. Thomas, Crain wrote, "thinks you have the capacity for greatness and that any aim short of the stars is too low."[6]

All Gipson needed was a good story. He had several ideas, some suggested by Crain and Thomas, though Crain was the first to admit the final decision was Gipson's: "Still and all, you are the lad who has to write the book and it is up to you to say which you want to do next."[7]

By spring, Gipson had decided on another novel, which would become *The Way of Jesse Gentry*, something of a sequel to *Hound-Dog Man*. Crain was delighted to hear of Gipson's decision and wrote Tommie, who had briefed him on the book-to-be: "It is grand news that Fred is off on a book idea of his own that both of you believe in . . . . A book that you dream up yourself and want to do is always to be preferred to one suggested by somebody else."[8]

In May, Gipson learned that six of his old Denver *Post* stories were to be included in an anthology to be published by Doubleday called *Rocky Mountain Empire*, including his "High Lonesome Place," which had been picked up by *Reader's Digest*. Gipson was always happy to see his stories get exposure, but that was about all he would get out of the deal. Since the stories had been published while he was on the salary of the *Post*, he had no hope for a piece of the book's profits, Crain wrote.[9]

As Gipson settled into his daily writing routine for the first time in a year, 20th Century Fox was making plans for the filming of *The Home Place*, which Hollywood had decided to call *The Return of the Texan*. That irked Gipson, but he learned that there was good reason behind the decision, even if the change would not do the book sales any good. In 1947, another novel had been published under the title *The Home Place*. That embarrassing fact had not come to light until after Gipson's book appeared.[10]

By the end of July, he was finished with the first draft of *The Way of Jesse Gentry* and queried Crain about the possibility of a book on trout fishing in the Rocky Mountains.[11] He had had a taste of that when he worked for the Denver *Post*, and he could sure stand a return to that country—on expense account—to do some more fishing and turn it into a book. Thomas was not enthusiastic about the idea. Fishing books, he said, were a dime a dozen, and Gipson's expertise at trout fishing could not compare with that of other writers who had been avid fly fishermen all their lives.[12]

At the end of August, Gipson took time off to go fishing while Tommie started a two-week "glamor program" from *Good House-*

keeping magazine.[13] And in the desert around Springerville, Arizona, 20th Century Fox began shooting the exterior scenes for *Return of the Texan*, roughly a thousand miles from the home place the Texan returned to in Gipson's novel. Although Gipson and others had tried to get the shooting done in Texas, for economic reasons the producers had opted for California and Arizona.

But Gipson could not put up much of an argument about the movie's location. After all, he had been paid $27,500 for the movie rights. His name would be on the screen credits, and at least the producers had come to Mason to see what the real country looked like.

Gipson's old friends on the *Standard-Times* were giving him good publicity. Grady Hill, who had given Gipson story assignments in the late 1930's, had gone to Hollywood to do a story on the filming of the movie. Hill was introduced to the director, Delmer Daves, a friendly, graying man who had met Gipson when the crew visited Mason County in July. "...I like that guy," Daves told Hill, assuring him he was aware of the conservation message in Gipson's book. "The great sensitivity [in *The Home Place*] will be retained in the movie."[14]

The venerable Walter Brennan, who had already won three Oscars would play Grandpa Firth in the movie. When Hill talked with him on the set, Brennan was still marveling at how hot it had been when they did the exteriors in Arizona. But he was excited about his role, too. He described the part as a "once-in-a-lifetime opportunity" that had that "Oscar feel" to it. "It has everything," he said. "Humor, pathos, and a walloping death-bed scene."[15]

Producer Frank P. Rosenberg had some other big names cast in *Return of the Texan*. Sam Crockett was played by Dale Robertson, who though not a Texan was close enough by Hollywood standards—he came from Oklahoma. The co-star would be Joanne Dru, who played the rich girl Crockett fell in love with. In *The Home Place*, Gipson's Crockett had three sons, but in the movie version, the family was cut to two boys, played by Lonnie Thomas, six, and Dennis Ross, eight.

Gipson finished his new book during the filming, and the manuscript was on its way to New York on October 9. He was pleased with it and confident it was as good as *Hound-Dog Man*, if not better. The letter from Crain a few days later came as a stunning surprise: "If somebody or other hadn't written a mighty good novel about a hound-dog man who lived in the Texas Hill Country, I wouldn't have any misgivings about selling *The Way of Jesse Gentry*." The book, Crain said, was more like a continuation of *Hound-Dog Man* than a sequel. A good piece of writing but not Fred Gipson-good.[16]

Soon, a letter from Thomas arrived. He, too, said he did not like *The Way of Jesse Gentry* and once again suggested an historical novel. "I feel an awful s.o.b. in writing a letter like this to a friend and one who has more creative skill and savvy than five generations of Thomases could have if each one spent fifty years in the editorial-middleman business," Thomas wrote.[17]

Tommie replied to Thomas five days later:

Dear Evan:

Well, it was a sad affair, but we buried Jesse Gentry yesterday. He was a good man, Jesse, with all his faults—and it was with heavy hearts that we laid him to rest. But we realize that the Lord giveth and the Lord taketh away and if providence in His wisdom has seen fit to lay a hand on Jesse, then the least we can do is give him a decent burial. Seriously, we were a little rocked back on our heels at the rejection but we fully respect yours and John's [Fischer's] opinion, so now we dust ourselves off and get to work on something else.[18]

An offer from Frank Wardlaw, the director of the University of Texas Press, whom Gipson had met in Corpus Christi in 1950, came at just the right time to fill the void left by the "passing" of Jesse Gentry, Tommie added.

Wardlaw had received a manuscript at the UT Press by J. O. Langford, who had homesteaded in the Big Bend country. Langford had been encouraged to write his reminiscences by Henry B. Du Pont, who had met the old man on a fishing and picture taking visit to the Big Bend and has been fascinated by his stories. Wardlaw, though interested in the material, considered it unusable as it was.

Du Pont called him and asked what could be done to get the book published. "Find a writer who can rewrite it and who can also draw out the things that can bring it to life," Wardlaw said. "All right, get one," Du Pont replied. "I'll pay whatever it costs."[19]

Wardlaw asked Gipson if he would be interested in the job for a flat fee of $2,000.[20] The idea appealed to Gipson, who had fallen in love with the Big Bend back when he was a newspaperman, but he wanted to meet Langford and read the manuscript first. After he had done that, Gipson agreed to take on the job. The project would not take long and would do for "wages" between novels.

The work was not quite as easy as he had thought it would be. Langford, though a true gentleman, had grown a bit cantankerous with age and wanted to keep the story word-for-word as he had written it instead of giving Gipson a free hand. Gipson got so angry he dropped the project. Trouble was, he had already spent the $2,000. Tommie took Langford's manuscript and did a couple of chapters herself, trying to imitate her husband's style. He read what she had done, redid it, and moved on to complete the job.

Wardlaw was delighted with the finished manuscript, though Gipson felt he could have done better. The book, *Big Bend: A Homesteader's Story*, received good reviews when it came out in 1952. Clifford Casey, of Sul Ross State College, critiquing the book for the *Texas Historical Quarterly* called it, "a beautiful little book from the front cover to the back end papers."[21]

In the meantime, Fred and Tommie, who more and more was his literary co-planner, continued to shift around in search of another book that would suit Harpers. They toyed with an idea for a Civil War book, but as Tommie wrote Thomas, ". . . we won't exclude any ideas that pop up."[22]

Crain was still worried the rejection of *The Way of Jesse Gentry* had had a serious effect on Gipson, though he was no less firm in his advice against the novel. Publishers, he said, were growing ever more conscious of economics. Novels were not making anyone much money, he said, suggesting Gipson might spend more time on magazine writing.[23]

Gipson had been trying to sell some magazine stories but with little success. He had one yarn, "Bad Day," that had been knocking around since the previous September. One publisher sent it back, commenting that it was not "top Gipson."[24] Finally, in February 1952, Gipson sent it to Allen Maxwell at the *Southwest Review*. Maxwell's reply on February 7 offered Gipson support for his drooping confidence: ". . . 'Bad Day' may be off-trail to some but strikes us as right on the beam. It's enlivened throughout with the good old Gipson touch—or touches—and adds up to an authentic and prime piece of Texana." The words of encouragement were about all the sale netted Gipson. The payment was only $40.

Despite his work on the Big Bend book, Gipson was in the midst of a literary drought. The only genuinely good news to come so far in 1952 was the completion of the movie based on *The Home Place*, which was due to premier soon.

One night in Austin, Gipson was drinking beer with Joe Small and writer Curt Bishop in one of the local watering holes. "Fred, where are they going to premier *Return of the Texan?*" Small asked.

Gipson looked down into his beer.

"Oh, I don't know. Some big place."

"Why don't you get them to do it here?" Small began. "One time why don't you convince them that an author is about as important to a story on the whole as an actor?"

Gipson and Bishop laughed. "Well, that shows how much you know about Hollywood. I'll appoint you a committee of one to see that this gets a world premier here," Gipson said.[25]

Neither Gipson nor Bishop thought there was any chance at all. With the exception of the visit by some of the Fox people to Mason the previous summer, Gipson had had virtually no connection with the filming of his book. But Small took the idea of a premier as a challenge. The next day, he started making telephone calls and writing letters. His conversation of the night before had not been idle beer talk.

A few days later, the manager of the Paramount Theatre in Austin called Small. "What do you want us to do?" he asked.

At first Small did not realize what the man was talking about. The manager explained: "We just heard from Dallas to cooperate with you in every way to have a world premier here in Austin."[26]

Small, a fair poker player who knew something about running a bluff, suddenly found himself involved in the planning of a world premier—as if that were something he knew how to do. He called in help, including Ruth Hunnicutt, a West Texas woman, who was working at the University's Radio House. Together, and with other Gipson friends, they started making plans.

In late February, Gipson got a letter from Small containing a memo headed "Return of Fred Gipson," which would have done credit to a political candidate's advance man. It contained Gipson's hour-by-hour itinerary for the day of the premier.

Landing the premier in Austin was a perfect coup, another much needed boost from Small, who was becoming almost like a brother to Gipson. Gipson visited him regularly in Austin, and when they were apart, they wrote letters. They reasoned that the publicity fallout from the movie's star, Dale Robertson, a currently popular actor, would be invaluable to Gipson.

The morning of the premier, Fox Movietone newsreel cameras were grinding away as the bobby-sock set at UT swooned over Robertson. The Texas Cowboys, a campus service organization, presented Gipson with a hound dog pup and a new hat. Mike and Beck had arrived at the campus on a fire truck with members of the cast. Robertson had ridden horseback from the Co-op on Guadalupe Street up the West Mall to the Main Building amid one of the biggest crowds ever gathered on the UT campus for something other than a panty raid or Oklahoma game pep rally.[27]

The hoopla was almost too much for Gipson, though he certainly realized its value. At one point, he pulled Small near him: "Hey Joe, I don't know where we're going or what we're doing . . . take me by the hand and lead me, will you?" That night, Gipson and Small got thoroughly drunk.[28]

The sober reality, though, was that Gipson was going to have to write again if he wanted there to be another world premier of a movie based on his work. The next project he had in mind, however, probably would not appeal to the moviemakers.

For years, he had known of an interesting old cowboy at Ozona, about eighty miles from San Angelo. He was no Hollywood cowboy. He was just a hard-working old boy who, though he had never shot up a saloon or faced a hanging for something he had not done, knew which end of the cow got up first. Gipson had learned long ago the difference between the cowboy of truth and the cowboy of fiction, and he believed the reading public would like to see the story of a real cowboy. The best candidate he could think of was Ed (Fat) Alford.

Gipson proposed the biography to Thomas, ". . . since I still seem baffled as to what to try next in the fiction line."[29] After some consideration, Thomas gave Gipson a green light on the idea.[30]

Alford could tell a story almost as well as Gipson. The only problem was in getting the old cowboy penned long enough to start talking and reach a financial agreement satisfactory to both of them. After a little "horse trading," a skill neither man lacked, they agreed Gipson would get the first $2,000 in royalties on the book, with eighty percent of the proceeds thereafter going to Gipson, twenty percent to Alford.[31]

Even after the money agreement was reached, Gipson still had a difficult time getting together with Alford. Tommie wrote Thomas at Harpers: "We keep not writing because there keeps on being nothing to write about. Most frustrating . . . . Right now Fred is in Dallas working on a possible *Reader's Digest* story on a research foundation somewhere around there. But when he gets back, he is going to make one more try at getting Ed corraled. If that fails, we'll just forget about that one."

If the Alford book did fizzle, she continued, her husband had seveal other ideas . . . a nature book for ten- to fourteen-year-olds, or maybe a novel that would be a thinly veiled account of his childhood on the home place. "There may be another idea or so that Fred liked, but these two are the ones that I seem to remember out of all the ones we've discussed and gnawed on lately," Tommie wrote.[32]

Gipson took a break in late May to go to Corpus Christi for the annual Southwest Writers Conference, billed as the second largest writers conference in the country. Gipson was on the lecture panel, along with J. Frank Dobie, Boyce House, Fritz and Emilie Toepperwein, Garland Roark, and others.[33] Gipson never needed much of an excuse to go to Corpus Christi, where he still had a lot of old friends from his newspaper days.

The purpose of the conference had been to help aspiring writers, but when he got back to Mason, Gipson found himself struggling like a rookie wordsmith with the research foundation story for the *Reader's Digest*. It worried Tommie, who wrote Charles Ferguson, one of the senior editors on the *Digest* and a long-time admirer of Gipson's work. She said Gipson was having trouble with the story and suggested Ferguson consider putting him on the payroll as a roving editor, the same sort of deal Donald Day had developed several years before.[34]

When Ferguson finally got the research foundation story a few weeks later, he liked it—heartening news to its author. There were only a few questions, and it looked like Gipson was going to hit the big-paying *Digest* again.[35]

Despite his worry about the worsening Texas drought, which considerably affected his grass-seeding plans, Gipson was keeping the Alford book on track. He had had several long interviews with the cowboy, using a wire recorder for the first time in his career, although he still found taking notes more comfortable.

In late August, Gipson got a letter from Ferguson. Incredibly, the *Digest* had decided against running the research foundation piece. Ferguson offered some suggestions on where else it might be sold and said he was sorry.[36]

On August 30, Gipson mailed Ferguson another story he had been working on, "Wild Cow Hunter." He remarked that Ferguson's suggestions on where to place the research foundation story was the first time an editor had tried to help sell a story he would not buy himself.

Within a month, Gipson had the Alford book pretty well wrapped up. Just about the time Gipson got the manuscript off to Harpers, Ferguson turned down "Wild Cow Hunter." Frustration turned to anger. Gipson banged out a reply to Ferguson: "The bald fact is . . . I just can't afford to write for *Reader's Digest*. No matter how much I might want to, I can't do it and eat."

He had spent eight weeks on the two rejected stories, in consideration of only a $300 "kill fee." He knew of at least six other potential *Digest* stories, but by the time he got one of those published, he would be "in the hole," he wrote.

"I wanted so badly to write for the *Digest* that I was willing to gamble for a while," he continued. "Well, now I no longer have the cash to gamble on. I've got to go back to writing the stuff that will pay off." The letter was beginning to sound piteous. ". . . I've written an occasional piece for the *Digest* for years and I think you'll agree that most of them were outstanding."[37]

Gipson's letter netted an answer from Ferguson to Tommie's earlier suggestion that he be put on salary by the *Digest*. Ferguson said he did not believe the prospect of usable stories was favorable enough to hire Gipson as a roving editor.[38]

Meanwhile, Gipson had tied together some of his old stories under the working title of *Uncle Vesper*. In the book, Vesper hired a boy away from the cotton patch one summer and spent a day telling him tall tales. Thomas had approved the idea in July, and Gipson mailed the first sixty pages within three weeks.[39]

The bad news continued and the drought worsened. On October 28, Thomas turned down *Uncle Vesper*. Tommie saw her husband growing gloomier. The well on their place was in danger of going dry if the drought did not break. So, it seemed to Gipson, was his talent as a writer. His land needed rain; he needed success.[40]

13

"You May Someday Come Up With Something Great"

By early 1953, Texas was suffering its worst drought since the Dust Bowl days of the mid-1930's, a period old-timers remembered with horror. Springs that had flowed forever quit. Stock tanks turned to smelly little pools or disappeared altogether. Crops went to hell and the grass—what little anyone had—died. Even ancient oaks, veterans of many major battles with dryness, gave up, dropped their leaves, and began to crumble.

Spring in Texas usually meant climatic warfare as cold fronts continued to charge into the state like a steady wave of shock troops to tangle with the moisture-laden warm air that drifted up from the Gulf of Mexico. The result was usually violent. Texans tried to take the hail, high winds, or tornadoes in stride, knowing they needed the rain and figuring nothing came for free.

But this spring, the rain was teasingly sparse—as was Gipson's income. People in Mason County presumed he was rich, having sold two novels, a movie, numerous magazine stories, and three non-fiction books. They were wrong. Most of the money had been sunk into the land, an investment that had yet to pay a tangible dividend. The only return had been the satisfaction of ownership.

Tommie, for the first time since World War II, was looking for work. For Gipson, there were a few tantalizing developments that in the end were no more promising than dry "heat lightning" at night.

That January, John Fischer had been promoted to editor of *Harper's* magazine, and Evan Thomas was named managing editor for trade books at Harper Brothers Publishers. Crain told the Gipsons that Thomas was thinking about two of Gipson's earlier novels—the once rejected *The Way of Jesse Gentry* and a book he had co-written in the late 1940's with John Latham—as paperback issues. The paperback book market was beginning to look like a potentially lucrative new trend in publishing, he said. The books could be sold for less than a dollar and, therefore, would go to a larger reading audience, he added.[1]

That notion was fine with Gipson. But in March, Harpers turned down the two books again. Worse than that, the advance on the Alford biography was dropped to $1,000, though Thomas had said he was satisfied with the book. Thomas suggested some minor editing changes and said Harpers would bring out the biography in the fall.[2] Gipson spent most of the dry spring making the revisions on the book. He tracked down Alford to read the galley proofs, but the old cowboy said he was not interested.

"Hell, you're writing this book. Say whatever you want to," Alford told Gipson.[3]

That summer, the land heated the instant the sun rose above the horizon. In the late afternoon when a cooling breeze could usually be expected, the air from the south was like a blast of air from a wood heater. Even at night, the temperature often did not drop below 80 degrees. Gipson began to long for the cool high country of the Rockies he remembered from his Denver *Post* days. There a man could pull trout out of snow-fed streams and enjoy air that was not full of dirt blown down from the Panhandle.

Despite the literary and climatic drought, life was growing: Tommie was pregnant again. Another kind of birth also was being discussed. The Smalls had come to see Tommie, and as usual, Joe and Fred had had long talks and long pulls on the bottle. One of the things they talked about was Small's plan to start a magazine to be called *True West*. Like J. Marvin Hunter's *Frontier Times*, it would be a pulp magazine devoted to non-fiction western stories. The two friends had dreamed about such a magazine for years.

"Fred, your name on *True West* would do us a lot of good. What about your editing it?" Small asked.

"Can we do it with me in Mason and you in Austin?" Gipson asked.

Small said he did not see why not.

"What can you afford to pay?"

They agreed on a monthly stipend of $100, an amount Gipson said would give him real stability for a change. A hundred dollars was a basic living; added to occasional book advances and royalty payments, it could even become a good living.[4]

Now, all Small needed was the money to get the magazine started. Back in Austin, he finally scraped up $7,300—much of it borrowed. The first issue of *True West* appeared in August 1953. Small and his wife, Elizabeth, handled the layout, advertising, circulation work, and most of the correspondence. Gipson edited the stories, sometimes virtually rewriting them, and mailed them back to Small. He wrote some stories outright for the magazine.

Cowhand, Gipson's biography of Alford, was published in September, with good reviews, if modest sales. The reading public was apparently more interested in the cowboy of legend than the cowboy of reality. Elmer Kelton reviewed the book for the San Angelo newspaper: "Gipson's book is one that will put a broad grin across the face of any West Texan who has ever lived and worked on a ranch or around ranch people. Mostly, it is humorous, crammed with chuckles and liberally sprinkled with belly laughs."[5]

The book was entertaining and written with entertainment in mind for the most part, but it did dwell on an irony: Although Alford had worked cattle, dug post holes, and climbed windmills most of his life, he had always done so for someone else. Like Gipson, in a way, he had not accumulated much of his own, except a lot of memories, good and bad. Also like Gipson, Alford had finally got himself a ranch—five sections in the New Mexico high country near the Arizona border. Alford would have liked more land, but it was a start. "And one foot in the stirrup is all an experienced cowhand ever ask of a bronc he's fixing to step across," as Gipson said in the book.[6]

Gipson's feelings of frustration were helped by the continuing inability to get the movie rights for *Hound-Dog Man* sold. On April 3, 1952, following the success of *The Return of the Texan*, Ida Lupino and Collier Young had taken an option on his first novel.[7] But now, more than a year later, the deal was still hanging fire.

At least Annie Laurie Williams had managed to get $800 from the Columbia Broadcasting System for one-time television rights to "My Kind of Man." The contract was signed June 30, 1953.[8] A television play based on the story was aired at 10:00 P.M., the following September 24, on CBS.

By early fall, *Cowhand* had sold 5,500 copies at $2.95 each, and condensation rights had been sold for $1,200. Harpers agreed to a $1,500 advance on a travel book that Gipson had proposed in July and okayed another biography—the story of the Lee brothers (Clell, Dale, and Ernest) of Tucson, Arizona, renowned mountain-lion hunters.

Despite copious correspondence, Gipson could never reach an agreement with the Lee brothers. Instead, he turned to a tale he had picked up years before when he worked for the Corpus Christi newspaper. Mike and Beck had enjoyed hearing him tell the story of a rooster, taken along in the chuck wagon on a trail drive, who had been befriended by the cowboys and saved from becoming a chicken dinner. When Gipson first heard the story of the trail-driving rooster from an old-timer in 1938, he had made a column out of it. Now he believed it would make a good children's book.

Gipson explained in the short foreword to his book, which was only eighty pages long, "I've added parts of tales told to me by other old-time trail drivers, most of them gone now . . . . For taking such liberties, I make no apologies. When you have two sons who demand more story detail than you can supply without 'stretching the blanket' a bit, then you stretch the blanket."[9]

As Gipson was wrapping up *Trail-Driving Rooster*, Crain reported that Avon Book Publishers would take *Trouble in the Hills*, the book co-written with Latham, if he made some revisions.[10] The idea did not appeal to Gipson, but he needed the money and decided to rework the manuscript, though a revision would be a lot of trouble.

On October 22, Harpers sent him a contract for the travel book,[11] followed shortly by the advance and another $1,500 for a paperback version of *Cowhand*. It was a sign of better times—a little literary shower to wet down the dust of drought.

Three days later Tommie lost the baby. They named her Martha Wynn, after Tommie's mother, and buried her in the old Gooch Cemetery beside her grandfather, Beck Gipson. For more than a week after the miscarriage, Tommie's condition was unstable, but by November 2, she was out of danger.[12]

The brightest spot in this dry, tragic year was the reception *Trail-Driving Rooster* got at Harpers. Crain himself crowed about it in a letter to Gipson on November 9:

> *Trail-Driving Rooster* has kicked up more of a shindy down at Harpers than anything you have shown them since *Hound-Dog Man*.
>
> Ursula Norstrom [Harper's juvenile editor] says you were obviously endowed by the Good Lord with whatever combination of talents it takes to write for kids, that you ought to have been doing it long ago.

I am happier about this than I would be about selling a novel, because I think the thing will pay off in itself . . . you have hit on a kind of writing you can do better than almost anybody currently practicing the art, and do it with somewhat less bleeding at the pores than is the case with your other kinds of books.

Crain's letter had a soothing effect on Gipson, like cold sweet milk on a burning stomach. His income all year had been modest and in pulses. All he could count on were the bills.

By March 1954, revision on *Trail-Driving Rooster*—including some toning down of material to get the book past children's librarians—was completed. Gipson was working on another project, a second try at a novel based on some of his earlier short stories. Gipson was getting so good at his craft that anyone reading the manuscript for *Recollection Creek* would have thought it had been written as a whole. After Harpers accepted the book in May,[13] Fred and Tommie started making plans for a western trip in the summer to collect material for the travel book that Harpers had agreed to.

The trip through the western half of the United States was something Gipson was anxious to do, and on Friday, June 18, the Gipsons pulled away from the home place in a green Studebaker loaded down with outdoor gear and fishing equipment. Tommie was at the wheel and would drive the whole trip so that Gipson could concentrate on watching the landscape and making notes for the book. Mike, thirteen, and Beck, eight, who had had to polish their boots before leaving, sat in the back.

The car rode low as Tommie headed down the dirt road for the highway to San Angelo. The family had somehow managed to pack camping equipment for both desert and cold mountain country, and dress clothing for social visits in the two types of climate. A rack on top of the car held the camping supplies; the luggage and Gipson's typewriter were in trunk.

Gipson had one last thought as they drove off from their dry farm. He hoped the hell it would rain while he was gone.

The Gipsons were embarking on a two-month trip that would cover eight thousand miles, a lengthy journey for a man who had been ten years old before he had ever left Mason County. The boys, not much accustomed to sitting still, were cramped, restless, and cranky by the time the Gipsons reached the Wynn's house in San Angelo, where they spent their first night.

Left to right: Fred, Mike, Beck, and Tommie in the early 1950's. (Courtesy Beck Gipson.)

Only a couple of stops on the trip had been preplanned: a pack trip near Pinedale, Wyoming, and a visit to a dude ranch owned by a friend of Joe Small. Otherwise, the Gipsons would stop and go where they wanted. Gipson wrote in the mornings and they traveled in the afternoons.

From San Angelo, they drove through the country Gipson had traveled so much as a reporter for Harte-Hanks—San Angelo to Fort Stockton, Alpine, the Big Bend, then to Carlsbad Caverns. By the time they reached the big cave, Tommie and Fred were grateful for the spaciousness of the famous cavern. The boys were packed so tightly in the back seat that they could not lie down to rest without facing each other and intricately arranging their limbs.

To keep their children's sheer energy from blowing up the car, Fred and Tommie played word games with them and had them on the lookout for Texas license plates now that they were out of state. At one point, an exasperated Gipson threatened to put a halter on each boy and make them run behind the car.

They began passing billboards advertising the movie, "Sadie Thompson." Tommie looked into the rearview mirror and saw Mike looking at her quizzically.

"Mother, who is Sadie Thompson?" he asked.

"She was a prostitute who brought about the downfall of a minister," Tommie answered.

Mike looked annoyed with himself for a moment. "Mother, I know you've told me, but I've forgotten. What's a prostitute?"

Beck was beginning to get interested in the conversation. He did not know what a prostitute was, either. Tommie tried to answer Mike's question as simply as possible, since Beck had not yet had the "facts of life" lecture.

"Well," she began, "a prostitute is a woman who sleeps with men for money."

Beck's blue eyes doubled in size. "Go—olly!" he said. "Which one gets the money?"[14]

The family visited the Grand Canyon, then doubled back through Arizona to Santa Fe, New Mexico, and Durango, Colorado, where they had lived during Gipson's stint with the Denver *Post*. In Salt Lake City, they swam in the Great Salt Lake and took a guided tour of the Morman Tabernacle. For Tommie, each stop meant washing underwear and socks, plus complicated packing and unpacking.

From Utah, the Gipsons headed into the high country toward Wyoming. Seeing the new country was immensely enjoyable; the tourist traps along the way were not. Gipson realized that a tourist was just a tourist. No longer was a traveler put up without question by strangers and treated as a neighbor: He was now considered a commodity.

Gipson was doing a lot of introspective thinking on the trip. He felt a gut-level lure to the remote places, almost as if he were part of them. He was beginning to think that only in an area of primitive isolation did life have any real meaning. At forty-six, he was having serious thoughts about the meaning of it all and nagging doubts about himself.

He poured out his feelings to Tommie and to the typewriter. "It is fairly obvious that the man of 46 who is still floundering, still blindly groping for the answers, is no longer very likely to find them anywhere.

"But when did reason and common sense have anything to do with emotion? For me, the wild places are like whiskey to an alcoholic, I'm forever being hounded by the craving to seek out and explore them. I'm also forever being frustrated by my inability to obtain the money and time necessary for such . . . ."[15]

For ten days, Gipson found that remoteness he craved in the Wind River Mountains. He was at harmony with himself and away from almost any sign of civilization. It was just he, Tommie, and the boys, a guide, and a couple of other groups alone in the wild mountains—no traffic, no dishonest people, no real evidence of land abuse, no pretensions.

There was time, too, for reflection about Mike, a source of pride and worry. All of the campers had caught trout, but it was thirteen-year-old Mike who landed the biggest, which left Gipson basking in the glow of fatherly pride. What worried Gipson was that he felt his son was a bit too much like him.

Most fathers want their sons to be in their image, but Mike, Gipson feared, was "too sensitive, too proud, too stubborn, too fearful of criticism and defeat, too inclined to beat his head against the same solid walls that anybody else would go around." That set Mike apart, making him all too aware of his fancied inadequacies and aloneness. "Having grown up that way," Gipson wrote in his daily manuscript-diary, "I understand all too well the frustration and hurt that he brings upon himself. Yet, for the same reason, I'm not able to be of much help to him."[16]

After touring Yellowstone National Park, the Gipsons headed west toward Portland, Oregon. From Oregon, they drove south through the giant redwoods of northern California. The brakes on the Studebaker started smoking as Tommie nervously negotiated the winding, steep road and tried to keep from getting run over by the speeding logging trucks. Finally beginning to cry from the strain, she pulled off the highway to rest a while and take a closer look at the huge trees. To get a better feel for the immensity of the centuries-old redwoods, Tommie and Fred and the boys lay down on a bed of pine needles to look straight up into the towering timber. After several minutes of absorbing the tree's beauty, Tommie was able to proceed.

They hit Eureka, California, about 10:00 A.M. The mountain driving had bothered Tommie, and now in city traffic, she was getting edgy again. She stopped for a red light next to a big truck. When the light changed, the truck moved out fast, blocking Tommie's view of the opposite lane of traffic. Unfortunately, the truck also blocked the view of a driver making a left turn from the northbound lane.

Gipson saw the car careening toward them. "Well, here it comes!" he had time to shout seconds before the impact, which scattered the contents of their cardboard storage box and jostled them. Miraculously, the only injury was to a fender, which was bent inward blocking the left front wheel. They had to have the car towed away to a repair shop. Though the car was insured, Gipson went ahead and paid for the body work with cash to save time.[17]

He had started out with $1,700, but that amount was dwindling rapidly. So was Gipson's enthusiasm for the trip. He was getting numb from travel and had no use for California other than as a place to sell his books to movie companies. There were too many people and most of them were on the hustle.

By the time they got to Tuscon, Arizona, the Gipsons had only $50 left, and another sixteen hundred miles to go. Broke and bone-tired, they arrived in Mason in mid-August, eight thousand miles of the West behind them and a manuscript nearly completed. The trip, despite its cost and headaches, had been educational for the boys and had had its good points. As Gipson remembered Mason County judge Marcus Grant saying, "You don't live but once, and if you don't go about it just right, that isn't often enough."[18]

Gipson had one more big trip he wanted to make: a journey to Africa. "Some day," he told Tommie and the boys, "we're going to Africa before I'm too old and before man's destroyed all the wildlife. I want to see the lions and elephants and rhinos and alligators and giraffes and gazelles and things."

Beck reminded his father that he could see all those things in the zoo at San Antonio. "It's not the same," Gipson countered. "They are caged and subdued there, with all the heart taken out of them. I know too well what that's like."[19]

The conversation, which he included in his manuscript, evolved into another glimpse inside Gipson's mind. Tommie asked if he felt caged, like the animals. Most of the time he did, he said. That was because he did not really fit in with the rest of the herd. Maybe, Tommie suggested, that was because he fought the rest of the herd too hard.

Maybe I have to fight it to exist, or rather, fight against its fool laws that don't fit nature. The law says, "Be meek, be kind, be gentle," but when you try it, the whole herd steps in your face, hurrying past to pay tribute to the arrogant, the cruel and the selfish, because he's the boy who wins. He's got the money, the power, the rich estates, the fine whiskeys, the beautiful women. He's bound to be somebody.[20]

Were those the things he really wanted, Tommie asked. Yes, he could have used a little more of those things, he said. He was beginning to feel a sense of loss: He had never gone to Africa, tracked down a killer jaguar, harpooned a whale, been a war hero, or visited the South Pole to watch the penguins. And he was afraid it might be too late to ever do those things.

That fall, Harpers was busy printing *Trail-Driving Rooster* and *Recollection Creek*, while Gipson finished his travel book, which he dubbed *The Road Leads West*. He sent the manuscript to New York by mid-November. For the first time since their marriage, Gipson had fought off Tommie's suggestions on a book. She thought *The Road Leads West* was ill-humored and, if anything, would discourage travel. But since she could not sway her husband, she hoped that Thomas could talk him into reworking the book into something fun to read.

Thomas did not like the book and did not mince words in saying so. Tommie had counseled rewriting; Thomas did not even recommend that. *The Road Leads West*, Thomas began, "just will not do . . . . The best thing to do with this manuscript is bury it."[21] A bull horn thrust into his mid-section would not have hurt as bad as that letter. Gipson looked on the book as a vehicle to say some things about himself and modern times. Now, not only were those things going to be left unsaid in print, but he was going to have to explain why his half year of effort had gone sour, just as most of the year had.

Thomas thought Gipson had reached a turning point:

The time has come for you to do one really big job of work. Dig out a piece of history of your own country and your own people and give it to us with all the skill and courage and sense of permanence and dignity of man on this earth that you are capable of.[22]

Gipson looked on the response from Thomas as a rejection, and this time, it made him mad. His working relationship with Harpers was in jeopardy—everything was in jeopardy. Crain tried to do his soothing work again. No need to worry about repaying the advance, he said. The contract would be torn up and the money applied to some future project. The whole venture, Crain suggested, should be looked on as a nice paid vacation. Harpers probably could have published the book, he said, but it was too full of Gipson's bitterness. It would have done nothing to further its author's career.[23]

For a month and a half, Gipson stewed over the rejection. He did not write Thomas, and his only correspondence from Harpers were ten author's copies of *Recollection Creek* and a letter from Ursula Norstrom asking a few eleventh-hour questions on *Trail-Driving Rooster* for galley changes.

In late 1954, the *Houston Post* was planning a special edition on Texas and asked Gipson to write something on Texas talk. Gipson was happy to do it, because it gave him a chance to cut loose with both barrels at those critical of the way Texans talked—or wrote.

One reviewer of *Cowhand*, Gipson wrote, had called his language, " 'Texanese,' and let on that the words I used were the off-brand sort a man ought to feel ashamed to be caught out in polite company with." But Gipson was not ashamed of his way of talking: "Texan is a soft, slow, easy-going sort of talk, not quite so flowery and pretty-sounding maybe as Spanish, but mighty easy on the ear. A man can sure be comfortable with it."

His late friend Laughing Jim, Gipson continued, could use the language better than anyone he had ever heard. Jim had never "been exposed to enough book learning to spoil his speech. He talked just like he wanted to and always to the point." An example of this, Gipson added, came when Jim was on trial after "a little difficulty" that had been settled "in a cutting scrape."

Testimony in the trial was not jibing, with lawyers for both sides clouding the issues with legal jargon. The judge, impatient after two days of trying to make out what was going on, finally called Jim to the stand to tell in his own words what had happened:

Well, Jedge, there wasn't really nothing much to it. This here bird drawed his sticker and reached for the back of my neck with it. This makes me mad, and I outs with mine and

133

steps inside his reach. Slips the blade into his flank and takened a walk around him. Cuts him till he quits hollering, then lets him fall. And I swear to God, Jedge, this was every little thing that takened place between us.[24]

Recollection Creek received good reviews, and Gipson finally revived his correspondence with Thomas. The fiction market was considered to be in a slump, but Gipson's new books were selling well. By the first of March, *Recollection Creek* had sold 5,634 copies.[25] By summer, total sales had increased by just shy of 2,000 copies, and *Trail-Driving Rooster* had sold 7,512 copies. *Hound-Dog Man* was still selling, with the total number of sales at 26,900.[26]

Though the sales of his first novel remained steady, efforts to sell the book to a movie studio continued with a frustrating lack of success. Fred and Tommie, and his movie agent, Annie Laurie, believed the sale of movie rights to *Hound-Dog Man* would be a real bonanza. *Hound-Dog Man* was his best book, Gipson felt, and a movie based on it—if handled the right way—would be a blockbuster, financially and cinematically. Initially, Annie Laurie had tried to get $100,000 for the *Hound-Dog Man* rights.[27] But for five years now, despite some offers that looked good for a time, *Hound-Dog Man* remained a ''property'' still in search of the right producer willing to pay the right price.

In January 1955, Gipson received a call from Jim Campbell, who had been in Houston visiting his mother. On his way back to California, he stopped in Mason. Campbell was a television salesman and distributor and had ambitions of being a producer. They visited again when Gipson was in Houston for an autograph party, and that summer, Campbell brought director Stu Heisler by to meet Gipson.

Campbell said the two men wanted to start producing Gipson's material for television, a fast-growing market. Gipson had continued writing short stories to supplement his book royalties. Most of those stories, they believed, were well suited for television productions. One script they read, ''Brush Roper,'' which had been accepted for publication by *The Progressive Farmer*, might even make a good weekly series. Television exposure of Gipson's material also might help in selling the *Hound-Dog Man* movie rights—something they hoped to be involved in as producers.[28]

Rights to ''Brush Roper'' were sold to the Hal Roach studios. Heisler would be the director for a television drama based on the story with the screen version to be written by Gipson. Walter Brennan, who had starred in *Return of the Texan*, was cast in the leading role, along with a young actor, Chuck Connors. Other members of the cast were Edgar Buchanan and Olive Carey.[29]

Gipson went to Hollywood to be a screenwriter. Well within three weeks, he was desperate for some Texas company. He called Joe Small and pleaded with him to come to California: "I sure need somebody to talk to."

The screenplay was finished and filming began on the show. Gipson and Small went to the sound stage to watch some of the action. When the two Texans walked into the big studio, Heisler was directing a scene in which a tree that a horse had crashed into was supposed to fall.

"No, cut!" he shouted. "You've got to look down here." At that moment, he saw Gipson and Small and gave up for the time being. As the three shook hands, Connors sneaked up to Gipson and caught him around the neck.

"So, you're the SOB that's caused all this trouble," he laughed. Brennan joined them as he launched into a slightly off-colored joke and everyone roared. Small thought the veteran actor was more entertaining off-screen than on if that was possible.

When the shooting resumed, Brennan was astraddle a "bronc" on a wooden sleigh pulled by a pickup truck. Taking in the top view, the camera made it look like Brennan was on a runaway horse.

"Can't I call him a sonofabitch just one time?" Brennan asked Heisler, hoping to inject some realism into the scene. "Well, go ahead and say it, but say it low," the director said. "Just go through the motions."[30]

The National Broadcasting Company aired the show at 8:00 P.M. on November 24. As the Gipsons watched the televised version of his story, Gipson squirmed at a scene in which a horse trotted along behind a Brahman bull that Grandpa (Brennan) had just roped. The horse, Gipson and any other real cowboy knew, should have squatted and pulled back. He told Tommie he hoped no intelligent roping horse was tuning in on the show.[31] But *Variety* gave it a good review: " ' Brush Roper' again proves . . . that the magic ingredients of video success are a good story, effective acting and solid directions."[32]

Gipson, however, was beginning to feel there was little connection between Hollywood and the rest of the world, especially his world. The wheeling and dealing was constant and confusing, even for a man who was the son of a respected mule trader. Being an informal Texan in that environment was part of the problem. Gipson was much more comfortable at home, and if not at home, at least with friends.

The camaraderie is what kept him going back every year to the writer's conference in Corpus Christi where, though he was expected to hold forth to aspiring writers, he got time for drinking and visiting with old friends. Writers from New York to California paid $25 to attend the 1955 Southwest Writers Conference to listen to Gipson and others.

"Every time I start to talk, I get in the awfullest messes," Gipson said at one of his sessions. "I begin to speak and think I know where I am going, and pretty soon find myself out on a limb. Then I think it's time to sit down. I seem to find myself in that position now, so I think I will sit down." And he did.

During another session, he said he was rankled by some of the reviews of *Recollection Creek*. Though most had been favorable, some had complained the novel lacked "message." Gipson felt no responsibility to slip a hidden meaning into his writing and being derided for not doing so made him angry. There was nothing wrong with a book's being entertaining, he felt.

"I seriously doubt that a book must have psychological implications and Freudian undertones . . . for it to be good," he told the conference participants. "The books that impress me most are those that are beautifully written."

Some aspiring author raised his hand and asked if a writer should write for money or for the sake of art.

"I think he should write for both," Gipson responded. "I personally couldn't do any writing at all unless I thought I was doing the best I could.

"If you always write the best you can, you may someday come up with something great."[33]

14

A Big Yellow Work Dog

Tommie knew it, Crain knew it, and Thomas knew it—somewhere inside Fred Gipson was literary greatness, not merely his already proven ability to write well enough to make a living. The problem was finding a way to pry out that greatness.

Gipson's agent and his editor both believed he needed to write a novel based on some particularly gripping segment of Texas history. That, they felt, could be his lasting work.[1] With that in mind, Tommie set out on a reading program, reviewing some of the books in her husband's library and acquiring other works of Texas history. Her plan was to soak up factual background and look for incidents that could be embroidered by Gipson and turned into a novel.

Tommie read *Pioneer Women in Texas* by Annie Doom Pickrell and passed on to her husband the story of a pioneer Texas couple who—because of constantly changing laws—had to get married five different times. Another story with possibilities was one about a group of boys who stole eggs to trade with Indians. Gipson reread the story of Herman Lehmann, outlined in J. Marvin Hunter's *Nine Years Among the Indians*, and studied John C. Duval's *The Adventures of Big Foot Wallace* and *Evolution of a State*, written by Noah Smithwick's daughter, Nana Donaldson.[2]

As much as Gipson loved to read, he was not able to spend all his time with a book. When he returned from Hollywood after working on "Brush Roper," he found the well on his place had gone dry. The drought was holding and now the underground water was beginning to play out. Fortunately, they had been able to sink a deeper well and hit water again. But that had cost money.³

The post oaks were turning and the first good norther was not far off in the fall of 1955 when Tommie and Fred worked out an outline for a children's book and mailed it to Ursula Norstrom at Harpers. Despite the contributions from Tommie's crash course in Texas history, the idea for this book was drawn from Gipson's own figurative well of family stories. That well seemed to stay full, no matter how regularly he went to it. Once they had worked out how they would make the pitch, Tommie wrote the letter for Fred:

Dear Miss Norstrom:
One of the most moving and powerful dog stories I ever heard was told by my grandfather. It was the story of a big yellow work dog who fought for two or three hours one night to keep a mad dog off of my grandfather on his way home on horseback. Since there was no known cure for hydrophobia, and since it was always fatal to human beings, and such a horrible death, there was nothing my grandfather could do but kill the dog that had saved him.
Is this too strong for a boy's adventure story? I've made a rough outline of the story and I could probably do the story in something like a month or six weeks, if you think it would go. However, if you think that ending is too brutal, you might have a suggestion for ending the outline I've worked up. Perhaps I'll wait to hear from you before I go to work on it.⁴

Two days later, Norstrom answered Gipson's query: ''We're really very glad to hear about this book. From the outline, it sounds as though it will be a very exciting as well as very worthwhile story.''⁵

Acceptance of the idea was highly satisfying to Gipson. The prevailing standard for juvenile books was a sore spot with him. Gipson felt most children's books were too ''stickly sweet.'' So much so, ''they'd gag a snake.'' Children, he knew, were not as naive as most adult book writers seemed to think. They realized life was not all cute, sweet, and nice.⁶

His juvenile book would be realistic. It would show life as it was and not as people thought it should be. He had in mind a couple of other books, but he would do the dog story first. As he had predicted in his letter to Miss Norstrom, the story went quickly. It was fun to write and seemed easier than anything he had ever done. When he finished a draft,

Tommie, who had earlier helped develop the structure of the story, edited and retyped it. He would then do some revision and she would retype it. Every time Tommie typed the manuscript, as familiar as she was with the story, tears came to her eyes at the end. In just three months, the project was finished.

The reaction to the manuscript by Crain, Norstrom, and Thomas was swift and incredible to Gipson. "Congratulations on *Big Yeller Dog*. It is *terrific*. We are very happy with it," wrote Norstrom. "I read *Big Yeller Dog* in one gulp last night and I think it is terrific. This is the first time you've really hit that top Gipson stride since *Hound-Dog Man*," Thomas wrote, adding that another reader at Harpers had cried after finishing the manuscript.[7]

None of his earlier books had got such a reaction, and he could not at first believe the reception *Big Yeller Dog* received. But Gipson was not going to pick a fight with success. It had eluded him too long, if indeed it had come now.

"I don't suppose either of you needs to be told by me that old Fred has hauled off and done it again," Crain wrote. "A great many people besides boys for a long string of years to come are going to be mighty grateful to you, Fred, for having written this." Crain said he could think of no reason the book would ever stop selling and predicted that Gipson's great-grandchildren would draw royalties on the story of the yeller dog. Three days after Thomas finished reading the manuscript, a check for $3,000 was on its way to Mason.[8]

"I'll have to confess," Gipson wrote Crain, "that I'm a bit flabbergasted at the reception of *Big Yeller Dog*, just about as much so as when something I do flops with everybody. But this way is a lot happier."[9]

Within a month, he was even more flabbergasted. For $7,500, *Collier's* bought serialization rights and planned to break the initial installment jointly with the first edition of the hardcover book, which Harpers had decided to bring out as an adult book rather than a juvenile. The firm also shortened the title to *Old Yeller* instead of *Big Yeller Dog*.

Thomas showed the manuscript to the editors at *Reader's Digest*, who accepted it for abridgement in their fairly new Condensed Books. The U.S. Edition alone, Crain happily reported to the author, would bring up to $25,000. "See what happens when you write a good book?" Crain wrote.[10]

The "good book"—written in less than ninety days with much less effort than usual—had already earned its stunned author, at least on paper, $35,000. That did not include royalties from hardback sales or from foreign editions, paperback editions, and movie rights, all likely possibilities. All this, and Harpers did not even have the galley proofs ready.

The movie question had Gipson worried. The last time one of his books created this much commotion, everyone seemed sure a movie sale would result. That had not happened yet, and the continued lack of success in selling the rights for *Hound-Dog Man* put Gipson in an uncomfortable position. Crain and Annie Laurie were more like family than literary agent and movie agent. Yet, Gipson was beginning to think Annie Laurie could have done better by *Hound-Dog Man*. Could he drop her as his agent and still stay on good terms with Crain?

Although Gipson continued to correspond with Annie Laurie concerning the movie rights of *Hound-Dog Man*, he also wrote Dick Patterson of the H. N. Swanson agency, a California firm that had been highly recommended. In February 1956, Gipson made up his mind: He would switch to the Swanson agency. He wrote Annie Laurie and the Swanson agency the same day. The letter he got back showed that Annie Laurie was hurt by his decision, but she did not put up a fight. To Gipson's relief, the move did not shatter his relationship with Crain.

The situation had been painful, but nothing compared to a different sort of anguish he was beginning to feel: Something was wrong with his upper back. He was not having discomfort; he was tortured by it. The pain, which pills and Scotch only dulled, began to get bad in March and continued to build throughout the spring.[11]

The *Old Yeller* galleys came in April. After he and Tommie read and approved the typeset version of the book, Gipson went to a doctor. The doctor, thinking the back problem might be related to the stress over the *Hound-Dog Man* movie rights and the split with Annie Laurie, prescribed pills to ease tension. He even passed on a brochure describing a special chair to make sitting easier for Gipson, who by necessity made his living seated in front of a typewriter.

By May, the pain had become so bad that Gipson could not even sit at the typewriter. It hurt to sit; it hurt to stand; it hurt to lie down. At times, he rolled in agony on the floor in front of a horrified Tommie. She had never seen anyone in so much misery.[12]

While its author suffered in Texas, the *Old Yeller* manuscript was making the rounds in Hollywood. In June, Swanson himself began negotiating with the king of children's entertainment, Walt Disney. After two days of intense discussion, a deal was cemented. The producer, who had started a national craze a few years earlier with his movie version of the Davy Crockett story, would make a movie based on *Old Yeller*.

Swanson wired Gipson. Two days later, when Gipson got around to replying, he and Tommie were "still floating around in the air . . . over the Disney deal."[13] Swanson asked $50,000 for the *Old Yeller* script and he got it.[14] The on-paper profits of the book were now more than $100,000.

"Isn't the movie sale something? Can you imagine all that money?" Tommie wrote Crain on June 20. Her husband's back had had him in such torment that he had not worked in three months, she said, which had given her time to get some work done around the house. The sale of serialization rights to *Reader's Digest* and *Collier's* had been meat and potatoes, bread and butter. The movie sale was pure gravy, which would take the pressure off her husband and give him time to do something about his back. The doctor in Mason had recommended a doctor in San Antonio who in turn recommended a specialist in Houston, she reported.

Crain said he believed Disney would do an excellent job of making a movie based on the book. The ensuing publicity, of course, would further sales of the soon-to-be-released hardback. "After all that hoopla the whole country will know about *Old Yeller* and about half the kids born in the next generation will read the book."[15]

Part of the arrangement negotiated by Swanson was that Gipson would do the screenwriting for Disney, who telephoned Gipson in Mason and personally invited him to Hollywood. But since the author of the novel was a neophyte when it came to camera angles and other technical matters, he would be assisted by veteran Hollywood script man Bill Tunberg.

Though his back was getting better, Gipson still suffered through occasional bad days. He would feel good just long enough to think he was cured and then endure back pain so intense he would think he was crippled.

Despite the bad back, Gipson became involved in another project, writing the text to accompany a series of primitive, almost cartoon-style drawings by cowboy artist Bill Leftwich of Pecos. Leftwich had done the drawings in 1949 when he was in Mexico with a United States team of cowboys and veterinarians sent to destroy cattle infected with hoof and mouth disease. The project had come to Gipson the way several other strokes of good fortune had in the past—through Joe Small and Frank Wardlaw.

Early summer saw a steady stream of good news for the Gipsons. The reviews of *Old Yeller* were glowing. Fannie Butcher of the *Chicago Tribune* wrote, "Occasionally, but very rarely, one reads a book with the increasing certainty, as one turns the pages, that a classic is unfolding before one's eyes. Readers of *The Yearling* had that memorable experience. Today's readers will have the same feeling as they turn the pages of Fred Gipson's story of 14-year-old Travis and the 'ugly old yeller dog.' ''[16] All the major reviewers were taking notice of the book. The *New York Herald Tribune* liked it as did *Saturday Review* and the *San Francisco Chronicle*. The word classic continued to surface.

In early July, British rights to reprint the book were sold, and by July 20, *Old Yeller* was into its second edition at Harpers. Too, the People's Book Club, which had issued *The Home Place* in 1950, now bought rights to *Old Yeller*.[17] The whole world was paying attention to Fred Gipson. Only those who were closest to him saw the price he was paying for success: The 48-year-old author of *Old Yeller* had developed an ulcer.[18] And his back was still plaguing him.

"Oh, if it hadn't been for Fred's ailment, these last two or three months would have been the best living we've had," Tommie wrote Crain.[19]

Old Yeller was not the only Gipson book getting attention. At that year's Texas Institute of Letters meeting, Gipson won the $100 Cokesbury Bookstore Award for *Trail-Driving Rooster*, and the $250 McMurray Bookshop Award for *Recollection Creek*. He was the first writer ever to receive two Institute awards in one year.

Despite all the glowing acclaim of his writing, Gipson's ulcer was still bothering him. Tommie believed her husband's ulcer was directly related to his nervousness about going to Hollywood. Gipson hated the idea of leaving Mason. He was uncomfortable even in Dallas, much less in the well-known hustle and bustle—mostly hustle—of Hollywood. Part of the tension was the uncertainty. "I'm on call to go to Hollywood for a six weeks assignment and as yet don't know when I'll be called," he said in a letter to a bookstore owner.[20] And he worried if he could make the grade as a screenwriter. He had stature now. But could he hold onto it in a different world, more than twelve hundred miles from his family and close friends? He flew to California on August 19, 1956, to find out.

At least the pay would be good: $1,000 a week. That, he figured, could make up for a lot of bother. Gipson was set up in a motel within walking distance of the Disney Studios. Disney, sympathetic to Gipson's continuing back troubles, had a couch moved into Gipson's office so he could lie down when the pain was bad.

Tunberg, an old pro at screenwriting, and Gipson got along quite well, especially after working hours when they found time to enjoy some drinks. Scotch, and the phenobarbital prescribed for the back pain and tension, left Gipson in a dream-like state much of the time. In the mixture, he found escape from the tension of the pressurized writing job, from the back pain, the loneliness, the growing and nagging fear that success could not be sustained.[21]

Disney had not built his empire by staying aloof from his projects. He monitored the progess on the script, which was causing some problems. In Gipson's book, the father of young Travis leaves on a cattle drive at the beginning and does not appear until the end. But since one of Hollywood's hottest stars, Fess Parker, was to play the role of the father, studio officials decided the cattle drive should be written in so Parker would get more footage in the film. The decision was reversed by Disney. "The cattle drive will have to go," he said. "We bought this book because we liked it. Why change it?"[22] The cattle drive—and thirty-five pages of script—were out.

The production staff had also decided that Gipson's ending of the book—when Travis is forced to shoot Old Yeller—was too brutal for children. Disney, who was seeking to inject more realism into his films, disagreed. The movie would end like the book. "The kids'll cry, but it's important for them to know that life isn't all happy endings."[23]

Gipson and Tunberg continued on the script while the author of *Old Yeller* was getting more miserable by the day. Tommie had stayed home with Mike and Beck, but Gipson had not been gone long when he called and said, "I'm so lonely I could die. When can you come out?" Tommie made arrangements to have the children taken care of and flew to California. She stayed two weeks, and then Gipson began worrying about how much it was costing. "I think maybe you'd better get home and save our money," he said.[24]

Tommie returned to Mason very worried about her husband. His drinking had become chronic. She was thankful he lived within walking distance of the studio. Even so, she was afraid her husband, floating along on alcohol and pills, might walk in front of a car.

Joe Small was worried, too. One Sunday afternoon he called Gipson, who at first pretended he did not recognize who was calling. "Well, goddamn, ole Joe Small," he finally acknowledged. "I'm so happy to hear from you. Can you come out? I'll pay your way if you can come out here. I never was so damn homesick and lonesome in my life. This damn place is not fit for a human being to live in. It's nothing but concrete and thieves."[25] Despite Gipson's offer, Small did not have time to go to Hollywood, and within three weeks, the Texas author was home. The screen version of his book was finished. Now it was time for the filming.

Gipson's ulcer, aggravated by the drinking, continued to worsen. Shortly after he got home, he was hospitalized. "He has a monstrous ulcer which has every chance of being cured if Fred's own fears and frustrations can be minimized," Tommie wrote a friend. But maybe there would be less pressure, she said, since *Old Yeller* had assured their income for at least five years.[26]

In November, as Gipson continued to recuperate from his Hollywood stint, *The Cow Killers*, his book based on Leftwich's experiences in Mexico, was published by the University of Texas Press. When the book was introduced at a party in Austin, Walter Prescott Webb joked good-naturedly that it was the only book he had ever heard of that was the joint effort of a "primitive artist, primitive writer and a primitive publisher."[27] The UT Press book, despite its quality, was overshadowed by the continuing success of *Old Yeller*.

Crain, worried about the novel's author, had an experience in December he knew would make Gipson feel somewhat better about life. Christmas was just a week away and Fifth Avenue was packed with New Yorkers trying to finish their shopping. Crain moved from bookstore to bookstore, his mood a mixture of impatience and exhilaration. None of the stores had the book he wanted: *Old Yeller*. He needed a few extra copies, but New Yorkers were still snatching them up faster than Harpers could keep them stocked. Finally, Crain walked into a store and saw a customer waiting at the cash register with a copy of *Old Yeller*. That meant the store still had a supply, he assumed. But he was wrong—the woman had bought the last copy of the book.

Crain gave up. After all, he knew the publisher. And he would write Gipson, who would get a kick out of it. He already knew the punch line he would use: "I'm dreaming of a Yeller Christmas."[28]

As Crain had predicted when *Old Yeller* was first sold to Disney, the movie people were producing a lot of publicity in advance of the film release. That and the general popularity of the book itself were generating heavy mail in two distinct categories. There were letters of adoration from young and mature readers alike and letters proposing "deals."

In the latter type of letter, the writers assumed Gipson had vast influence with Hollywood and the publishing world and could help them sell their "work." They also believed he was breathlessly awaiting their offers of stories he could turn into books—as long as they got part of the action.

Most of the time, he returned the stories and book manuscripts unopened. Almost always, though, he added a cover letter. Sometimes he even read the stories: "I have read with interest your dog story of

Tippy," he said in one letter. "Unfortunately, for me, it does not set off the proper 'electric' shock that makes me want to write the story." To another writer: "In the first place, while I might wish to be an editor for Walt Disney, the fact remains that I am not and never have been; and I wish there was some way to stop the spread of that foolish and unfounded rumor, which can only embarrass me if it ever gets back to Walt."[29]

Tommie handled the heavy load of fan mail, passing the letters on to her husband and writing the replies. The mail came from all over the U. S. and from some foreign countries.

"Mr. Fred Gipson," one person wrote, "I would like to say this from the bottom of my heart. I am sure that your writing has made the world a better place to live in, as it has softened so many hearts." A boy from Brooklyn wrote: "I like the way you make the words up. I like saying 'Old Yeller' better than saying 'Old Yellow.' Like the book *Old Yeller* very much."[30]

By the spring of 1957, Gipson was beginning to feel better than he had in a long time.[31] The drought was broken. His badly parched Mason County acreage drank up the rain, and he hoped for a good grass crop—finally. Nature was at last cooperating in the scheme of things again if the federal government could just be straightened out.

A form letter from Senator Lyndon Johnson, asking the opinion of landowners in Texas on pending legislative matters, drew a heated response from Gipson, who had first run into Johnson when he worked for Congressman Kleberg back in the late 1930's. He began the letter, "Dear Lyndon," and then recounted for Johnson how he had bought land in 1950, including eighty acres of "badly abused cropland" that he had taken out of production "and began trying to restore its fertility by seeding it to grass and legumes."

For the first six years he had made little headway against the ravages of drought. Now, he complained, he did not qualify for the Soil Bank program because he had taken the land out of production. Then he pointed out he had paid almost $10,000 in income taxes the year before, "more than enough to build up the fertility of my soil, without anybody's help . . . . It burns the hell out of me to see my tax money go into the pockets of owners who inherited ten to twenty times as much land as I'll ever own, yet who didn't have the foresight to take care of the land."[32]

In March, one of the Disney publicity people had asked Gipson to write a story on the background of *Old Yeller*. Gipson replied he

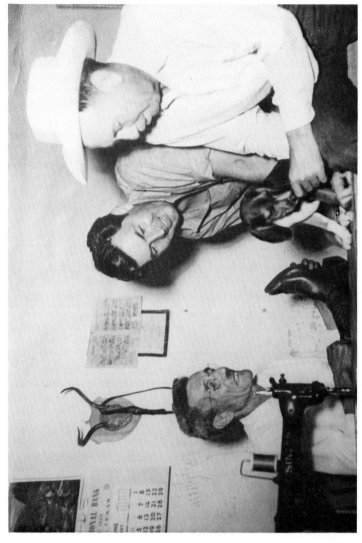

Left to right: Bootmaker Frank Polk, Fess Parker, and Gipson during Parker's visit to Mason in June 1957. (Mason County *News*, courtesy Mrs. Frank Polk.)

was just "too nervous" to do any writing in polished form, but he wrote several pages of notes.[33]

When he went to Hollywood, he wrote, he had been determined that he would allow no "desecration" of his book by the Disney staff. But Disney told him that the fourth chapter in the book, which featured an action-packed fight with a bull, would have to go. Such a scene would be too hard to put on film, he told Gipson.

To Gipson's thinking, however, the scene was perhaps the most dramatic in the whole book and from the first story conference on, he protested the decision. Later, he persuaded Disney into letting him write in a runaway mule scene to recapture some of the excitement he felt was lost when the bullfight scene was rejected.

"But for the steadying influence of my friend and co-screenwriter, William Tunberg, I very likely would have called it quits," he said in the letter to the Disney promotion department.[34]

The filming of *Old Yeller* finally got under way, though three weeks behind schedule because of bad weather and the unpredictability of the animal stars.[35] The movie would have more four-legged stars than humans: Old Yeller was being played by Spike, a 115-pound dog found at the Humane Society; in addition, there would be a coon, a bear, twenty-five hogs, cows, wolves—a veritable menagerie.

Spike, though, was the lead animal actor. He was chauffeured around in his own station wagon, had a makeup man, a hairdresser, and a double to stand in for the rough scenes. And he gained five pounds after getting the part. All the animals were well cared for. Animal handlers, veterinarians, trainers, and Humane Society observers made up half the production crew.

Assembling the cast of animal performers was no trouble. The problem came in the production. Early in the movie, for instance, was to be a scene showing a surprised squirrel running down a log as two frogs jumped into a pond. Cameramen hid inside two specially constructed hollow boulders to shoot the action. Trainers placed the squirrel and frogs in position.

Cameras whirred and a crew member fired a rifle, producing a loud crack that was supposed to excite the three small actors into action, but nothing happened. Nor did shouts, food bribes, or all the people gathered around make them move. Finally, in desperation, the crew placed cages containing other squirrels and frogs a foot or two off camera. The closer proximity of company did the trick—the squirrel and the two frogs became animated. A five-minute scene had taken four hours to film.[36]

Gipson had told Disney that coons loved corn so Disney had had fresh roasting ears hidden in the middle of the cornfield on the set that the masked varmints were supposed to raid. But when the cameras rolled, the coons had shown no interest at all in the corn. They would not do their bit until the trainers placed fresh shrimp inside the corn shucks. Later, when Disney kidded Gipson about the incident, the Hill Country writer had a ready excuse: Disney obviously had not acquired country coons. Only a city coon would know anything about shrimp.[37]

Then there had been the problem of how to make a normally docile cow mean and agitated. When Old Yeller got near her, she was supposed to get quiet. But she stayed quiet all the time, no matter where Old Yeller was. Finally, with the permission of the Humane Society, a small wire was fixed to her leg. When it was necessary for her to be riled, a harmless but irritating electric charge was sent through the wire. When she was to be gentle, the current was cut off.[38]

During much of the filming of *Old Yeller*, Gipson was in Mexico fishing with Joe Small in an effort to cure the nervousness that still was plaguing him. He had always felt a strong lure south of the Rio Grande and had made several previous trips with friends. Tommie and Fred had even talked about living in Mexico for the summer, but he had balked at that idea. Tommie believed he would not mind living there, but had a troublesome suspicion he would prefer to go alone.[39]

While in Mexico, Gipson and Small had put the finishing touches on a scheme Gipson was going to broach with Disney: a television series based on stories from Small's *True West* publications. Gipson would do much of the writing.

Despite Gipson's on-and-off torture from back pain and steady drinking, Small had been delighted to see something new emerging in his longtime friend: self-confidence. Gipson had never had that before. Even Gipson half-way admitted it in a letter to Thomas: "If I hadn't had my ears beaten down so many times in the past, I'd start getting cocky about *Old Yeller*."[40]

Still, some self-doubt lingered. He had yet to summon the courage to think about another book. That would come later, when his nerves were fully settled and he was completely under control. He knew he had more books in him, but he now was forever barred from mediocrity. Any future book would have to be as good as *Old Yeller* or better—not a particularly comforting thought.[41]

15

"Helpless As a Tied-up Calf"

Small and Gipson had not stopped talking since the plane left San Antonio. They hashed over every point Small would try to make with Disney in selling him on a television series based on his fact Western magazines. Gipson had told Small that Disney was easy to get along with, but Small was still nervous.

The two Texans got to Disney's studio a few minutes early. When Disney arrived, he ushered them into his office and situated them in front of his massive desk. Disney then addressed the two in language none of his childhood fans would have believed.

"Now, goddamn it, we don't want any bullshit . . . ." he began, stunning Small. "You're Fred, you're Joe and I'm Walt. Let's forego the bullshit."

Only then did Small realize he was dealing with a true genius—someone who could out-countryboy a countryboy.

Disney was interested in the series idea. He had read copies of *True West* and had seen the statistics that showed how the seventh issue of the new magazine had broken out of the red, a rarity in the magazine publishing business.

As the three men talked, Disney kept his empire running, periodically being interrupted for telephone calls that gave both Small and Gipson insight into the producer's success. Someone could not get a truck moved, and the matter had been referred all the way to Disney. "Tell that _____ to get that truck out of there, or I'll come down and move it myself." Small and Gipson figured Disney was not kidding.

Fred (*right*) and his good friend Joe Small, c. 1960.
(Photo by L. A. Wilke.)

They talked until lunch time. "How about coming down and eating lunch with me?" Disney asked. "Let's continue the conversation and I'll show you around a little bit." They ate in the commissary at a big table marked "Walt Disney."

The deal was practically finalized, via gentlemen's agreement. Disney would do a couple of shows based on *True West* stories for his weekly Sunday television program. If the programs were successful, the following season he might try a TV series.[1]

Tommie had made the trip, too, along with Beck, who got a first-class tour of Disneyland. The next day, the Gipsons and Small heard the theme music of *Old Yeller* and saw a rough version of the film. Everyone was pleased with the acting and photography, but Tommie thought Spike was too fat for Old Yeller.[2] They also visited with Fess Parker, who had grown up in San Angelo and attended the University of Texas. In June, he had spent a week in Mason fishing with Gipson and Frank Polk.[3]

Later that summer, after returning from California, Tommie and Fred had a long and pleasurable visit with J. Frank Dobie in Austin. They drank beer and talked about one of Dobie's Longhorn stories as a possibility for the *True West* television series. Dobie readily gave permission for Gipson to retool it for Disney.[4]

As fall came, Gipson was as content as he had been in a long time. Release of the movie was expected soon, and the first three weeks of October saw almost ten inches of rain fall on the home place. All the water tanks on the place were full and one patch of grass he had barely been able to keep alive now stood shoulder high.

A Swedish publisher had just bought the rights to reprint *Old Yeller*. Gipson wrote Crain that he would use the money to buy grass seed, since all the rain would make for a lush winter growing season. "I'm clearing brush from some 30 acres more and then seeding it in after the first frost," he wrote. "With the moisture we now have, it won't require much rain in the spring to get it up and off to a good start. Maybe one of these days, I'll get to see some of this country growing the oceans of grass that once grew here."

In the same letter, Gipson also briefed Crain on his television-writing efforts, explaining he had decided to try his hand at it since he had no book in mind. Tommie was doing some research that might develop into a couple of historical novels, he said, but how soon he started on those depended on how long it took to get the television project finished. "I probably shouldn't have let myself get into this television stuff . . . that type of work has never appealed to me," he wrote. "On the other hand, should they click, I'll always have a place to go with any story that I feel will whip up into a good show."[5]

The rainy weather had Gipson in an expansive mood. Since most of the people he would like to talk with were far from Mason, he wrote letters. Although Tommie had been handling most of his correspondence, he reported to Crain himself. And now he wrote Small, dating the letter "A Rainy Sunday," that Bill Anderson at Disney Studios had liked Part 1 of "Old Sancho," Dobie's Longhorn story that he had reworked for television. But Anderson was withholding comment until he saw the second part, which Gipson had mailed the previous Tuesday.

"So here I sit, wanting to go fishing, only it rains, rains, rains all the time, till I'm about to mildew. Ain't it wonderful!

"Would like to go catch a fish, though, before cold weather sets in. But if it'll rain, let her fall. Can . . . [go] fishing next year or sometime."[6]

By November, Gipson still had not been able to go fishing and still had not heard from Hollywood about "Old Sancho." Disney was in Mexico City. Anderson told Gipson he had just managed to stuff the scripts into his boss's briefcase before he left. Disney had promised to give him a report, Anderson said. Gipson, however, was not too bothered about the delay—he had already been paid for both parts.

Gipson told the Smalls to hold open a weekend in December "as a time you can't go nowhere else, on account of you're gonna be up here. Will let you stew around, wondering why, until we get everything in the clear, which it nearly is now."[7]

The surprise he alluded to was a special pre-premier showing of *Old Yeller*, which was being arranged by Gipson and the movie distributors, Buena Vista Films. The private screening, for about a hundred of the Gipson's closest friends and relatives, would be in the Odeon Theater in Mason. Tommie would feed the crowd before the film, and afterward there would be a party worthy of the event at the home of Judge Marcus and Mildred Grant.

An even earlier screening, a sneak preview, came December 3 at the Texas Theater in San Angelo. Rowley United Theaters was having its annual convention in San Angelo, and the occasion gave movie managers from three states an idea of the hopeful hit to come. When Gipson was introduced to the conventioneers at a luncheon in the Town House Hotel, San Angelo Mayor H. E. McCulloch called him an "old West Texas boy who had gone places." That night, after the movie was shown, the audience stood and applauded. Some in the crowd wiped back tears.[8]

Friends of the Gipsons from all over Texas went to Mason for the December 14 private screening. The movie was shown at 10:00

P.M. and got the same reaction it had in San Angelo—the guests loved it. Gipson cracked that that was only because he was buying the whiskey, but there were real tears in the eyes of many of the viewers, and most of them had already read the book.

The party after the December 14 screening was the first of many, and Gipson soon had had enough. Not that he minded drinking, but as he told Tommie, he had had a "belly full" of social occasions. He refused to go to a Christmas dance for which Tommie had bought an expensive backless dress. Even Tommie grumbled to a friend that she had just as soon Christmas season be confined to three days the next year.[9]

After seventeen years of marriage, Fred and Tommie had found and explored their differences. And they knew what they had in common: Both needed rest and solitude.

On New Year's Day 1958, the Gipsons were well aware that the swirl of events surrounding the opening of *Old Yeller* had them down. They were edgy and sharp with each other and neither was feeling particularly well, despite the prospect of what seemed so bright a future. Her husband had been troubled by his stomach for years, and now Tommie was worrying that she had developed an ulcer. Also, her doctor had discovered a growth on her thyroid that needed to be checked.

For years, the couple had worked as a team. But Gipson was beginning to rankle at even the suggestion that Tommie's help was anything more than editing. Fueled by his basic insecurity, which even the success of *Old Yeller* had not completely smothered, the role of Tommie in his writing began to worry him.

Husband and wife often differed over Gipson's casualness with the language. So Tommie was delighted when Dobie, after reviewing the "Old Sancho" script, sided with her. "You earned my undying gratitude on your observation that there's no need of being vulgar with language in order to be easy with the audience," Tommie wrote Dobie.[10]

Their usual writing-editing technique, Tommie explained, was for Gipson to use all the "ain'ts" and "thems" he wanted in his first draft. Then Tommie cut as many of those words as she could, ". . . without removing the color and naturalness." The problem, and Tommie acknowledged it to Dobie, was that the writing ". . . actually *is* Fred's, and I'm something of an upstart to be giving him sass."[11]

153

Small, too, had offered advice on the way "Old Sancho" should be handled. Dobie saw Small's suggestions and concluded he was pressing for too much sentimentality in the story. "I am reminded of Abraham Lincoln's retort upon being besieged by various people to follow God's way in picking his generals and in otherwise conducting the Civil War," Dobie wrote. Lincoln had said he was perfectly willing to take God's way if he just knew what it was. "The only writer I want Fred to trust in this business is himself."[12]

True to everyone's expectations, the movie version of *Old Yeller* was another Disney box-office success.[13] In Houston, people waited in lines several blocks long to see the movie. Six policemen were called in to handle the traffic around the theater. The crowds were attributable not only to the quality of the movie and the book, but also to some clever promotion, including a special showing of the movie for dogs at the Metropolitan Theater in Houston. Numerous Bayou City dogs took their humans to see *Old Yeller*, where they could get three dog bones for a quarter—with butter for an extra nickel.

Cowboy cartoonist Ace Reid of Kerrville, an admirer and drinking buddy of Gipson's, took his wife to see *Old Yeller*. "We . . . blubbered through the whole dang thing. Six people drowned in the first three rows," he wrote Gipson.[14]

Crain wrote that he had seen the movie and, like almost everyone else, thought it had been well done. Meanwhile, the book was continuing to sell. A copy had been ordered for the White House, he reported, which meant a second President was reading Fred Gipson.[15]

Eight days later, Crain got a call from 20th Century Fox, which evidently had not heard that Gipson had changed movie agents. That did not bother Gipson's literary agent-friend, however. What 20th Century wanted, and the company sounded firm on it, were the rights to *Hound-Dog Man*. The success of *Old Yeller*, Crain opined, was finally enough to convince a film company that *Hound-Dog Man* could be just as good as, if not better than, *Old Yeller*.[16] Gipson accepted the news matter-of-factly. He had heard it before, and though he had made a little money in various options on the property, every proposal had fizzled.

What did excite the author of *Hound-Dog Man* and *Old Yeller* was the weather. The drought had begun to break the spring before, but now there was absolutely no doubt. Practically every day that winter there had been a fine, steady, soaking rain. With so much moisture in the ground, Gipson planned to seed twenty more acres of old field in grass. He had already bulldozed the brush from another twenty acres, terraced it, broken it, and seeded it, which meant that every drop of rain was on Gipson's side. Even if Texas was to endure

Fred surveying his beloved native Texas grass, c. 1960. (Courtesy Beck Gipson.)

another dry spring, he believed, there was now enough underground moisture to keep the grass growing.

Already, his land could pass as an agriculture experimental station. Grasses on the place included blue panicum, buffel, blue buffel, King Ranch bluestem, Gordo bluestem, sorghum, almum, eastern gamma, Indian grass, and several varieties of lovegrass. Gipson figured lovegrass, which could not be found anywhere else in the area, would turn out to be the best grass for Mason County. The blue panicum, he knew, did not do too badly, but it was hard to get established and could not stand dry spells. Eastern gamma, which was native to the county, was a good grass, but the seeds were extremely hard to harvest because they took a long time to mature.[17]

He felt good about his land and the improvements he had made on it, but other things were bothering him. In a week, one of Disney's producers would be coming to Mason to work with him on the television show. Gipson hoped it would be someone he could get along with. If not, he was prepared to call the whole thing off, despite his friendship with Small. Too much of his time, he believed, was being sunk into the project. That worry was compounded by a suspicion that Disney's interest in the project had waned.[18]

Gipson also was concerned about Tommie. In January, she had said all she needed to snap back from the rigors of the busy schedule in December were rest and a permanent. But she still was not feeling well, and further medical tests in Austin had indicated the growth on her thyroid would have to be removed. Gipson's father and sister Ethel had died at comparatively young ages of cancer; an unspoken fear for Tommie haunted him. He and Tommie had had their problems, but he did not think he could live without her.

The operation was March 5. Dr. Raleigh Ross of Austin gave Gipson the news while Tommie was still in the recovery room: The growth was malignant. Bestsellers, rain, tall grass . . . and Tommie had cancer. A specimen was sent to a laboratory for more detailed analysis, with a promise from the doctor of an in-depth report on Tommie's prognosis in a few days. Gipson sank into a deep state of despair.

The next report, however, was much better. The lab tests showed that though the thyroid had contained a malignant tumor, the tumor had been contained. The whole thyroid had been removed, the doctor explained, and he did not think the cancer would spread. Pills to do the work of the thyroid and periodic checkups were all that was necessary, he said.[19]

Gipson's concern for Tommie and his worries about the television project were having an effect on what little writing he tried. Despite the overwhelming success of *Old Yeller* and all the movie publicity, three of his short stories were turned down by magazines. For once, he did not really need the money but the rejections were a serious assault on his pride.

At least the *Hound-Dog Man* saga seemed near a happy ending—after almost a decade. The offer from 20th Century Fox had been genuine. H. N. Swanson wrapped up the details, which included purchase of the movie rights and a screenwriting job in Hollywood again. Other screenwriting jobs seemed likely.[20] Gipson had not grown any fonder of Hollywood, but the money was good. Too good not to go.

Tommie had recovered and kept the home place running during the summer of 1958 while her husband was in Hollywood. One of the first problems she had to handle came in the mail a short time after Gipson left. She looked at the letter again and started laughing. The news it contained was no real laughing matter, but it still struck her as funny. The letter was from Allen Maxwell at *Southwest Review*, and was something she would have to take up with Fred.

On June 2, Maxwell explained, he had received a letter from the editor of *Boy's Life* magazine, the official publication of the Boy Scouts of America. It reflected the embarrassment of an obviously red-faced editor. The magazine had had a writing contest and the winner had been a young Eagle Scout who submitted a short story called "Ye Old Coon Hunt." The judges had been greatly impressed by the quality of the writing, the editor said. As the winning story, the scout's entry had been published under his by-line in *Boy's Life*.

Not long after publication of the story, *Boy's Life* got a letter from a thoughtful reader. The reader said he remembered a good story in *Reader's Digest*, sometime during the war, about a coon hunt. The piece was called "My Kind of Man" and was written by a Fred Gipson. The resemblance between "Ye Old Coon Hunt" and the Gipson story was startling, the reader said.

Someone on the *Boy's Life* staff quickly got a copy of the *Reader's Digest* story and compared it in horror to the story published in their magazine, ostensibly written by an honor scout. The stories were almost word for word the same. The boy had changed a few words here and there, possibly thinking that justified such literary thievery. So, with figurative hat in hand, *Boy's Life* was asking the real author of the story what he wanted done.[21]

The *Boy's Life* staff sweated a bit while Tommie and Gipson talked it over. Tommie wrote Maxwell and said she was referring the matter to Crain, just in case, but added, ''As far as we're concerned, there's no point in taking any action.'' She continued:

> All I can say about that little boy scout is that while he may not have a well-developed sense of property, he certainly is a good literary critic. He couldn't have chosen a finer story to copy. And it's most gratifying that it won first place.[22]

On June 26, Gipson wrote *Boy's Life*, explaining he planned no legal action. He urged that the boy be made aware of the seriousness of his offense, in case that had not already happened. ''Least of all do I want to crush down a boy for making one bad mistake,'' he said. ''I remember too well how, at his age, I was making just about all the mistakes in the book.''[23]

The loneliness of life in Hollywood away from his family and the home place was wearing on Gipson again. His co-workers and friends were trying to do what they could to keep the Texas writer happy. His secretary and her husband invited him to their house for dinner. Their place was so modern, he reported to Tommie, that he had had a hard time keeping from walking through glass doors and walls. And he added, ''They live close to such people as Frank Sinatra, which evidently means a lot. But shabby as our little shanty is, in comparison, I'll take it and the extra room. Damn so many people, all huddled together.''[24]

A week or so later, Tommie flew to California, arriving on Wednesday, July 2. Gipson had to work the next day, but on Friday, the Fourth of July, the couple spent the day lounging around the motel's swimming pool. That Saturday, they had dinner with actor Jeff York, the six-foot-six giant who had played in several Disney films, including *Old Yeller*. Sunday, Fess Parker and a friend took the Gipsons sailing out of Newport, below Anaheim, in his forty-six-foot boat. The breeze was perfect and hundreds of sails dotted the rich green water of the bay. Gipson manned the tiller for a time, easing the sleek racing boat past a ponderous Chinese junk with paper-looking brown sails.[25]

When Tommie flew back to Texas, she wrote her husband to report how the place looked and brought him up to date on the progress of his grass. The letters from her always cheered him and helped him, at least for a few moments, forget about the high emotional price he was paying for a good salary.

''I want so desperately to get enough money ahead that I don't have to fool with this sort of thing any more,'' he wrote.[26] His financial status was not bad as it was. Crain had recently reported that *Old Yeller* was still earning its author $500 a week. And from his other agent, Gipson learned he had a good chance at getting another screenwriting job.

In his letter about the not-so-good Boy Scout who had lifted "My Kind of Man," Gipson had admitted to past mistakes himself. Now, Crain believed his client was making a new mistake by getting too involved in screenwriting. "I hope he doesn't decide to settle down . . . writing scripts for Hollywood," Crain wrote Tommie. "After all, he's already had one ulcer."[27]

With the *Hound-Dog Man* script finally finished, and with a reprieve on further screenwriting work until after the first of the year, Gipson came back to Texas. In January, Russell Tinsley, outdoor editor of the Austin *American-Statesman* and a native of Mason County, came to interview him. For Gipson, the interview was a forum he could use to complain about Hollywood. "I don't like Hollywood, but I sure like the pay," he told Tinsley. In fact, he continued, he no longer cared much about "modern society." He preferred the outdoors instead. "I'm the best bass fisherman in Mason County," he said, adding, "but I know five or six fellows I'd have to whip before they'd recognize that title."

Gipson also talked to Tinsley about Mike, who was in his last semester of high school. "Some of the Gipson talent is wearing off on his off-spring," Tinsley wrote. "Teachers in Mason High School already recognize some of that touch for telling a story in his oldest son . . . ."[28]

Both of his sons gave him a lot of fatherly pride, however. They could fish almost as well as he could, they helped out around the place, and both were doing well in school. But Mike's interest in writing was worrisome. Fred and Tommie knew firsthand how tough the writing life could be. Still, they believed that if Mike really wanted to be a writer, some day he would be.

At least Mike had never aspired to a career as a rock'n'roll singer, like Fabian, the teenage idol who had been picked to star in *Hound-Dog Man*. Elvis Presley, the first choice for the role, had been drafted into the Army. Neither Gipson nor Crain was happy with the casting of Fabian, but as Crain grudgingly admitted, once a property was sold, it was in the hands of the producer.[29]

The job Swanson arranged for Gipson that spring was based on the same business principle. Gipson would be paid $1,250 a week to produce a screenplay based on someone else's work—*The Travels of Jaimie McPheeters* by R. L. Taylor. As he worked to retool Taylor's novel for the screen, Gipson grew more nervous about Fox's treatment of *Hound-Dog Man*. For a time, it had even looked as if the movie would be given another title, but Gipson wrote Tommie that he had heard the original title would be kept. Also, he reported, Stuart Whitman had been cast to play Blackie Scantling.

Gipson, meanwhile, was becoming something of a celebrity himself in Hollywood. He was invited to appear on the television quiz show *What Are the Odds*, which in his case would deal with the chances of writing a best-selling book—a way of gambling he knew well.[30]

Unlike many of the egocentrics of the film industry, Gipson was not trying to create an image. His reputation was developing through behavior that was entirely natural and long-standing. At parties, he drew crowds with his homespun storytelling abilities, but he was always ready to listen, too. And he was not particularly worried about doing something different.

One day after a good rain he noticed a group of excited children around a concrete drainage ditch near his Culver City apartment. He went to see what they were doing and learned they were finding coins washed from storm sewers. He took off his shoes, rolled up his pants and joined them in the search.

In a letter to Tommie, he tried to explain why he was still whipping himself so hard to make money. Largely, aside from the family, the reason was his love of the land.

> I know that it would be easier on us if I did not want more land or want to improve what we have. And quite often I've spent money which we may never see again. And yet, if you'll look back on the money we've made, the only thing we have to show for it is a house, a little land, and what improvements we've made on them. When not spent on those things, it's gone anyhow.[31]

That summer, shortly before filming of the movie was to begin, Fox undertook a major rewrite of the *Hound-Dog Man* script. Though Gipson had had a hand in the first effort, the revision was handled by someone else. In early July, Tommie drove to California with her mother. When they arrived, they found Gipson in a powerless rage. He said the new treatment prostituted his book—a book he believed was better than *Old Yeller*.

Tommie thought her husband's fury was almost funny at first, until she started seriously studying the script. Some of the changes wrought by the rewrite were unbelievable to her. In the novel, the action had occurred around Christmas, when Blackie Scantling spent most of his time hunting coons. The script, however, had been altered so that the filming could be done in summer. That blue-pencil climate change created other irritating problems: No one would buy summer pelts, even if it were legal to take them that time of the year, and a scene in the book where a child fell into the river and Blackie worried he would catch pneumonia would not make sense in summertime.

What Gipson and Tommie found even more galling was the deletion of the word "coon" from the script. After all, the novel was about a coon hunter, and coon hunting was very much a part of the book. Gipson called producer Jerry Wald to complain about the new script, especially the deletion of any reference to coons. Wald had told Gipson the word "coon" had been cut after the studio received a letter complaining that the word was a racial slur.

"We're not discussing Negroes—we're talking about raccoons," Gipson said. "They have nothing to do with Negroes—not a Negro involved in the whole story."

The screenplay now had Blackie Scantling as a possum hunter. Gipson told Wald that did not make sense.

"What do you call a possum, a coon?" Wald asked.

"No, I don't call a possum a coon. I call a possum a possum," Gipson replied.

"And what's a coon?" Wald asked.

"A raccoon," Gipson said. "And it's always called 'coon' by all those who hunt 'em, including the Negroes, all over the South. Negroes would be the first to laugh at you if there was any such damned excuse."[32]

Wald agreed to reinstate the word "coon" and urged Gipson to point out any other mistakes he saw in the rewrite. Still, Gipson was so put out with the treatment of his story that he checked with Swanson to see if his name could be removed from the screen credits. Swanson talked him out of it, explaining that a screenwriter got paid on the basis of accumulated credits. Most people did not notice the screen credits anyway, Swanson said, and those whose attention he did value would understand the situation.

Tommie went over the rest of the script and wrote Wald a letter over her husband's signature saying she had discovered more than ninety errors prior to Scene 161. Beyond that scene, she said, there was little point in her making any suggestions, since an entirely new ending had been tacked on the story. Past that point, she wrote, "the whole script seems fake, like something about two other people."

"As the script now stands," she continued, "it is neither fish nor fowl—and I can hardly resist the pun there. It is neither good Backwoods, good Musical Comedy, nor good Soap Opera. As it is, it's offensive to millions of naturalists of the South and Southwest; and yet not appealing to the more urban musical comedy audiences. Filmed from its present script, it can only be done in knowing contempt for the intelligence of the movie audience.''[33]

The result of the letter was a meeting on a Sunday morning with the film's director, producer's assistant, and dialogue advisor. Tommie and the three movie men pored over the script from 10:00 A.M. to 6:30 P.M., stopping only for lunch. Most of the time, Gipson sat on a nearby couch, unable to take much part in the proceedings for fear of falling into a blind rage. The meeting amounted to a nature lecture by Tommie, who had to explain to the Hollywood types how cows gave down their milk, that wells did not have a hand pump and a windmill, that Hill Country folk did not build big, fancy barns, and that a woman did not just get up and casually pluck and bake a turkey for breakfast.

The day was over well before they reached the end of the script, which Tommie said "combines Gunsmoke with Stella Dallas."[34] Wald's associates had taken copious notes during the meeting, but Gipson glumly realized there was no real way to head off what he felt would be a disastrous movie.

Filming began July 27. Tommie and her mother departed for Texas two days later, leaving Gipson behind to finish the *Jaimie McPheeters* script. At El Paso, Tommie stopped to telephone novelist Tom Lea. Her husband, she said, was deeply hurt. Lea was sympathetic. "When you go to Hollywood," he said, "you have to know you're going there for money and forget about everything else." In Hollywood, he said, someone with a good story was ". . . as helpless as a tied-up bull calf with a cutting knife coming at him."[35]

By late August, even the money was not enough to keep Gipson in California any longer. With only half the *McPheeters* script done, and his ulcer acting up badly, Gipson came home. The producers said they would get someone else to finish the job.

A short time later, Tommie opened a letter from the Swanson agency. It said Gipson was still owed $625 for a half week's work. But of that amount, $105.48 had to be deducted for the federal income tax, $1.65 for the Screenwriter's Guild pension fund, and $517.87 for California non-resident tax. Those three deductions added up to exactly $625. However, some money still needed to change hands: Gipson owed his agency $62.50—ten percent.

Fortunately, Tommie managed to keep the letter away from her husband, and the next day, she mailed the check for the ten percent commission. "But don't worry about us," she wrote. "We have the homestead paid for."[36]

The *Hound-Dog Man* experience and the unsuccessful *Jaimie McPheeters* effort had Gipson's emotions backed up to the jagged edge of a nervous breakdown. His ulcer was still burning his belly and he had begun to suffer with gout.

The movie was released in November. There were no rave reviews. John Bustin, film critic for the Austin *American-Statesman*, panned the movie but showed sympathy for Gipson. Bustin concluded that nothing in the movie "manages to get across the pleasant unpretentious charm of Gipson's original novel; so it all ends up as a mediocre and often quite tedious effort of small consequence."[37]

Then, as if a hack Hollywood screenwriter were plotting the scenes and camera angles of Gipson's life, at a time when he was already near mental collapse, things got worse. Two recent Texas A&M graduates started building a hog pen on the adjoining ranch. Their idea, based on the latest theories in animal husbandry, was to raise hogs on concrete. Keeping hogs on concrete instead of in the usual muddy pens was the clean, "Space Age" way to raise hogs, they believed. In the middle of the concrete pen was a rotating sprayer, which kept the hogs cool (replacing mud). The constant spray would wash the hog excrement down a large drain, where the highly fertile sludge would be stored before it was spread on the fields to enrich the soil.

For years before man had blasted satellites into space or invented new ways to raise hogs, the Gipson family had been able to sit on the porch of their house and enjoy the cool south breeze in the spring and summer. But after the neo-technological hog pen went into operation, the once pleasant south wind carried a horrid smell to the Gipson place. The odor was worse than bad—it was a smell that attacked, often sending its victims reeling in nausea.

An already angry and sick Fred Gipson became livid with new rage. The land he had worked so hard to own, and then to revitalize, was now going to be made unlivable by the stench of hog manure.[38]

Gipson shortly before he underwent shock treatment in 1960. (Courtesy Beck Gipson.)

16

Dreams

Gipson pulled out of bed at 4:00 A.M. Years ago in Corpus Christi, there were times when even the clanging of a cheap alarm clock could not stir him. But he and the whole world were different now. There was no reason to rise before dawn. He had no real work to do—could not do it if he had to—and he was not getting up to go hunting or fishing or to help herd goats. He just could not sleep any longer, though he would have welcomed the escape.

Before she went to bed, Tommie had built a pot of coffee. All Gipson had to do was plug it in and wait for it to brew. As the coffee began to percolate, he got the bottle of Scotch. When the pot quit steaming, he poured a cup, laced it with Scotch, and began another day of dying. The caffeine in the coffee gave him alertness; the Scotch, freedom from reality.

Three hours later, Tommie got up and came into the kitchen to cook breakfast. Because Gipson usually ate well, Tommie did not think of him as an alcoholic, but the man she had lived with for more than two decades had gradually changed. He was a man who had grown to hate the world, becoming more depressed, more jittery, more hostile every day.[1] The doctors were trying to solve his obvious medical problems. The ulcer and the gout seemed to be responding to treatment, but not Gipson.

Gipson drank more Scotch and coffee, skipping lunch. He talked, cried some, and denounced all the stupid bastards and crooked sons of bitches in the world. Beck, who was home for the day, listened and sympathized. He, like Tommie and Mike, desperately wondered what could be done to help.

The day outside matched Gipson's dreary mood and helped contribute to it. He had always found comfort in getting outdoors, but even that had become less effective in the face of his overwhelming despondency. Now, though talk was about other things, Gipson was struggling with the biggest decision he had ever had to make. He did not even know if he could make it. He wanted Tommie to do it for him but, at the same time, realized it was too awesome a burden to pass off on her.

Shock treatment. The doctor had said it matter-of-factly, explaining it was often very helpful in treating acute depression. A patient was given drugs to relax him, then wheeled into a clean, white room where he was strapped to a table, had a rubber protective device placed in his mouth, and small electrodes attached to his head. There was no memory of pain afterward, the doctor assured.

At 3:00 P.M., knowing that his brother was having a bad day, Charles dropped by, offering to play Beck and his father a game of canasta. Gipson played but had trouble finding the cards. During the game, he thrashed the problem over with his brother. Finally, he called Tommie into the room. He would face the uncertainty of shock treatment rather than continue as he was.

They left for Galveston the following Tuesday, February 16, 1960. At Fred's request, Tommie took a long, slow route, made slower by the many stops for water to go with her husband's Scotch. Gipson looked over at Tommie. ''I know this may sound dramatic and maybe completely foolish, but if I should come out just a complete idiot—or if I shouldn't come out of it at all—will you make sure the boys get the ranch?''[2]

The year before, financially flush despite Gipson's health problems, the Gipsons had purchased a 320-acre ranch on the Llano. The only improvement on it was a 100-year-old rock and log house. Fishing in the river was good; deer and turkey were plentiful. Though modest in size by Texas standards, it was a beautiful ranch. The Gipsons started referring to the place as the river ranch.

As they drove south, Tommie tried to reassure her husband. If there were even a millionth of a chance something could happen to him, she would not let him go through with the shock treatment. During a break in their discussion, Tommie went over their current financial status in her mind. Only two more payments were left on the ranch, and two more payments were due from Fox for *Hound-Dog Man*. They had $20,000 in savings and sufficient funds in their checking account for the year's living expenses, with enough left over to buy some cattle and make some improvements to the ranch. Gipson would not have to write another word for at least two years, which would free him from much of his stress.

They reached John Sealy Hospital in Galveston about 5:00 P.M. and Gipson was admitted that night. Tommie got a motel room. The next day, she talked with the doctors handling Gipson's case, then returned to Mason. The shock treatments would begin a week later, the doctors had said.

Shortly after she got back to Mason, Tommie got a telephone call from Dr. Joe Franz, a history professor at the University of Texas. What he had to say brought tears to her eyes. The nominating committee of the Texas Institute of Letters wanted Gipson to be the Institute's next president. Tommie stammered for a moment and then told Franz of her husband's impending shock treatments. Franz said Gipson could have right up to the last minute before the Institute's March 4 meeting to make up his mind if he wanted to accept the office. "We all love that husband of yours," he told her.[3] Tommie wrote Gipson with the news, and later, after talking it over by telephone, they agreed he should accept the honor. A week later, she went to Houston and delivered an acceptance speech for him at the Institute's annual banquet.

On March 17, Tommie wrote Crain to tell him about Gipson: "At this stage, I can't really tell if he is improving at all. I think there is no way of knowing . . . but it is rather a heartbreaking experience, and it won't be over the minute he steps through the front door of the hospital on his way home."[4]

Gipson was discharged from the hospital near the end of March. He had changed, no doubt. For one thing, he was very grateful to be home and very appreciative of Tommie. The medical advice was for him to take it easy and not make any major decisions for at least a month; another doctor said to take six months. But within a year, the doctors said, Fred Gipson should be like new. Tommie already believed the gamble had paid off. Her husband was pacific, subdued.[5]

Summer started with the usual hot winds blowing in from the Mexican desert. And the Gipsons took a major step toward the ranching business. They bought an old bull named Fritz and fifteen head of black Angus cows due to calve before the first cold norther. The family plan was to keep the heifers and sell the steers, until the herd numbered twenty-five to thirty. Tommie was excited about the acquisition of the cattle. For her, the only problem was falling in love with them, which would make it hard when it was time to sell.

Gipson, meanwhile, continued to improve. He was even talking about writing again. Several ideas for historical novels were kicking around in his head. Over the Fourth of July holiday, Gipson made up his mind. On July 5, 1960, Tommie wrote Crain: "It looks like we're back in business, as of this morning. Fred hatched off an idea for a sequel to *Old Yeller* which I think can't miss."

The book would be loosely based on the story of Herman Lehmann, the man Gipson had seen shoot a steer with a bow and arrow years before at Katemcy. He would mix Lehmann's childhood capture by the Apaches with the adventures of another dog, who could be Old Yeller's pup—both figuratively and literally.[6]

When Gipson started thinking about what to call the new book, the boys' black and tan Lacey hound came to mind. Mike had got the dog as a pup from Sammy Martin, a high-school friend. He and Beck had named the stubbed-tail pup, Sam, in honor of Mike's friend. Gipson, admiring the dog's scrappy nature, especially when it came to eating, added "Savage" to the name. Since the dog had become very much a part of the family, making him the hero of his next book seemed only natural.

Life was definitely better around the home place. Gipson's health was back and he was working again. But the matter of the odoriferous hog pen across the way continued to rub him raw. Every time he saw either of the two owners, he complained about the smell and the lack of neighborliness in not doing something about it. The confrontations grew more intense. The old anger—though narrower in focus—was building again.

Tommie wrote the State Health Department. That agency said there was nothing it could do. Finally, the Gipsons retained a San Angelo law firm to handle the matter. A lawyer told them the only possible remedy was to file a damage suit.[7]

Something had to be done. The pressure was building to a dangerous level. Gipson drove into Mason one morning to go to the post office and found one of the hog pen owners inside. An argument developed. Gipson threw a punch, which the younger man deftly dodged. He was not fast enough, however, to avoid a well-aimed kick by the fifty-two-year-old novelist, who landed a boot to his neighbor's backside. The sheriff reluctantly filed on Gipson for "fighting in a public place." Gipson had a doctor's appointment in Austin that day so he was not arrested. The justice of the peace, a long-time friend, said Gipson could come by any time to take care of the fine.

After seeing the doctor, Gipson stopped by to visit another old friend, a former district judge, who told him there was not much hope of any legal satisfaction in the hog pen case. Furious at the news, Gipson decided to "lay out" his fine in jail and make a public issue of the matter. He instructed Tommie to tip off every newspaperman they knew about the story. Maybe the publicity would put more pressure on the owners of the hog pen.

One of the owners was from an old-time Mason County German family and had just been married to a woman from another well-known family. Tommie tried to reason with Fred: The man he had kicked had a lot of friends and relatives. The ridicule, which Gipson hoped would fall on the family and the man who built the pen, could easily backfire. Finally, Gipson changed his mind but complained bitterly to Tommie that she had allowed his public emasculation.

After the fight, the man whom Gipson had kicked went to Gipson's brother-in-law, Ned Polk, and talked with him. Polk went to Tommie and said the whole situation had to cool down, or there could be a killing. Hoping to settle the matter, Polk got the owners of the hog pen to offer to sell Gipson their place for $21,000. But Gipson felt the land was not worth that much money. Tommie at first disagreed, but when she looked closer at the land, she realized her husband was right.[8]

For some time, Gipson had been thinking about building a new house on a bluff overlooking his beloved Llano. The problem over the hog pen was beginning to look like a valid justification for leaving the home place, though it riled Gipson to be forced from his home—even for a more modern house—by a man he viewed as an inconsiderate neighbor.

By August, hog pen worries aside, Gipson was making good progress on his *Old Yeller* sequel. Mike was working on the ranch at home before starting school again in the fall, and Beck was already in football practice, in the hands of his coaches almost twelve hours a day.[9]

In March, Gipson had not been able to deliver his own inaugural speech as the new president of the Texas Institute of Letters. By fall, though, he was in good enough health to accept an invitation to address a group of librarians and Parent Teachers Association members at Municipal Auditorium in Austin on November 19. His talk, which he had written in advance, was entertaining but full of double-barreled blasts of personal philosophy. There were many children in the audience, and he seemed to aim his remarks more at them than at the adults.

Parents, librarians, and writers of children's books, he said, were too preoccupied with "protecting" children.

> But who are we fooling? Not children. A child may not like such hurts, but they are willing to accept the truth. In fact, eager for the truth.

With a little explanation and guidance from grownups children will quickly understand and accept the facts of nature—that you can't have life without death. That every living creature, including man, kills to live. It's grownups that seem not to want to accept these facts. So they cut out all the truth, vigor and vitality of books before they hand them to the child to read.

He talked more about books and how he wrote his, stressing that what he did for a living was "complex and difficult work, with no absolute rules to go by." Every part of a story, he said, presented a different problem to a writer. "Each . . . might be solved a dozen different ways, yet all must add up to the whole. That's why writers go crazy, trying to solve such problems."[10]

But at his typewriter back in Mason, he had not been having much difficulty with the latest book. Tommie wrote Crain in early December that her husband was "coming along nicely" on the book and was within two to four weeks of finishing the first draft. Her estimation proved a bit optimistic but by January 17, 1961, Gipson was down to the last chapter. Though busy "killing Indians" on his typewriter, he was talking book ideas and planning a hunting trip to Mexico. A month later, *Savage Sam* was finished and in the mail to Harpers.[11]

Gipson hoped he had put together a good book but was nervous about its reception in New York. He had not written a book in almost five years. He had traveled a rough road since *Old Yeller* and was scared his strain and mental anguish would show through in *Savage Sam*. He need not have worried. Crain and Thomas both were delighted with the manuscript, a vote of confidence that did much to bolster the shaky ego of its author: ". . . you can't know what a vast relief it is to find that I've turned out a story that you and Evan feel is worth all the trouble incident to making it nearly as perfect as possible."[12]

Crain had called *Savage Sam* "a bearcat of a story," saying he hated to put it down after he started reading it. Nelle Harper Lee, author of *To Kill a Mockingbird*, had happened to be in Crain's office when he got the manuscript. She picked it up and read three chapters and surrendered it only reluctantly to Crain when she had to leave, he said.[13]

Though pleased with the reception for his latest effort, Gipson was still fuming over a column that had appeared in the Victoria *Advocate* a few weeks earlier. "Fred is the holder of a contract with Walt Disney Enterprises which is reported to pay him $40,000 per year for the rest of his life just on the chance he might turn out something of interest for the entertainment king," the *Advocate* reported.[14] The only contract Gipson had ever had with Disney involved *Old Yeller*, and it certainly did not provide a lifetime salary. He pounded out an angry letter to the paper, complaining about the embarrassment to him and to Disney.

In early May, the Gipsons flew to New York to discuss some suggested revisions on the manuscript. Though Thomas had been to Texas during Gipson's treatment at Galveston, it had been a long time since they had seen Crain. Gipson was not offended by the proposed changes and said he thought he could do them in a short time. He was inspired: The book was not even published and Disney was going to buy the movie rights for $25,000.[15]

Thomas and Crain were happy that the new book had already been bought by Disney, but they and John Fischer, still one of the top men at Harpers, were alarmed that Gipson might return to Hollywood to work on the screen adaptation of *Savage Sam*.

"Aside from the major questions of his health and happiness," Fischer wrote Tommie after they were back in Mason,

> there is a practical, money type consideration. I could give you a list of promising writers as long as your arm who went to Hollywood and disappeared, as if they had stepped into the La Brea Tar Pits. You can start with Ben Hecht, Gene Fowler, Charles MacArthur . . . and go on from there.
>
> Fred is a writer, not just a promising one, but already one of the best. He is not a Hollywood character, thank God. Hollywood never did any writer any good, and to many it has done a great deal of harm. The bait in a coyote trap never is a sane proposition for the coyote, no matter how big the chunk may be.[16]

Gipson finished the manuscript revision on *Savage Sam* by the end of May and, on June 2, headed to Corpus Christi with Mike for the annual writers conference. In *Savage Sam*, Gipson had kept the memory of *Old Yeller* alive by having Sam be Old Yeller's pup. Now, in real life, he was watching with a mixture of fear and pride—the beginning of a new writer in the Gipson family. Twenty-one-year-old Mike was trying to organize one hundred pages of notes that he had collected from a young Hungarian refugee, a friend he had met at the university. Mike had interviewed his friend at length about his experiences during the unsuccessful 1956 uprising against the Soviets in Hungary and thought he could write a dramatic, exciting book about him.

Tommie wrote Crain about Mike's project, which reminded her of Fred's struggles to get his information on Colonel Zack Miller in order some twenty years earlier. "I'll bet [Mike] is learning right now that the writing of a book is a bigger task than he thought it was, which is one of the first things to learn in the profession of authorship," Crain replied to Tommie.[17]

The task had certainly paid off this time for Mike's father, who received a $4,500 advance from Harpers for *Savage Sam*, along with the payment from Disney for the movie rights, in July. With the book out of the way, Gipson concentrated on plans for the new home on the river. One Sunday in August, after working for hours trying to make a rough drawing of the house he wanted, Gipson finally admitted, "Mama, I guess I just ain't no architect."[18]

Joe H. Bell of San Angelo was retained to design the house. The plans he drew called for a house sixty feet above the Llano, with a cantilevered balcony on the river side, and a twenty-two-foot deck suspended on steel beams over the creek that ran into the Llano. The house would be of cedar and red sandstone, much of it from old fences piled on the place a century before. There would be a nine-foot fireplace, and six rooms, including an office for Gipson. The house would "cost like smoke," as far as Gipson was concerned, but it would be worth it. He would be able to enjoy a beautiful view from almost any room, he would be free of the hog pen smell, and he would have a fine place to work and to entertain his friends.

Gipson was planning to return to Hollywood—against everyone's advice—to work on the *Savage Sam* script at $1,250 a week for at least eight weeks.[19] Before he went to the West Coast again, though, he was going with his friend Bob Snow on a bear and lion hunt in Mexico. Snow, a veteran state game warden, had been hunting cats and bear in Mexico since the days of the Mexican Revolution. He was a man, like Gipson, who could tell a good story over a bottle of tequila around the campfire.

They headed out in mid-September for the 300,000-acre San Miguel Ranch, south of Del Rio. As they left, Gipson told Snow, "My wife and my doctor have me on the wagon now, but if they think I'm going to stay on, they're just crazy!"[20]

Tommie noted in a letter to Gipson's doctor that her husband had been "on the wagon" about three weeks but had already slipped back into many of his old, self-destructive ways, despite his recent successes. "I can't learn to be quiet about alcohol," Tommie wrote.

Gipson by the Llano at his river ranch. (Photo by McKnight Studio, courtesy Beck Gipson.)

Gipson on porch of the river ranch. (Photo by Mike Cox.)

"I never bring up the subject, but, boy when Fred does, I give it all I've got . . . . [That's] when he really turns on me with resentments he's built up from before the womb." Despite her complaints about his drinking, however, she was already beginning to miss him.[21]

In Mexico, Gipson was finding adventure but not necessarily the kind he wanted. Snow's dogs had not picked up any bear scent, which was not surprising, since bears were becoming rare in North Mexico. They did jump one mountain lion, but it escaped to a rugged rimrock in a canyon, where the dogs could not follow.

The action started when a wild range hog wandered into their camp one night, looking for garbage. Snow's eight hounds jumped the big boar, instantly discovering they had cut off a bigger slice than they could get down. The old boar tore into the dogs, slashing viciously with its teeth and tusks. When it was over, which did not take long, all eight dogs were cut up, and so was a young Mexican who had tried to break up the fight, though his injuries were minor. Gipson and Snow spent the rest of the night stuffing entrails back into the dogs by lantern light.

They did have good luck shooting quail, which they ate around the campfire while they swapped stories. When Gipson got back to Mason, he was saddlesore and tired, but he had had his first taste of adventure in quite some time. And almost everything that had happened, he reasoned, could some day be used in his writing. He was seriously considering moving the setting of his writing south to Mexico, with his next hero being a small Mexican boy.[22]

On October 29, Gipson flew to Hollywood to begin the screenwriting job on *Savage Sam*.[23] Tommie made two trips to California to stay with her husband, who, as usual, quickly got homesick. On both occasions, Tommie appointed Mike, who had dropped out of college in October to devote full time to his book, honorary "mother" of Beck. In a letter to Donald Day before she left on one of her treks, she explained that Mike was ". . . wildly ambitious and yet has this feeling that he can never, never live up to what he has set up for himself. Well, he told me about this dream . . . the night after he had handed me six weeks of manuscript . . . . He dreamed that he was back in school, doing the broad jump with other boys, only, this time, he could fly a little. Not really take off and fly, but every time he jumped he flew a little.

"Isn't that wonderful? He feels that he is on his way. He knows he can't really spread his wings and fly yet, but he knows he has begun."[24]

The screenwriting, which took longer than expected, dragged on through early April 1962. The Gipsons stayed in a modest apartment on an access road off the Golden State Freeway. The sound of traffic was constant, but at least they had an upstairs apartment that afforded a view of the mountains in the distance—when they were visible through the smog. They had rented the apartment in January, moving in during a cold rain. When the rain stopped, hordes of noisy children appeared in the neighborhood like so many rain lilies, including a four-year-old who came to the Gipsons' front door wearing a grey Confederate uniform about three sizes too large. He told them he had a daddy but lived with his mother. The little boy called everyone "Uncle" or "Daddy," Tommie reported in a letter to a friend. One morning the little Confederate showed up and asked if "Grandpa" was home. Tommie thought that was pretty funny, until he greeted her with a friendly, "Hi, Grandma!"

The child added some brightness to the apartment, a refreshing change from the gloominess of Gipson, who continued to complain about his aches and pains (a sore jawbone from a bad dental job long before and his continual back trouble). But more than his physical complaints, Tommie worried about her husband's continuous fear and anger. Tommie argued that there was too much joy in life to constantly dwell on one's problems. Life, she told him, should not be wasted.[25]

Though Gipson had been treated royally by Disney during the *Old Yeller* screenwriting, their relationship was not as smooth this time. Gipson's drinking had become more chronic. As they left California, however, Gipson vowed to Tommie that once he was away from that "Godawful place and back to God's country," he would slow the heavy drinking. But a month after they were back in Mason, her husband's drinking still had not slowed. Tommie did not want it to happen, but saw that they were headed for divorce. She told Gipson she had already contacted a lawyer, who had recommended a psychologist in San Angelo. Gipson agreed to see him.[26]

After *Savage Sam* had come out in February, the mail brought a steady stream of good reviews. Riding the crest of good publicity on his book, Gipson was invited to write a story for the *New York Times Review of Books* on children's writing. He made his case again for realism in children's books and offered the world a sip of his philosophy: "I think that born into each one of us is a memory of times long past, a sort of ancestral hunger for the call of wild places and the driving urge for an uninhibited freedom to do whatever we're big enough to do."[27]

Savage Sam leaps at an Apache warrior (Rafael Campos) and is restrained by frontiersman Beck Coates (Brian Keith) in scenes from the Walt Disney movie *Savage Sam*. The screenplay by Fred Gipson and William Tunberg was based on Gipson's best-selling novel. (©MCMLXII Walt Disney Productions.)

By Father's Day, Gipson was badly depressed again. It was Beck's birthday, but he was attending a church function in Seguin, and Mike was back in Austin. Tommie and Gipson were at home alone in Mason, playing gin. When Tommie would win a hand, her husband would break into sobs. Tommie was trying to think of a way to lose, in hopes of making Gipson feel better.

A hundred miles away on Lake Travis west of Austin, Joe Small and his wife Elizabeth were entertaining Cactus and Jewel Pryor at their lake house. Small did not have a telephone at the lake place but had an arrangement that his neighbor, who had a phone, would contact him in case of emergency. When the neighbor walked over and told Small he was wanted on the phone, Small knew there was trouble. The caller was Bert Gerding, a detective lieutenant with the Austin Police Department.

"Joe, something bad has happened." Gerding paused.

"What is it?" Small asked, his body tightening, his mouth going dry.

"Mike Gipson has just shot himself."

"Oh, my God, no! Is he dead?"

"Yes, Joe. You've got to do me a favor. I can't . . . people in the police department are supposed to be pretty hard . . . but I haven't got the courage to call Fred Gipson. You've got to call him."[28]

Gerding, a policeman who had nearly become a doctor instead of a law enforcement officer, had asked Small to introduce him to Gipson about a year before. They had become casual friends.

When Small called, Tommie answered the phone. He asked to talk with Gipson. Tommie called her husband to the phone, puzzled at the strange tone of their old friend's voice.

"Fred, get ready for something bad. Now, it's just really bad," Small began.

Gipson's voice changed. "Who's it about?"

There was silence for a moment when Small said it was about Mike.

"Well, what has that rascal gone and done now?" Gipson asked.

Small could think of no other way to do it. He blurted the news: Mike had shot himself in the heart with a .22 caliber pistol. Small, fighting back his own tears, offered the Gipsons the use of his house until the funeral.[29] A short time later, Charles drove his brother and Tommie to Austin.

Mike left behind two stunned and bewildered parents, a younger brother, and dozens of friends. The Gipsons buried their eldest son in the Gooch Family Cemetery, beginning a struggle with crushing grief and a search for the reason why. Tommie was able to write Crain and Annie Laurie on July 2: "We can only guess at Mike's reasons, of course, but we feel sure that we know some of them."[30]

Mike had been depressed over the slow progress on his book. The Thursday before his death, he had come home and found a letter he had sent Crain returned; he had misaddressed it. In the letter, Mike had proposed sending four or five chapters of his book to Crain for use in trying to get an advance from a publisher. The returned letter was another delay on a project in which he was deeply involved.

After lunch that day, Mike and Beck had gone into town to buy cow feed. When they returned, they unloaded the feed at the barn and then walked over to a nearby shed. Inside, chained to a post, was Savage Sam. He had been beaten to death. When Tommie saw her two sons come back into the house, she noted Mike was without color. She asked what was wrong, but he could not speak. "I'll tell you later," Beck managed to get out. Mike left almost immediately for Austin, still unable to talk. Tommie never saw him alive again, and the family never learned who killed their dog, or why.[31]

The following Saturday, Mike had gone to a party and then returned to his apartment on Speedway near the University campus, where he stayed up late talking with his black roommate. Sunday afternoon, an attractive Jewish girl Mike was serious about said that her parents intended to take her out of school unless she stopped seeing him. This development, coupled with the senseless killing of his dog, the frustration of writing, and a general disgust with the way racial and religious prejudices were affecting his life, apparently led Mike to his final decision.

Mike went out for a while, then returned and asked his roommate where his pistol was. The roommate, sensing Mike's desperation, had moved it, but Mike found the weapon. The roommate rushed downstairs to summon a mutual friend. They heard the shot before they got back upstairs.

Mike had written a note to the girl and had used ink from his typewriter ribbon to leave his fingerprints on it, apparently to make sure no one thought his death was anything other than self-inflicted.

Two days after Mike's suicide, a letter to him arrived from Crain. He said he would do all he could to sell Mike's book.

To get the tragedy out of his mind, Gipson turned to his work, trying to put together a series of his old pulp stories into a quick book. It kept him occupied without forcing him to do original writing, which he did not think he could do. Another way to keep going was to drink, which he had never really stopped doing, despite treatment and the best advice of his doctors.

That drinking put a building strain on his marriage, a problem even before Mike's death. Still, Tommie had hope. "Maybe I'm just having some optimistic days about Fred, but for quite a while now, he's been so fine with me that I'm beginning to think we'll be all right. You know how badly I want that," she wrote a friend.[32] At least they were both still trying to preserve their twenty-two-year marriage. Though both had reservations about doing so, they were still seeing the psychologist in San Angelo.

Tommie had the dream in July. Mike, handsome as ever, drove up outside their home with a girl in his car and announced that he had eloped. "So that's where he's been," Tommie heard herself saying. Then she was awake and crying.[33] Mike was gone, and she and Fred were going to have to try very hard to make sure they did not lose each other, too.

17

Along Recollection Creek

The aqua Mustang bounced down the unpaved road, raising a trail of reddish dust. Each hard bump sent a snake of pain up Gipson's spine. Mourning doves were feeding on the sides of the road. The approach of the Mustang sent them into the air, their sudden departure a blurred explosion of white and gray. A covey of quail tried to outwalk the car, then turned on their toy soldier-like legs and marched into the long-stemmed lovegrass in the adjoining field. A territorially-minded paisano looking for lizards ran across the road just past the bone-dry creek crossing. The sleek bird seemed to wait for Gipson every day.

The ranch was only a quarter of a mile wide, and Gipson soon passed through the cattle guard that marked the main entrance to his property. Above the gate was a sign placed there by friend Holmes Jenkins. It read:

> Recollection Creek
> Fred Gipson

The mailboxes stood in a row under two giant live oaks on the unpaved extension of FM 1723, about two miles from the river house. The rural carrier usually delivered the mail by noon. Sometimes Gipson would run into a neighbor getting his mail and the two would talk. If no one was around, Gipson might just start reading his mail as he sat in front of the box. There was not much traffic on the road.

On Thursdays, there was always a Mason County *News* in the box. He got the monthly newsletter from Dunlop's Feed Store, bank statements, bills, letters from his agency and friends. But what he looked most forward to were the letters from children who had read one of his books.

Gipson averaged about thirty fan letters a month. They came from all over the world, since *Old Yeller* had been published in virtually every major language. He had had a stock reply printed, but if a letter was particularly sad or amusing, he would answer it personally. He smiled when he remembered one letter from a boy who said, "Dear Mr. Gipson: I have been told by my teacher to write to my favorite writer. I don't know whether you are alive or dead. If you're dead, just forget it."[1] Sometimes, when he was so lonely he did not care much about living, a letter like that would cheer him.

An old friend had told him that time and circumstance had about played out on both of them. At sixty, Gipson figured he had some time left, but he was inclined to agree about circumstance.[2] He and Tommie had barely managed to keep their marriage going for more than a year after Mike's death. His memory of that day in August 1963 when she left for San Angelo was only a blur. He had been drunk and they had had a bitter argument. Still, in hopes that things might work out, Tommie had not actually sued for divorce until January 1964.[3]

"Thank you for leaving the water in the well," he telephoned her when the property settlement was reached.[4] In truth, however, he had gotten the better end of the deal. He kept the 320-acre river ranch with its new home and the royalties from his books. Tommie got most of the library and cash from the sale of their old place to Gipson's nephew and his wife.

Early one Sunday morning not long after Tommie had filed for divorce, Gipson had been driving by the old home place when he saw an orange glow in the windows. He knew that his nephew and family were at church. Gipson ran to the door, opened it, and was knocked backward by the rush of heat. The place was engulfed in flames. As he watched helplessly, the house he had worked so hard to build virtually book by book, the house where his children had grown up, was reduced to charred lumber and scorched, cracked rock.

A year later, his mother died in a Mason nursing home. It seemed as if everything he had ever had, and everyone he had ever loved, were gone. Walter Prescott Webb, who used to come up to his old place for a sip of whiskey and long talks about things like grass and mules, had been killed in a car wreck. Not long after that, J. Frank Dobie had died in his sleep in Austin.

At least Gipson still had friends like Frank Wardlaw and Joe Small. Small did not come out to the ranch much any more, but Gipson visited him practically every time he went to Austin and they talked a lot on the telephone. When Small's continuing success with his western magazines had been the subject of an Associated Press story, Gipson had sent his friend a hand-written letter:

Dear Mister Small Hostail—
I red in a paper where you got independent rich by printing pieces on old rags.
Well, I got some old rags stuffed away (some people call them "dirty wash") what need airing . . . .
Anyhow, what I want to know is how to get in-dependant rich printing pieces on old dirty rags, if you ain't too stingy to tell me. And I want to know reel quick, on account of I don't want to waste much time and hard work. What I want to do is get right at spending the money.
And what I want to spend the money on is whiskey and wild wimmen. Can you think of anything better?
Would you come explain it all to me reel quick? You can find me up here on the banks of the Llano River.
Be nice if you'd bring a jug along.
Mr. Fred Gipson, Esquire
(or is it Inquire?)⁵

The tone of the letter was humorous, but Gipson was not kidding when he suggested Small bring something to drink. He made regular trips to Fredericksburg to buy Legacy Scotch by the case.
The fear Gipson lived with now was that, as his friend had said, all his circumstances had dried up. He had a gnawing feeling that whatever ability he had left as a writer had been killed with the same bullet that ended Mike's life in 1962. That day in June had been the start of what basically had been a downhill slide.
There had been good moments, though. In June 1963, shortly before the Gipsons' separation, the movie version of *Savage Sam* had pre-miered at the Odeon Theater in Mason. The Gipsons used the occasion to show off their new ranch home. The San Angelo paper covered the event thoroughly, ending the main story prophetically:

He [Gipson] admits he hasn't done much writing since work on the house began and that he probably won't get much done anytime soon . . . . With nine major novels and four motion pictures to his credit, as well as numerous short stories and children's books, Gipson deserves a little leisure time.[6]

After the divorce, Gipson had started a couple of books but had not finished them. However, *Ford Times* had commissioned him to do a story on the Big Bend, and *The New York Times* ran several book reviews he wrote. In 1966, the *Times* asked Gipson to interview Peter Hurd, whose portrait of Lyndon B. Johnson had been rejected by the President.

Gipson drove to New Mexico and met Hurd at his Sentinel Ranch near San Patricio. They got along only on a polite basis the first day as both tried to show how much they knew about the other's work, succeeding only in showing how little they knew.

They rode horseback into the nearby mountains the next day, climbing till Gipson's nose leaked clear fluid, and his arthritic bones started making more noise than his creaking saddle. The two men—one who made his living painting with oils, one who painted with words—talked about life and began to get to know each other. When silence settled between them, it was not uncomfortable. It gave Gipson time to think.

On the side of that mountain, he was closer to heaven than a lot of men get. His religion centered not so much on the notion of a heaven above as a heaven on earth. The sight of wind moving through tall, native grass—that was heaven to Gipson. A quail's call, a wild turkey's gobble, or a bell-voiced hound trailing a coon was Gipson's choir on high. His peace was on earth, in the enjoyment of the land, its creatures, its weather. Several years earlier, when he was given an award for *Old Yeller*, he had written an acceptance speech he could not give in person. He listed the wild things he loved: a flight of mourning doves at sunset, the splash of a feeding bass.[7] Basic, eternal things he knew would be there long after he was gone. That was his religion.

When the *Times* rejected the story Gipson wrote about Hurd, he wondered if he would ever again be a successful writer. He fretted about his writing style, that its simplicity was outmoded in a time of explicitly sexual novels. His writing lacked sophistication, he told friends. His sister Stella argued with him about it once, telling him that if the world needed anything, it was more simplicity.

Oh, Gipson still had ideas—and offers from publishers. In June 1968, the San Angelo *Standard-Times* sent a reporter to Mason for an interview with Gipson who said he still had some book topics in mind.[8] What he needed, he said, was a secretary (preferably female) to stay at his ranch and help with his writing and some translating he would need done.

184

Gipson wanted a translator because he believed his chances for the future were in Mexico, a country which had fascinated him since the first time he and some friends went to whoop it up in the border dives back in the late 1920's and early 1930's. He liked the Mexican people, too, and felt a special kinship with those living in extreme poverty. His Spanish was better than that of most Texas gringos, but he felt he would need help with the language to get the maximum benefit from the rich harvest of raw folklore he believed lay south of the Rio Grande.[9]

So, Gipson packed his Mustang with a change of clothes and a bottle of Scotch and headed south, no less an adventure-seeking maverick than any other cowboy who ever saddled up and headed for a country steeped in wildness and romance. He even thought about moving to Mexico but realized he could not stand being away from Mason County for long.

"A writer has to replenish himself," he had told an interviewer a few years before. "I find when I stay [on the ranch] too long I get stale and have to get out and mix with people."[10]

On one trip to Mexico, Gipson found someone he believed was the answer to everything he needed in life: someone who could offer female companionship, help him with his plans to write novels based on Mexican folklore, and stimulate his muse in general. She was Angelina Torres, a pretty English tutor he met in Mexico City. He helped her get a six month's work visa and brought her back to Texas to live with him at the ranch.

Beck, meanwhile, who had graduated from high school the year of his parents' separation, dropped out of Texas Tech University during his second year to join the Army. At Tech, he had met a girl from Ballinger, Texas, Carolyn (Cookie) Cook, and they had fallen in love. One morning in June, with only three minutes to talk, Beck had called her from a pay telephone at Fort Polk, Louisiana, where he was in basic training. He asked her to marry him and she agreed. The rest of the three minutes was spent planning their wedding and honeymoon. They were married in Ballinger on July 7, 1967.

Now, five months later, Gipson was thinking about a wedding of his own. Beck had been transferred to Fort Wolters at Mineral Wells to undergo helicopter flight training. Gipson called his son one night and told him he had decided to marry Angelina on December 17. Beck got a weekend pass so he could be there.

When Beck and Cookie reached Mason, Gipson was still fuming over what had happened the day before. He had heard the sound of a vehicle approaching the ranch house and looked out to see a green Border Patrol jeep. He knew immediately what had happened. Someone—he figured he knew who—apparently had tipped the immigration authorities that Angelina's visa had expired.

As the two uniformed officers walked toward his house, Gipson reached into a closet and grabbed a shotgun. When he opened the front door, he held the shotgun on the two officers at stomach level. Gipson asked them what they wanted and was not surprised when they said they had come to pick up Angelina Torres. What the tipster had not explained to the Border Patrol was that Gipson planned to marry her, which would automatically make her a United States citizen. The two officers, realizing they were on thin ice legally and safety-wise, walked slowly back to their jeep and left.

The day of the wedding, Gipson and the few guests he had invited were nervous that the officers might come back armed with a warrant. The tension was heightened because right up until the last minute, several of Gipson's friends were trying to talk him out of marrying.

But Gipson had not had a better six months in a long time. Miss Torres seemed like the answer to all his problems, and he was going to marry her. Gipson would have preferred the blessing of his family and friends but did not much care what people thought about his marriage, realizing almost gleefully that it would give his neighbors something to gossip about for weeks.

Despite his recent libertine ways and the local talk it inspired, Gipson was fairly well accepted in his community. Back in 1958, during the Mason County centennial, signs were erected outside town that read: "Mason, Texas, Home of Fred Gipson, Author of *Old Yeller*." Although everyone in the county knew that Gipson was a writer, not everyone understood exactly what that involved. "Don't you ever work none?" an old farmer had asked him one time.[11]

But Gipson, growing self-conscious and defensive about his ways, had put up a protective barrier of irascibility that made a lot of the people in Mason feel he was shutting them out. Their reaction to that fueled his insecurities. He began to feel he was more of a black sheep than he was, though there was no doubt he was considered more of a celebrity outside Mason County than in it.

Gipson's marriage, despite his hopes for it, did not blossom. He and Angelina had had some fine moments together, but problems soon developed. Six months after the ceremony, the marriage was over. The divorce settlement cost him about $5,000, but Gipson was philosophic about the failed marriage—he was sorry it had not worked, but he had enjoyed it while it lasted.[12]

What had Gipson far more worried than the divorce was his son. Now that Beck had learned how to fly a helicopter, he had orders for

Vietnam. If Beck did not make it back, Gipson knew what little chance he had for the future would die with his son.

Cookie and her parents, Clifford and Norma Cook, spent a lot of time at the ranch. Cookie also made several trips to San Angelo to be with Tommie, who was attending Angelo State University and planning to marry her old friend Joe North, a recent widower. But generally, Cookie stayed at the ranch with Gipson.

Despite his being constantly on edge about Beck, for the first time since *Savage Sam*, Gipson started another book. It would be called *Little Arliss* and would feature the exploits of the youngest of the two brothers who first appeared in *Old Yeller* and then had survived capture by Indians in *Savage Sam*.

Following his long-standing routine, Gipson would get up before dawn each day and write. Then he would drive to Mason for breakfast. When Cookie got up, she would retype what he had written. Later, she would cook lunch and around one or two o'clock, Gipson would take a nap. When he got up, they would talk over what he had written, the news of the day, and life in general, sitting for hours over drinks on the deck overlooking the Llano.

The two developed a close father-daughter relationship. Gipson taught Cookie how to use a fly rod for bass fishing. Even though he was a man in his sixties with a bad back, Cookie could barely keep up with him as they walked up and down the Llano or the James River.

They went to a lot of movies, either in Mason or Fredericksburg, and took several long trips into Mexico. On one trip, they went to Monterrey and then on a mule ride at Horseshoe Falls. They toured all the small villages within a day's drive of the city where Gipson had honeymooned years before. If he saw someone who looked interesting, he would stop and talk to them, spending hours in cafes and cantinas with Cookie at his side.

When they got back to Mason, Cookie got up one morning expecting to do more typing on *Little Arliss*. But when she went into Gipson's study, she could find no trace of the manuscript. Cookie asked Gipson where the book material was, and he said in a tone that invited no further questions, "I have a speaking engagement in Lamesa." After he returned from the trip to the High Plains, he never mentioned the book. The book was dead; the subject closed.[13]

In May, the engine on Beck's helicopter failed and the craft crashed into a bay. Beck managed to swim two hundred yards to shore, towing his copilot who was a poor swimmer. He was hospitalized with a back injury. A month later, the decorated survivor made it back to Texas. He served out the rest of his enlistment as a flight instructor at Fort Wolters.

On August 18, 1970, at the Fort Wolters base hospital, Cookie gave birth to a son. They named him Benjamin Cook Gipson—after both grandfathers. Becoming a grandfather and having his son safely back from Vietnam gave Fred Gipson renewed optimism about life.

That fall in Mexico, he bought a wooden chest with hand-wrought fastenings. When he got back to Mason, he went to Frank Polk's boot shop and had a leather square tacked on the top of the chest. Carved into the leather were the words "Ben's Treasure Chest." Then Gipson began filling the chest with things he thought his grandson ought to have: a tusk from a wild hog, gold coins from Mexico, interesting rocks. He kept the chest by the door at the ranch house and urged guests to contribute whatever they considered special.

Gipson had traveled through Mexico to San Salvador, looking for someone else to help him start writing again. He even ran newspaper ads in Spanish, seeking someone willing to work with an employer "in the house of his family in the United States." The notebook he used to keep track of his expenses for income tax purposes was labeled, "Search of help."[14]

The next woman Gipson brought to his ranch was not as his bride-to-be. She was an employee who provided the professional services he needed, as well as companionship. This arrangement, as were others like it, was short-lived.

When Beck got out of the Army, he and Cookie returned to Lubbock, where both finished work toward college degrees at Texas Tech. After graduation, Beck went to work with a commodity brokerage in Dallas. Both the school work and the new job had been interrupted by frequent emergency trips to Mason, as Gipson began to rely more on his son for help. Once in mid-1971, Beck had had to make a hasty flight to Mason in a friend's chartered plane and meet with Joe Small's attorney to get his father out of a spurious lease arrangement involving the ranch.

During the time Beck was in Dallas, Gipson could look forward to a call between 6:30 and 7:00 A.M. every morning, since Beck started work early at the brokerage and had access to a WATS line. He knew his father was getting increasingly lonely. Gipson even resorted to catalogues with pictures and mailing addresses of women. One bore the slogan, "Be lonely no more." Three thousand names could be had for $7.[15]

In January 1973, he left on another Mexican odyssey in "search of help." He drove to Del Rio, with stops in Nueva Rosita, Monclova, Satillo, Buenavista, and then to Tampico on the Gulf of Mexico. By spring, Gipson was back in Mason County. His search had been unsuccessful. Like Coronado and his elusive quest for the Seven Cities of Cibola, Gipson was looking for something he was not likely to find. He needed more than a bilingual secretary and female companionship. He needed what he could never have again—good health.

The trees were just beginning to bud on Gipson's river place when Bill Warren, book editor of the Austin *American-Statesman* drove to Mason for an interview. A sixty-five-year-old man who looked nearly eighty greeted Warren. Gipson's mustache was now cottony white, the lines of his face were dug deep, as rugged as the Llano River Canyon. The flesh beneath Gipson's neck hung like the loose skin on a gobbler's throat. Gipson walked slowly with the help of a wooden cane. Arthritis was adding to the agony of his bad back.

The years of hard work and hard drinking had stacked up and were pulling Gipson down. A man was lucky, Gipson believed, if he did not get old enough to realize that "the best of what was going to happen to him had already happened." That was one of nature's cruelest jokes: The body went to Hell, while the mind wanted to hold back and try again for something better. "It was like a man was pushed backwards downhill, seeing the top getting farther from him, but always seeing it, always wishing he could go back."[16]

Several years earlier when typing notes for a novel he never wrote, he had had those thoughts. Now increasingly, he knew he had been right. Still, he was interested in getting back into book writing. "I have some ideas for two or three things, but I need someone to write them down for me—someone who'll let me breathe down his neck," Gipson told Warren.[17]

Gipson may have had trouble getting in the mood to put words on paper, but it was never hard for him to talk with friends. He liked to drive to cartoonist Ace Reid's 250-acre ranch near Kerrville on the opening day of deer season to spend the night sitting around a campfire, drinking Scotch and telling stories.

Reid had a hunter's cabin in a draw near a spring where unpolluted water trickled from a limestone cliff. A few paces from the spring was a big sycamore log. Nearby was a circle of blackened rocks long used for campfires. Gipson and Reid would sit on that log in front of the fire all night long—Gipson sipping Legacy mixed with the spring water, Reid working on a fifth of Jack Daniels.

Reid had a couple of old Longhorn steers that would amble toward the fire, moonlight glinting off their curved horns. When light started showing in the east, Gipson would get up, walk to his car, and head back to his ranch.

Gipson's earliest memories centered on a fireplace. Now, as he struggled with loneliness, the big fireplace in his ranch house gave him comfort. It brought back that feeling of warmth that had nothing to do with the burning logs—a feeling of security he believed came from an inherited, primitive memory. Whenever it was even remotely cool, he would have a fire going which he insisted on starting with bear grass, the way his father had taught him. Lighter fluid or crumpled paper would have been more convenient but not true to nature. Having enough wood on hand to get through the fall and winter became one of his major preoccupations in life.

Sometimes Gipson could forget his assorted aches and pains. He left his cane at the ranch house the night he went with the Wardlaws, along with a friend of Mrs. Wardlaw's who was a graduate student in Austin, to the Ramblin' Rose dance hall at Llano. Gipson and the graduate student danced to country western songs until closing time. The management of the famed nightspot put a spotlight on Gipson at one point, announcing that he was the famous writer from Mason.

Word quickly spread in Mason that Gipson had been at the Ramblin' Rose. The next weekend, Wardlaw was back at Gipson's ranch. His friend had gone on an errand, so when the telephone rang, Wardlaw answered it.

"Is Fred Gipson there?" a woman asked.

"No, he's not here now," Wardlaw replied.

"Well, who are you?" she asked.

Wardlaw answered her question.

"Oh, you were with Fred last weekend at the Ramblin' Rose, weren't you?" she said.

Yes, he had been at the Ramblin' Rose.

The woman, who had not identified herself, then blurted: "Who was that woman?"

"Oh, she was a University of Texas coed," Wardlaw replied, smiling gloriously at the thought of what that would do for the local gossip mill.[18]

Gipson had known for a long time that he was a favorite topic of local talk, and that some of the eight persons on his party line were not above listening in occasionally. One time, Gipson was using his best Hill Country language to cuss someone in a phone conversation with Wardlaw, who reminded him that someone might be eavesdropping.

"I don't give a damn, it's good for them to hear it," Gipson said.[19]

Fred beside the nine-foot fireplace at the river ranch. Fires, indoors and outdoors, were always a source of comfort for Gipson. (Photo by McKnight Studio, courtesy Beck Gipson.)

Gipson said what he wanted to say, always had. Wardlaw admired the fact that his friend lived life as he wanted to, with very few illusions. His health was bad and he was not doing any writing, but he was his own person.

Once, when he noticed a guest throw a beer bottle across one of his stock tanks, Gipson practically ran him off the place. "Now go get it," he told the visitor, who sheepishly retrieved the empty bottle.[20] He did not like to see the land—his or anyone else's—abused in any fashion.

Wardlaw considered Gipson one of his closest friends. What he liked about him, other than his proven abilities as an author and his independence, was his love of nature, his closeness to the land. The university press director believed Gipson's knowledge of nature was natural, and he realized that sounded redundant on the surface. But his friend's store of knowledge seemed almost inborn. Gipson knew that a coon does not wash every bite of food before eating it, that a cow gets up hind feetfirst while a horse gets up front feetfirst, that catfish do not bite when the moon is shining, that a jack rabbit will not run into a hollow log and that wolves eat acorns.

To Wardlaw's thinking, Gipson was not a twentieth-century man, though he had been born eight years after its beginning. He belonged to the previous century—virtually everything he did supported that, even the way he cooked.

Gipson could cook beans or catfish or *cabrito* better than anyone Wardlaw knew. His secret ingredient for beans was an apple—not peeled or cut up, but a whole apple immersed in the simmering beans. In frying catfish, Gipson had two principle philosophies: The bacon grease he used was not hot enough until a kitchen match thrown in the pot exploded; and the proper amount of salt and pepper was "way too much," because the heat fried off the spices. Barbecuing *cabrito* was an all-day affair. The result, in the opinion of anyone who tried it, was the best job of goat cooking north of the Rio Grande.

As his health permitted, Gipson continued to travel and accept speaking engagements. In March 1970, he had gone to Dallas for the annual meeting of the Texas Institute of Letters. At the meeting, he and Dallas *Morning News* book critic Lon Tinkle were named fellows of the Institute—only four other members had ever been accorded that honor.[21]

On September 20, 1971, he drove to Killeen to be the featured speaker at the dedication of that city's new library. For such talks, he scribbled notes on envelopes. On one, he wrote, "I'm a writer—or once was. New story? Got plenty in mind, but so tied up with pain of arth., need somebody to do ass-busting work I used to do. Can't pay competent salary—but need [some]one to gamble with me—Got any ideas?''[22]

The American Library Association invited him to speak at its 1972 convention in Chicago, but he was unable to go. In 1973, he tried to interest the Disney studios in *Little Arliss*. The studio replied on July 2 that the script was ''colorful'' but had no solid story line.

Several years earlier, Sam H. Henderson, a professor at North Texas State University in Denton, had written a booklet on Gipson as part of a series being done on Southwestern writers by the Steck Publishing Company. *Savage Sam*, he wrote, ''. . . in no way hints that any kind of final summing up of his achievement is in order. The astonishing quantity and variety of Gipson's writing should indicate that a man of his wide range of interests and creative energy can be productive of much more.''[23]

But the fire was out.

Stella stood on the porch of her brother's river ranch. The creek below talked softly. Beyond the Llano's curve, the moon had climbed, laying a silver shroud over the Gipson ranch house. It was about nine o'clock, August 14, 1973.

A fish slapping the water with its tail interrupted Stella's quiet contemplation. Only a few days earlier, Gipson and Wardlaw had been sitting on this porch, arguing over the size of a catfish Holmes Jenkins had caught. Gipson had ended the argument by pulling out a new pair of fish scales he had bought about three weeks before, after a fish caught by Jenkins had grown with each telling of the story.

Stella had got the telephone call about five hours earlier. Cookie's parents had come for a visit. When they got to the ranch house, Gipson's Mustang was in the garage. As frequent guests at the ranch, the Cooks knew they were welcome to walk on in without knocking. Since Gipson did not greet them, they assumed he was taking his regular afternoon nap. They sat in the living room waiting for him to get up but began to get nervous as time passed. Finally, Cliff Cook went to peek inside Gipson's bedroom. Seconds later, he rushed to the telephone and called for an ambulance. His next call was to Gipson's friend and doctor, J. G. Bodenhamer, of Mason.

Cookie's father knew, however, that nothing could be done for his friend. Gipson was dead. Not far from his hands was a paperback book he had been reading. Dr. Bodenhamer said he had had a cerebral hemorrhage and a justice of the peace ruled death by natural causes.

When the family and close friends began discussing funeral arrangements, Beck's first thought had been to bury his father on the land he had loved so much and had worked so hard to be able to buy. But state law prohibited that, he learned. The family plot at the Gooch Cemetery, where Mike and his infant sister were buried, was full. The only way to bury Gipson there would have been to get a lot in the new section of the cemetery across the road from the other Gipson graves. Wardlaw suggested that Gipson's resting place belonged in the State Cemetery in Austin, near his friends Dobie and Webb.

Governor Dolph Briscoe was contacted at his Uvalde ranch and agreed to issue the necessary proclamation allowing burial in the State Cemetery. More than a hundred persons gathered at 11:00 A.M. on Friday, August 17, for Gipson's graveside rites.

Several months before, Gipson had asked Wardlaw to say something at his funeral, as Wardlaw explained, ''. . . in the unlikely event that he should predecease me.'' Wardlaw, his voice faltering with emotion, fulfilled his friend's request and told those gathered at Gipson's grave:

> It is natural to think of Fred Gipson's writing as having many important roots in common with the work of his friends J. Frank Dobie, Roy Bedicek, and Walter Prescott Webb . . . . Most of the work of these three older men was shaped in many important ways by their closeness to the land, to the natural world, to the people who made the West. Fred Gipson's certainly was. Walter Webb compared Fred's work to that of Mark Twain in its universality of appeal to people of all ages and places. He once expressed to me the belief that *Old Yeller* stood perhaps the best chance of achieving immortality of any book yet written in Texas—and this from the author of *The Great Plains*. Webb may well have been right.[24]

Gipson's grave is next to Webb's. The red granite marker bears a simple legend, the kind of unpretentious eloquence the man beneath it had breathed into his writing: ''His Books Are His Monument.''

Appendix A

Published Works By Fred Gipson

BOOKS

Big Bend: A Homesteader's Story. With J. O. Langford. Austin: University of Texas Press, 1952. 2nd ed. rev., 1973.

Cowhand: The Story of a Working Cowboy. New York: Harper & Bros., 1953. 2nd ed., College Station: Texas A&M University Press, 1977.

The Cow Killers. Austin: University of Texas Press, 1956.

Curly and the Wild Boar. New York: Harper & Row, 1979.

Fabulous Empire: Colonel Zack Miller's Story. Boston: Houghton Mifflin Co., 1946. Condensed in *Holiday*, September 1946, p. 65.

The Home Place. New York: Harper & Bros., 1950. Condensed in *Philadelphia Bulletin* Book-of-the-Week *(The Sunday Bulletin)*, April 29, 1951, p. 1. Serialized in *The Idaho Farmer*, beginning Oct. 16, 1952, p. 31.

Hound-Dog Man. New York: Harper & Bros., 1949. Condensed in *Omnibook Magazine*, June 1949, p. 104.

Little Arliss. New York: Harper & Row, 1978.

Old Yeller. New York: Harper & Bros., 1956. Serialized in *Collier's*, June-July 1956. Condensed in *Reader's Digest Condensed Books*, 1956.

Recollection Creek. New York: Harper & Bros., 1955.

Savage Sam. New York: Harper & Row, 1962.

The Trail-Driving Rooster. New York: Harper & Bros., 1955.

MAGAZINE ARTICLES AND STORIES

"All This and Game, Too!" *Sports Afield*, February, 1947, p. 26.

"Angels Work Overtime." *Rocky Mountain Empire Magazine* (Denver *Post*), Feb. 22, 1948, p. 2.

"Bad Day." *Southwest Review*, vol. XXXVII (Autumn 1952), p. 325.

"Bad Hog." *Rocky Mountain Empire Magazine* (Denver *Post*), Feb. 29, 1948. p. 8.

"Bad Trouble on Panther Branch." *Dime Western*, December 1944, p. 63.

"The Banana Snitchers." *The Progressive Farmer*, October 1948, p. 48.

"Bandits of Rio Tonero." *True*, Aug. 22, 1944.

"Bass Go For Editors." *Western Sportsman*, September 1946, p. 15.

"Bear in Harness." *Rocky Mountain Empire Magazine* (Denver *Post*), June 27, 1948, p. 5.

"Big Coon on Little Willow." *Outdoors*, April 1944, p. B-8.

"Big Goat Deal." *Rocky Mountain Empire Magazine* (Denver *Post*), Aug. 22, 1948, p. 3.

"Big Jim's Sixgun Solo." *Ace-High Western*, November 1941, p. 59.

"The Big Melon Bust." *Rocky Mountain Empire Magazine* (Denver *Post*), March 7, 1948, p. 2.

"Bird Woman." *Rocky Mountain Empire Magazine* (Denver *Post*), March 28, 1948, p. 2.

"Black Cat Bachelor." *The Progressive Farmer*, August 1947, p. 16.

"Blessed Are the Meek," *The Westerner*, October 1945, p. 15.

"Blizzard Range Fugitives." *Dime Western*, August 1943, p. 98.

"Blizzard Trail." *Southwest Review*, vol. XXX (Spring 1945). Reprinted in *True West*, Fall 1953, p. 20.

"Blood Drinker." *Triple Western*, date unknown. In Fred Gipson Papers.

"Blue Whistler." *The Southern Sportsman*, December 1936, p. 21.

"Bounty Hunter From Hell." *Dime Western*, May 1942, p. 84.

"Bring On Your Roast Dog!" *The Westerner*, December 1943, p. 31.

"Brush Roper." *The Progressive Farmer*, June 1956, p. 56.

"The Bulldogger." *Rocky Mountain Empire Magazine* (Denver *Post*), Sept. 20, 1953, p. 36.

"Buried Treasure." *Liberty*, Nov. 23, 1946, p. 22.

"Chum." *The Westerner*, December 1946, p. 18.

"The Circle A Invasion." *Dime Western*, October 1942, p. 96.

"Come and Get It, Law Dog!" *10-Story Western*, February 1943, p. 50.

"Coon Hunt in the Blackjacks." *Rocky Mountain Empire Magazine* (Denver *Post*), Feb. 15, 1948, p. 2.

"Coooooon!" *Southwest Review*, vol. XXXIII (Winter 1948), p. 52.

"The Cowboy Who Broke the Killers." *Argosy*, May 1955, p. 51.

"The Cow Killers." Published in two parts in *True West*, June 1957, p. 20, and October 1957, p. 24.

"Cowmen, Guard Your Sheep." *Star Western*, June 1942, p. 54.

"Cow Pen Reveries." *Rocky Mountain Empire Magazine* (Denver *Post*), Feb. 8, 1948, p. 3.

"Cow Work Is Work." *The Westerner*, July 1943, p. 9.

"The Cu-Ne-Va Ghost." *Rocky Mountain Empire Magazine* (Denver *Post*), Sept. 19, 1948, p. 3. Reprinted in *True West*, April 1956, p. 29.

"Cyclone Ropers." *The Westerner*, June 1944, p. 16. Reprinted in *The Western Horseman*, June 1950, p. 10.

"A Damn' Bad Man!" *Dime Western*, August 1942, p. 71.

"Dark of the Moon." *Rocky Mountain Empire Magazine* (Denver *Post*), March 21, 1948, p. 8.

"The Day Fat Alford Blushed." *Rocky Mountain Empire Magazine* (Denver *Post*), May 24, 1953, p. 6.

"Devil River Gets An Outcast." *10-Story Western*, May 1945, p. 44.

"Dinner Bucket." *Scene: Magazine of the South and West*, May 1947, p. 21.

"The Doctor's Payoff." *Rocky Mountain Empire Magazine* (Denver *Post*), Dec. 19, 1948, p. 3.

"The Dog That Came to Dinner." *The American Weekly*, Jan. 12, 1958, p. 4.

"Drifter Makes a Hand." *10-Story Western*, July 1943, p. 52.

"Dull Afternoon on a Ranch." *Rocky Mountain Empire Magazine* (Denver *Post*), June 13, 1948, p. 5.

"Fat Had an Itch." *Argosy*, May 1954, p. 40.

"Fracas in the Rocks." *Rocky Mountain Empire Magazine* (Denver *Post*), Jan. 18, 1948, p. 2.

"Feud Busters at Cedar Gap." *10-Story Western*, May 1943, p. 8.

"First Buck." *The Southern Sportsman*, November 1936, p. 12.

"Fisherman's Luck." *Rocky Mountain Empire Magazine* (Denver *Post*), Feb. 15, 1948, p. 6.

"Fishing Time on the Llano." *Rocky Mountain Empire Magazine* (Denver *Post*), April 11, 1948, p. 3.

"A Fool and His Money." *Farm and Ranch*, date unknown. In Fred Gipson Papers.

"For the Love of 'Nigger'!" *The Southern Sportsman*, September 1941, p. 8.

"Ghost in the Chisos." *Rocky Mountain Empire Magazine* (Denver *Post*), May 2, 1948, p. 3. Reprinted as "Ghosts of the Chisos" in *Frontier Times*, Fall 1958, p. 20.

"Gift Horse." *Western Sportsman*, January-February 1951, p. 8.

"Gobbler That Walks Alone." *Outdoor Life*, August 1942, p. 50.

"Graveyard Gobbler." *Adventure*, June 1944, p. 34.

"The Grub Liners' Grizzly." *The Westerner*, December 1942, p. 22.

"Gun Boss of the Phantom Range." *10-Story Western*, July 1944, p. 100.

"Gun Riot at Wolf Run." *Ace-High Western*, September 1943, p. 8.

"Gunsmoke Stops a Tumbleweed." *.44 Western*, March 1942, p. 35.

"Gun Wait." *10-Story Western*, October 1942, p. 90.

"The Gusher That Snowed." *Rocky Mountain Empire Magazine* (Denver *Post*), April 18, 1948, p. 2.

"Half-interest in Hell." *Big-Book Western*, April 1943, p. 56.

"Handshake with a Bull Elk." *True West*, Summer 1953, p. 13.

"The Hanging of Bob Augustine." *True*, December 1945, p. 51.

"Hard Luck Hits Town." *Dime Western*, February 1942, p. 78.

"Hard-Pressed Sam." *Southwest Review*, vol. XXII, no. 2 (Winter 1936), p. 177.

"Heap Big Pow Wow." *True West*, August 1956, p. 18.

"Hell and Holy Water." *Adventure*, September 1947, p. 52.

"High Lonesome Place." *Rocky Mountain Empire Magazine* (Denver *Post*), Feb. 1, 1948, p. 3. Condensed in *Reader's Digest*, June 1951, p. 125. Included in *Rocky Mountain Empire* by Elvon L. Howe, ed. (Garden City, N. Y.: Doubleday & Co.), 1950.

"Hill Country Coon." *Adventure*, December 1942, p. 72.

"Horse-Killing Steer." *Rocky Mountain Empire Magazine* (Denver *Post*), April 4, 1948, p. 3.

"Hound-Dog Men Are Born." *Southwest Review*, vol. XXXI (Fall 1945), p. 54. Retitled "A Hound-Dog Man" and condensed in *Reader's Digest*, February 1946, p. 93.

"If It Moves, Rope It!" *Cavalier*, March 1956, p. 28.

"I Hate Snakes." *American Weekly*, Feb. 18, 1958.

"Indian Trader Talks Back." *Rocky Mountain Empire Magazine* (Denver *Post*), Aug. 29, 1948, p. 2.

"Injuns Is People." *The Southern Sportsman*, May 1941, p. 11.

"Is Your Child a Turtle-Biter?" *Rocky Mountain Empire Magazine* (Denver *Post*), date unknown. In Fred Gipson Papers.

"It Sure Beats Me." *Liberty*, March 24, 1945, p. 33.

"Joe Bauldauff's Bear." *Rocky Mountain Empire Magazine* (Denver *Post*), Aug. 6, 1950, p. 2. Included in *Rocky Mountain Empire* by Elvon L. Howe, ed. (Garden City, N. Y.: Doubleday & Co.), 1950. N. Y.: Doubleday & Co.), 1950.

"Journey into History." *Rocky Mountain Empire Magazine* (Denver *Post*), July 11, 1948, p. 4.

"King of the Wild Country." *Dime Western*, date unknown. In Fred Gipson Papers.

"Lady Jack Whacker." *Rocky Mountain Empire Magazine* (Denver *Post*), Aug. 8, 1948, p. 2. Included in *Rocky Mountain Empire* by Elvon L. Howe, ed. (Garden City, N. Y.: Doubleday & Co.), 1950.

"La Senora Maggie." *Rocky Mountain Empire Magazine* (Denver *Post*), May 23, 1948, p. 2.

"Last Escape." *Rocky Mountain Empire Magazine* (Denver *Post*), Jan. 11, 1948, p. 3. Condensed in *Reader's Digest*, March 1949, p. 35. Included in *Rocky Mountain Empire* by Elvon L. Howe, ed. (Garden City, N. Y.: Doubleday & Co.), 1950.

"Last of the Fighting McCauleys." *Star Western*, October 1943, p. 62.

"The Last of the Wild Ones." *15 Western Stories*, July 1944, p. 25.

"Last Roundup on the Bell." *Rocky Mountain Empire Magazine* (Denver *Post*), May 9, 1948, p. 3. Included in *Rocky Mountain Empire* by Elvon L. Howe, ed. (Garden City, N. Y.: Doubleday & Co.), 1950.

"Left-handed Fiddlers Mean Trouble." *Dime Western*, October 1944, p. 48.

"Like Hell, You're Dead!" *Frontier Times*, May 1965, p. 24.

"Lonesome Man." *Collier's*, May 1944, p. 19.

"Long Tom: The Wild Gobbler." *Southwest Review*, vol. XXXI (Fall 1945), under pseudonym of Mike Beck.

"The Lost Fingers of Mack Hughes." *True West*, April 1955, p. 14.

"Loyal Valley Renegade." *10-Story Western*, December 1942, p. 36.

"Luck." *The Branding Iron* (Mason High School Annual, Mason, Texas), 1924.

"A Man's Business." *The Progressive Farmer*, June 1957, p. 36.

"Massacre at Dead Man's Pass." *10-Story Western*, June 1943, p. 94.

"McDade's Holiday Cleanup." *True*, December 1944, p. 15. Reprinted in *True Western Adventure*, Spring 1957, p. 43.

"The Meanest Man in the World." *Dime Western*, April 1944, p. 23.

"Melon-Patch Killing." *Southwest Review*, vol. XXX (Spring 1945), p. 211. Condensed in *Reader's Digest*, May 1945, p. 75. Reprinted in *Story Art*, Spring 1949, p. 16.

"Mesquite Murphy—Injun Hunter." *The Westerner*, February 1943, p. 10.

"Minnie's Yellow Treasure." *Rocky Mountain Empire Magazine* (Denver *Post*), Nov. 14, 1948, p. 2.

"Moral Victory." *Rocky Mountain Empire Magazine* (Denver *Post*), Nov. 14, 1948, p. 2.

"My Favorite Animal Story." *Farm and Ranch*, December 1947, p. 32.

"My Kind of Man." *Southwest Review*, vol. XXX (Autumn 1944), p. 15. Condensed in *Reader's Digest*, November 1944, p. 73. Included in *21 Texas Short Stories* by W. W. Perry, ed. (Austin: University of Texas Press), 1954; *Modern Feature Writing* by DeWitt Reddick (New York: Harper & Bros.), 1949; *Son-Of-A-Gun Stew* by Elizabeth Matchett Stover, ed. (Dallas: Southern Methodist University Press), 1945.

"My Son Is Dead." *True West*, Fall 1953, p. 25.

"Natural Born Hunter." *Southwest Review*, vol. XLVIII (Winter 1963), p. 15.

"Nesters Ain't Wanted." *Star Western*, July 1942, p. 69.

"Not a Matter of Fish." *The Southern Sportsman*, August 1941, p. 8.

"No Town for a Tinhorn." *Dime Western*, February 1943, p. 76.

"One Dull Day." *True West*, December 1963, p. 9.

"One War—One Ranger." *.44 Western Magazine*, January 1944, p. 8.

"Orphans of the Owlhoot." *10-Story Western*, June 1944, p. 34.

"Outlaw Till Sunset." *10-Story Western*, August 1942, p. 91.

"Over the Hill." *Liberty*, January 1946, p. 26.

"Over the Hill With Death." *Ace-High Western*, January 1942, p. 35.

"Paycheck in Hell." *10-Story Western*, August 1942, p. 66.

"Pioneer Recalls Hard Times of the 50's and 60's." *Home Color Print Co. Magazine*, date unknown. In Fred Gipson Papers.

"Pistol Passport for Llano Invaders." *Star Western*, November 1943, p. 40.
"Possum Money Comes Easy." *The Progressive Farmer*, February 1948, p. 42.
"Prankin' Man." *Rocky Mountain Empire Magazine* (Denver *Post*), May 16, 1948, p. 2.
"Rabbit Hound." *The Progressive Farmer*, October 1953, p. 62.
"Rangeland Word Wrangler." *Rocky Mountain Empire Magazine* (Denver *Post*), July 4, 1948, p. 4. Reprinted in *Writer's Digest*, September 1949, p. 34.
"Ranger Keep Travelin'." *10-Story Western*, January 1945, p. 27.
"Rio Grande Rebel's Last Stand." *Dime Western*, June 1944, p. 65.
"The Ruination of Restless Soloman." *Adventure*, December 1947, p. 58.
"Sad Sam." *Southwest Review*, vol. XXXI (Autumn 1946), p. 333. Condensed in *Reader's Digest*, October 1946, p. 123.
"Saturday Afternoon in Town." *Rocky Mountain Empire Magazine* (Denver *Post*), March 14, 1948, p. 2.
"Sermon in Stones." *Adventure*, October 1941, p. 68.
"A Sheriff For to Be." *.44 Western Magazine*, May 1942, p. 41.
"Show-off Roper." *Southwest Review*, vol. XXXIX (Winter 1954), p. 77.
"Signed On At Murder Camp." *Dime Western*, May 1943, p. 94.
"Sixguns, Salvation—and Sin!" *10-Story Western*, July 1942, p. 38.
"Some Hoss Thieves Is Different." *10-Story Western*, September 1942, p. 59.
"Star Spangled Justice." *10-Story Western*, April 1944, p. 87.
"Stepson of the Owlhoot." *Dime Western*, November 1942, p. 92.
"Tenderfoot Tower." *Big-Book Western*, February 1944, p. 96.
"Texas Writer Blasts His Critics, Defends 'Back Yard' Language." *Quill*, November 1957, p. 29.
"That Damn' Chongo!" *Dime Western*, June 1942, p. 86.
"That Sloe-Eyed Gal of the Blackjacks." *Texas Ranger*, March 1936, p. 18.
"Them Reckless Lee Boys." *Rocky Mountain Empire Magazine* (Denver *Post*), June 20, 1948, p. 5. Included in *Rocky Mountain Empire* by Elvon L. Howe, ed. (Garden City, N. Y.: Doubleday & Co.), 1950.
"They Grow 'Em Tough on the Llano." *Star Western*, August 1943, p. 42.
"Throwback." *Southwest Review*, vol. XXXI (fall 1945), under pseudonym of Tommie Gipson.
"Tiger Red and Windmill Pipe." *True West*, Spring 1954, p. 17.
"Timid Soul." *Farm and Ranch*, June 1948, p. 12.
"Togo the Faithful." *Rocky Mountain Empire Magazine* (Denver *Post*), July 25, 1948, p. 2.
"The Toughest Man in Texas." *Star Western*, June 1942, p. 135.

"Town of Beer and Sorrow." *Southwest Review*, vol. XXXIV (Spring 1949), p. 189. Reprinted in *True West*, April 1959, p. 25. Included in *The Best of The West* by Joe Austell Small, ed. (New York: Julian Messner, Inc.), 1964.

"The Tracks of Big Foot Wallace." Publication facts unknown. In Fred Gipson Papers.

"The Trailer of Wildcat Creek." *Dime Western*, December 1943, p. 78.

"Trail Trouble." *Frontier Times*, Spring 1958, p. 39.

"Trapped Tenderfoot." *True West*, August 1957, p. 27.

"Uncle Dude Loses a Million." *Rocky Mountain Empire Magazine* (Denver *Post*), July 18, 1948, p. 4.

"Ungrateful Bear." *Reader's Digest* (British Edition), June 1960, p. 216.

"The Valley of Missing Herds." *New Western Magazine*, July 1942, p. 42.

"Water to the Desert." *Rocky Mountain Empire Magazine* (Denver *Post*), May 30, 1948, p. 4.

"Wee Willy and the Goosey Dun." *Frontier Times*, Fall 1962, p. 37.

"When Buster Came Back." *Rocky Mountain Empire Magazine* (Denver *Post*), Aug. 1, 1948, p. 4.

"Whittlin' Banker." *Rocky Mountain Empire Magazine* (Denver *Post*), Nov. 14, 1947.

"Why I Go Back to Big Bend." *Ford Times*, November 1964, p. 61.

"Wildest Show on Earth." *Rocky Mountain Empire Magazine* (Denver *Post*), Jan. 4, 1948, p. 5.

"Wild Hogs Are Different." *The Progressive Farmer*, June 1955, p. 52.

"Wild Places Calling." *True West*, June 1956, p. 18.

BOOK REVIEWS IN *The New York Times*
American Tall-Tale Animals by Adrien Stoutenburg. May 5, 1968.
Backtrack by Milton S. Lott. Nov. 28, 1965.
Crimson Moccasins by Wayne Dyre Doughty. July 10, 1966.
The Destiny Road by Charles Morrow Wilson. May 9, 1965.
The General's Boots by Neta Lhones Frazier. May 9, 1965.
Gold Dust and Petticoats by Barbara Benezra. May 5, 1965.
The Golden Eagle by Robert Cushman Murphy. Aug. 8, 1965.
Horse Tradin' by Ben K. Green. June 11, 1967.
Hunger Valley by Edmund S. Fox. May 9, 1965.
Joshuway That's the Way by Rhoda Woolridge. May 9, 1965.
Little Kingdom by Hughie Call. Aug. 23, 1964.
Lobo by McKinlay Kantor. July 3, 1957.
Prisoner of the Iroquois by John Tomerlin. May 9, 1965.
The Sound of Axes by Fredrika Shumway Smith. May 9, 1965.

The Summer Land by Burke Davis. Sept. 12, 1965.
The Telling by John Weston. March 13, 1965.
Trace Through the Forest by Barbara Robinson. May 9, 1965.
Wagon Scout by Jane Annixter and Paul Annixter. May 9, 1965.
Whichaway by Glendon and Kathryn Swarthout. Nov. 6, 1966.

SCREENPLAYS AND TELEVISION SCRIPTS
Brush Roper. With William Tunberg. Hal Roach Studies, 1955.
Old Yeller. With William Tunberg. Walt Disney Productions, 1957.
Sancho the Homing Steer. Walt Disney Productions, 1962.
Savage Sam. With William Tunberg. Walt Disney Productions, 1962.
The Travels of Jaimie McPheeters. Based on the book by R. L. Taylor. Avon Production, Inc., 1959.
Wild in the Country. With Shelby Elam. Jerry Wald Productions, 1958.

MISCELLANEOUS WORKS
"Change of Heart." *The Daily Texan* (University of Texas at Austin), Sept. 20, 1935, p. 3.
"A Dissertation on 'Coon Hunting'." *The Daily Texan* (University of Texas at Austin), Nov. 22, 1935, p. 2.
"Getting To Work." *People's Choice Book Club Newsletter*, vol. VII, no. 9, 1950.
Introduction to *Cowpokes Wanted* by Ace Reid (Kerrville, Texas: privately published), 1961.
Introduction to *Mason and Mason County: A History* by Stella Gipson Polk (Austin: Pemberton Press), 1966.
Introduction to *Songs of the Saddlemen* by S. Omar Barker (Denver: Sage Books), 1954.
Introduction to *Stirrup High* by Walt Coburn (New York: Julian Messner, Inc.), 1958.
Introduction to *Treasury of Frontier Relics* by Les Beitz (Conroe, Texas: True Treasure Library), 1966.
"Monarch." *The Daily Texan* (University of Texas at Austin), Nov. 3, 1935, p. 6.
"New Boots for the Bullfight." *Daily Texan Centennial Supplement* (University of Texas at Austin), March 1, 1936, p. 6.
"The Story of the Story Teller Told." *The New York Times*, May 13, 1962.
"Sweet Potatoes." *The Daily Texan* (University of Texas at Austin), Sept. 22, 1935, p. 5.
"The Talk." The Houston *Post*, Jan. 30, 1955.

Appendix B

Unpublished Works By Fred Gipson

Fred Gipson produced a voluminous amount of material during his writing life. Much of it has survived, though some early papers were destroyed in a fire that gutted Gipson's first ranch house near Mason in 1964. In 1965, at the urging of the late R. Henderson Shuffler, who at the time was directing Texana collection efforts at the University of Texas, Gipson donated many of his manuscripts and letters to UT. When the Humanities Research Center was organized, the papers were placed there. After Gipson's death in 1973, many of his remaining papers—manuscripts, correspondence, files, newspaper clippings and assorted other documents—were donated by his son, Beck Gipson, to the HRC. The Gipson papers fill thirty-nine large file boxes.

The unpublished manuscripts listed here are contained in the Gipson papers or mentioned in correspondence. All are typescript. The number of pages and date written have been included when possible.

BOOKS
"A Cowboy For to Be." 71 pp.
"The Devil to Pay." 223 pp.
"The Road Leads West." 331 pp., 1954.
"The Way of Jesse Gentry." 245 pp., 1951.

SHORT STORIES AND ARTICLES
"And Grandma's Pet Coon Churned." 11 pp.
"The Anger of Anton Jabosky." 15 pp., 1955.
"Big Money." 11 pp.
"Bright Red Calico Shirt." 1958.
"Bronc Riders Are Made." 3 pp.
"Brush-wild Cow." 2 pp.
"Buckskin Stepson." 47 pp.
"Buffalo Rider." 5 pp.
"The Dancing Heifer." 3 pp.

"Dog Swap." 8 pp.
"The Fisherman Got Away!" 8 pp.
"Fishing Is a Man's Business." 13 pp., 1954.
"Fort Mason (Historical Pageant)." 23 pp., 1958.
"Fox in the Ditch." 8 pp.
"Gift Dog." 12 pp., 1952.
"Give a Cowhand Enough Rope." 9 pp.
"Good Neighbor Policy." 4 pp., 1947.
"High Ride." 2 pp.
"Jay Wouldn't Listen." 21 pp.
"Nobody's Dog." 13 pp.
"The Retirement of Pearl Jackson." 10 pp.
"Speaking of Bad Men." 2 pp.
"The Speech." 18 pp.
"Sweet Cream for Arabella." 6 pp.
"Tales of Mason County." 7 pp.
"The Tales They Tell." 3 pp.
"Trapped in a Boghole." 4 pp.
"Turkey Hunt." 3 pp.
"We Used to Go Fishing." 15 pp.
"Wild Cow Hunter." 1952.

Notes on the Text

Abbreviation Key:
ALP — Alex Louis Papers.
AMP — Allen Maxwell Papers.
BGP — Beck Gipson Papers.
EGGP — Eunice Green Giddens Papers.
FGP — Fred Gipson Papers.
JSP — Joe Small Papers.
SGNP — Stella Gipson North Papers.
TGNP — Tommie Gipson North Papers.

The first reference within each chapter to correspondence between two persons includes the full names of each correspondent. Only last names are used in subsequent references, except for Tommie Gipson. All references to Gipson, without a first name included, are to Fred Gipson.

CHAPTER 1.

The Home Place

[1]Beck's father, John Gipson, left Ireland with his wife to immigrate to the United States. Mrs. Gipson, however, died aboard ship and was buried at sea. After arriving in Galveston, Gipson, an educated man who spoke four languages, settled in Franklin County, in East Texas, and began ranching. He was past middle age when he married a younger woman, Eve Sanders, with whom he had five children. Their third child, born October 9, 1872, was a son they named Beck.

In 1879, John Gipson got a job as a school teacher in the Northeast Texas community of Mount Vernon. Before the family reached their new home, however, Gipson became ill and died. Mrs. Gipson made it to Mount Vernon with the children, but within a month she also was dead. Several other families had made the trip with the Gipsons and divided up the Gipson orphans to raise as their own. Beck had no formal education but learned about life as he moved from family to family—to people who kept him in exchange for work.

Emma's father, von Christopher Benjamin Deishler, was a German. He came to the United States for two reasons: grief over the death of his French-born mother and impending induction into the Prussian army. He reached the Texas coast about 1860 at age fourteen with virtually no possessions except a German song book bearing the names of his family.

A year later, Deishler's sentiments concerning the military changed and he lied about his age in order to join the Confederate Army. After the war, he married Sarah

207

Ann Doyle, whose parents had come to Texas in a covered wagon from Tennessee. The Deishlers had six children. The eldest was Emma Mayberry, born December 14, 1874, in Cherokee County.

Beck and Emma met in Winnsboro and were married November 7, 1894. A short time later, they moved to nearby Hunt County where their first child, Jennie, was born.

(Mason County Historical Commission, *Mason County Historical Book*, pp. 89–90; Mason County *News*, Oct. 22, 1936.)

[2]Author's interview with Beck Gipson, June 2, 1979.

[3]Author's interview with Bess Gipson Polk, May 5, 1980.

[4]Family legend has it that before the Gipsons left the coastal country, they packed an alligator egg in their trunk. When they got to Mason, the egg hatched, "producing what was probably the first and only alligator ever born on the Llano." Frank Wardlaw told this story in his eulogy at Gipson's funeral on August 17, 1973.

[5]Stella Gipson Polk, "A Personal Reminiscence," *The Highlander*, May 6, 1976.

[6]Fred Gipson, Corpus Christi *Caller-Times*, Dec. 3, 1938.

[7]Fred Gipson, Corpus Christi *Caller-Times*, Dec. 11, 1937.

[8]Corpus Christi *Caller-Times*, June 13, 1937.

[9]Polk, "A Personal Reminiscence."

[10]Fred Gipson, Corpus Christi *Caller-Times*, date unknown, FGP.

CHAPTER 2.
Barefoot Boy
[1]Stella Gipson Polk, *Mason and Mason County: A History*, pp. 86–87.

[2]Fred Gipson, "Dinner Bucket," *Scene Magazine*, vol. 1, no. 3 (May 1947), p. 21.

[3]Fred Gipson, Corpus Christi *Caller-Times*, Nov. 13, 1938.

[4]Stella Gipson Polk, "My Brother—Fred Gipson," *True West*, July-August 1974, pp. 16–18.

[5]Fred Gipson, "Papa's Straw Hat," *Southwest Review*, vol. XLVIII, no. 3 (Summer 1963), pp. 220–223.

[6]Fred Gipson, Corpus Christi *Caller-Times*, April 27, 1938.

[7]Author's interviews with Fred Gipson, May 16, 1971, and with Stella Gipson Polk, Jan. 22, 1977.

[8]Fred Gipson, Corpus Christi *Caller-Times*, June 20, 1937.

[9]Fred Gipson, Corpus Christi *Caller-Times*, Aug. 28, 1937.

[10]Fred Gipson, Corpus Christi *Caller-Times*, May 19, 1937.

CHAPTER 3.
I Reckon He'll Just Be a Hound-Dog Man
[1]Fred Gipson, Corpus Christi *Caller-Times*, June 14, 1938.

[2]Fred Gipson, Corpus Christi *Caller-Times*, Dec. 25, 1937.

[3]Renwicke Cary, San Antonio *Light*, March 17, 1964.

[4]Fred Gipson, Corpus Christi *Caller-Times*, April 16, 1937.

[5]Fred Gipson, Corpus Christi *Caller-Times*, date unknown, FGP.
[6]Fred Gipson, Corpus Christi *Caller-Times*, April 5, 1938.
[7]Ibid.
[8]Fred Gipson, Corpus Christi *Caller-Times*, Feb. 6, 1938.
[9]Stella Gipson Polk, "My Brother—Fred Gipson," *True West*, July-August 1974, p. 18.
[10]Fred Gipson, Corpus Christi *Caller-Times*, March 23, 1937.
[11]Polk, "My Brother—Fred Gipson."
[12]Fred Gipson, "Fishing Time on The Llano," *True West*, September-October 1963, p. 38.
[13]Fred Gipson, "First Buck," *The Southern Sportsman*, November 1936, p. 13. Other information in chapter 3 was obtained, in part, in interviews by the author with: Charles Gipson, April 8, 1977; Stella Gipson Polk, Jan. 22, 1977.

CHAPTER 4.
"Seize the Opportunity"
[1]Fred Gipson, Corpus Christi *Caller-Times*, Nov. 23, 1937.
[2]Fred Gipson, Corpus Christi *Caller-Times*, Oct. 31, 1937.
[3]Author's interview with Eunice Green Giddens, Feb. 28, 1977; *The Branding Iron*, vol. II (1925).
[4]Fred Gipson to Dorman Winfrey, Sept. 11, 1962, FGP.
[5]Fred Gipson, Corpus Christi *Caller-Times*, May 18, 1937.
[6]Fred Gipson, Corpus Christi *Caller-Times*, Oct. 22, 1937.
[7]Author's interview with Stella Gipson Polk, Jan. 22, 1977.
[8]Fred Gipson, Corpus Christi *Caller-Times*, Nov. 5, 1938.
[9]Fred Gipson, Corpus Christi *Caller-Times*, Dec. 24, 1937.
[10]Corpus Christi *Caller-Times*, April 8, 1938.
[11]Other information in chapter 4 was obtained, in part, in interviews by the author with: Mrs. Arch Carter, April 7, 1977; Eunice Green Giddens, Feb. 28, 1977; Beck Gipson, June 2, 1979; Charles Gipson, April 8, 1977; Stella Gipson Polk, Jan. 22, 1977.

CHAPTER 5.
"One Thing and Then Another"
[1]Fred Gipson, Corpus Christi *Caller-Times*, Nov. 22, 1937.
[2]Fred Gipson, *Daily Texan*, date unknown, FGP.
[3]Fred Gipson, *Daily Texan*, Nov. 11, 1935. On Sept. 20, 1936, the *Daily Texan* carried a story by Mrs. Marcelle Hamer, librarian in charge of the Texas collection at the UT Library, that probably caught Gipson's eye: "Of histories of Texas, there are plenty. Travel books are numerous. Book stores in every city . . . are featuring Texas books . . . . When will someone write a Texas novel, one that will stand as a classic along with the history of the state?

"The writing of history requires a long association with the subject and careful study. To write a novel, one must have a close acquaintance with the places and the people, in order to reflect ways, thoughts, turns of speech that interpret the character of a people or the spirit of a place."

[4]Stella Gipson Polk, *Mason and Mason County: A History*, p. 87.

[5]Fred Gipson, *Daily Texan*, Feb. 23, 1936.

[6]Fred Gipson, *Daily Texan*, Nov. 3, 1936.

[7]Fred Gipson, *Daily Texan*, Dec. 18, 1936.

[8]Fred Gipson, *Daily Texan*, Jan. 15, 1937.

[9]Fred Gipson, *Daily Texan*, Dec. 17, 1936.

[10]*Daily Texan*, April 15, 1936.

[11]*Daily Texan*, Dec. 6, 1936.

[12]Author's interview with Stella Gipson Polk, Jan. 22, 1977; Mason County *News*, Oct. 22, 1936.

[13]Author's interview with Polk. Other information in chapter 5 was obtained, in part, in interviews by the author with: Margaret C. Berry, March 1977; Charles Gipson, April 8, 1977; Stanford Leach, April 1977; Allen Maxwell, March 4, 1977; Dr. DeWitt Reddick, April 18, 1974; Joe Small, May 14, 1974.

CHAPTER 6.
"All Newspapermen Are Crazy"

[1]Fred Gipson, Corpus Christi *Caller-Times*, Feb. 21, 1937.

[2]*Valley Morning Star* (Harlingen, Texas), March 16, 1967.

[3]Author's interview with Tommie Gipson North, June 2, 1979.

[4]*Daily Texan*, Jan. 21, 1937.

[5]Fred Gipson, Corpus Christi *Caller-Times*, Aug. 24, 1937.

[6]Ibid.

[7]Fred Gipson, Corpus Christi *Caller-Times*, Feb. 25, 1937.

[8]Fred Gipson, Corpus Christi *Caller-Times*, July 18, 1937.

[9]Fred Gipson, Corpus Christi *Caller-Times*, May 3, 1937.

[10]Author's interview with Grady Hill, April 7, 1977.

[11]Fred Gipson, Corpus Christi *Caller-Times*, Oct. 8, 1937.

[12]Betty Baugh Van Eman to Mike Cox, April 23, 1977. In possession of the author.

[13]William C. Barnard to Mike Cox, Sept. 17, 1977. In possession of the author.

[14]Gipson had become a South Texas celebrity. He was invited to judge beauty contests and rode in the Corpus Christi annual Buccaneers Day parade.

[15]Fred Gipson, Corpus Christi *Caller-Times*, Oct. 17, 1937.

[16]Fred Gipson, Corpus Christi *Caller-Times*, Oct. 27, 1937.

[17]Fred Gipson, Corpus Christi *Caller-Times*, Sept. 26, 1937.

[18]Fred Gipson, Corpus Christi *Caller-Times*, Dec. 12, 1938.

[19]Fred Gipson, Corpus Christi *Caller-Times*, date unknown, FGP.

[20]San Angelo *Standard-Times*, Jan. 31, 1939.

[21]Author's interview with Hill.

[22]Fred Gipson, Corpus Christi *Caller-Times*, Nov. 20, 1937.

[23]Corpus Christi *Caller-Times*, June 9, 1937.

[24]Fred Gipson, Corpus Christi *Caller-Times*, May 20, 1937.

[25]Author's interview with Tommie Gipson North, April 20, 1974.

[26]Fred Gipson to Tommie Wynn, July 2, 1939, TGNP.

[27]Gipson to Wynn, n.d., TGNP.
[28]Gipson to Wynn, Sept. 23, 1939, TGNP.
[29]Gipson to Wynn, Oct. 3, 1939, TGNP.
[30]Gipson to Wynn, n.d., TGNP.

CHAPTER 7.
Bill Manning: Literary Agent of the Southwest
[1]Fred Gipson, Corpus Christi *Caller-Times*, Feb. 9, 1940.
[2]Fred Gipson, Corpus Christi *Caller-Times*, Feb. 7, 1940.
[3]Fred Gipson to Tommie Wynn, n.d., TGNP.
[4]Author's interview with Tommy Gipson North, July 23, 1979.
[5]Author's interview with North.
[6]Gipson to Wynn, Nov. 23, 1939, TGNP.
[7]Gipson to Wynn, n.d., TGNP.
[8]Author's interview with Joe Small, May 14, 1974.
[9]Author's interview with Small.
[10]Author's interview with North.
[11]Fred Gipson, "Around Our Place," Oct. 5–11, 1941, TGNP.
[12]Fred Gipson, "Around Our Place," Sept. 20–28, 1941, TGNP.
[13]Fred Gipson, "Around Our Place," Oct. 5–11, 1941, TGNP.
[14]Fred Gipson, "Around Our Place," Oct. 12–18, 1941, TGNP.
[15]Fred Gipson, "Around Our Place," Nov. 2–8, 1941, TGNP.
[16]Author's interviews with North and Small. Other information in chapter 7 was obtained, in part, in interviews by the author with: Norris Davis, March 31, 1977; Tommie Gipson North, April 8, 1977 and July 23, 1979; Joe Small, May 14, 1974.

CHAPTER 8.
"My Kind of Man"
[1]Author's interview with Tommie Gipson North, April 8, 1977.
[2]Fred Gipson, *Daily Texan*, Sept. 20, 1936.
[3]Fred Gipson, "My Kind of Man," *Reader's Digest*, November 1944, p. 73.
[4]Author's interview with Tommie Gipson North, June 3, 1979.
[5]Fred Gipson, Corpus Christi *Caller-Times*, April 11, 1937.
[6]Fred Gipson, "Around Our Place," Nov. 9–15, 1941, TGNP.
[7]Fred Gipson, *Daily Texan*, June 21, 1936.
[8]Fred Gipson, *Fabulous Empire: Colonel Zack Miller's Story*, p. viii. Other information in chapter 8 was obtained, in part, in interviews by the author with: Fred Gipson, May 16, 1971; Tommie Gipson North, April 7, 1977 and June 3, 1979.

CHAPTER 9.
Fabulous Empire
[1]Fred Gipson, *Fabulous Empire: Colonel Zack Miller's Story*, p. vii.
[2]Gipson, *Fabulous Empire*, pp. vii–ix.
[3]Author's interview with Fred Gipson, May 16, 1971.

4Author's interview with Tommie Gipson North, April 8, 1977.
5Lucile Sullivan to Mike Cox, Sept. 25, 1978. In possession of the author.
6Fred Gipson to Alex Louis, October 1945, ALP.
7Fred Gipson, Corpus Christi *Caller-Times*, June 14, 1938.
8*Southwest Review*, vol. XXX, no. 3 (Spring 1945), p. 297.
9*Southwest Review*, vol. XXXI, no. 1 (Fall 1945), pp. i–ii.
10Allen Maxwell to Fred Gipson, May 1, 1946, AMP.
11Gipson to Maxwell, May 4, 1946, AMP.
12Gipson to Louis, June 2, 1946, ALP.
13Gipson to Louis, Aug. 20, 1946, ALP.
14San Angelo *Standard-Times*, Sept. 1, 1946.
15*Texas Week*, Oct. 12, 1946, p. 32.
16Gipson to Maxwell, Oct. 14, 1946, AMP.
17Ibid.
18Other information in chapter 9 was obtained, in part, in interviews by the author with: Fred Gipson, May 16, 1971; Allen Maxwell, March 4, 1977; Tommie Gipson North, April 8, 1977.

CHAPTER 10.
$25,000!
1Author's interviews with Tommie Gipson North, April 20, 1974 and April 8, 1977.
2*The Progressive Farmer*, August 1947, p. 41.
3Despite the many times he wrote about Charlie Sanders, only once did Gipson ever refer to Sanders by his full name—in a column he did for the Corpus Christi *Caller-Times*.
4"Show World," Austin *American-Statesman*, May 13, 1973.
5Fred Gipson to Allen Maxwell, Nov. 9, 1946, AMP.
6Gipson to Maxwell, Nov. 18, 1946, AMP.
7*Southwest Review*, vol. XXXI, no. 4 (Fall 1946), p. 425.
8Maurice Crain to Fred Gipson, March 13, 1947, FGP.
9Donald Day to Fred Gipson, April 22, 1947, FGP.
10Day to Gipson, Sept. 3, 1947, FGP.
11Fred Gipson to Elvon Howe, Feb. 2, 1948, FGP.
12Author's interviews with North.
13Author's interviews with North.
14Crain to Gipson, June 14, 1948, FGP.
15Crain to Gipson, June 18, 1948 and June 26, 1948, FGP.
16Crain to Gipson, July 22, 1948, FGP.
17Fred Gipson to Joe Small, June 1948, JSP.
18Crain to Gipson, June 23, 1948, FGP.
19Author's interviews with North.
20Maxwell to Gipson, Aug. 31, 1948, AMP.
21Fred Gipson to Elizabeth M. Stover, Aug. 25, 1948, AMP.
22Gipson to Maxwell, Nov. 1, 1948, AMP.
23Crain to Gipson, Nov. 27, 1948, FGP. The British edition eventually was titled

212

Circle Round the Wagons.

[24]*Book-of-the-Month Club News*, December 1948, pp. 6–8.

[25]Ibid., p. 8.

[26]John Fischer to Fred Gipson, n.d., FGP.

[27]*Saturday Review of Literature*, Jan. 22, 1949, p. 18.

[28]Crain to Gipson, Jan. 15, 1949, FGP.

[29]San Antonio *Express*, Jan. 23, 1949.

[30]San Angelo *Standard-Times*, date unknown, FGP.

[31]Other information in chapter 10 was obtained, in part, in interviews by the author with: Fred Gipson, May 16, 1971; Allen Maxwell, March 4, 1977; Tommie Gipson North, April 20, 1974 and April 8, 1977.

CHAPTER 11.

"We'll Just Have to Grow the Grass Back"

[1]Author's interviews with Joe Small, May 14, 1974 and March 9, 1977. Charlie Sanders died a few years later and was buried in the Gooch Family Cemetery not far from the old home place. Sanders lived on as Blackie Scantling, however: by 1977 *Hound-Dog Man* had gone through twenty-five editions.

[2]Fred Gipson, "A Town of Beer and Sorrow," *Southwest Review*, vol. XXXIV, no. 2 (Spring 1949), pp. 189–191.

[3]Fred Gipson to Elizabeth M. Stover, Sept. 21, 1949, AMP.

[4]Gipson to Stover, Oct. 31, 1949, AMP.

[5]Maurice Crain to Fred Gipson, Sept. 30, 1949, FGP.

[6]Crain to Gipson, Oct. 24, 1949, FGP.

[7]Evan Thomas to Fred Gipson, Oct. 24, 1949, FGP.

[8]John Fischer to Fred Gipson, Oct. 25, 1949, FGP.

[9]Thomas to Gipson, Jan. 15, 1950 and Crain to Gipson, Jan. 24, 1950, FGP.

[10]Crain to Gipson, March 4, 1950, FGP.

[11]Crain to Gipson, March 13, 1950, FGP.

[12]Crain to Gipson, March 24, 1950, FGP.

[13]Thomas to Gipson, April 24, 1950, FGP.

[14]Thomas to Gipson, April 21, 1950, FGP.

[15]Fred Gipson, Corpus Christi *Caller-Times*, Dec. 29, 1937.

[16]Fred Gipson, *The Home Place* (1950), p. 223.

[17]Crain to Gipson, June 2, 1950, FGP.

[18]Pamela Barnes to Fred Gipson, May 1, 1950, FGP.

[19]Crain to Gipson, June 2, 1950, FGP.

[20]Fred Gipson to Allen Maxwell, July 20, 1950, AMP.

[21]Ibid.

[22]Crain to Gipson, July 24, 1950, FGP.

[23]Crain to Gipson, Aug. 3, 1950, FGP.

[24]Dean Chenoweth, Corpus Christi *Caller-Times*, Sept. 17, 1950.

[25]Gipson, *The Home Place*, p. 5.

[26]Crain to Gipson, Sept. 27, 1950, FGP.

[27]Donald Day to Fred Gipson, Sept. 11, 1950, FGP. Other information in chapter 11 was obtained, in part, in interviews by the author with: Charles Gipson, April

7–8, 1977; Fred Gipson, May 16, 1971.

CHAPTER 12.
The Well Almost Dried

[1]Dean Chenoweth, Corpus Christi *Caller-Times*, Sept. 17, 1950.
[2]Amarillo *Globe-News*, June 6, 1954.
[3]Fred Gipson to C. L. Lundell, November 1952, FGP.
[4]Fred Gipson, *The Home Place* (1950), p. 81.
[5]Maurice Crain to Fred Gipson, Oct. 6, 1950; Nov. 21, 1950; Jan. 27, 1951; FGP.
[6]Crain to Gipson, Jan. 19, 1951 and Jan. 27, 1951, FGP.
[7]Crain to Gipson, Feb. 5, 1951, FGP.
[8]Crain to Gipson, May 5, 1951, FGP.
[9]Crain to Gipson, May 21, 1951, FGP.
[10]Crain to Gipson, June 4, 1951, FGP.
[11]Gipson to Crain, July 30, 1951, FGP.
[12]Evan Thomas to Fred Gipson, Aug. 7, 1951, FGP.
[13]Gipson to Crain, Aug. 27, 1951, FGP.
[14]Grady Hill, San Angelo *Standard-Times*, Sept. 16, 1951.
[15]Hill, San Angelo *Standard-Times*; 20th Century Fox Film Corp., "Vital Statistics on *Return of the Texan*," 1951.
[16]Crain to Gipson, Oct. 11, 1951, FGP.
[17]Thomas to Gipson, Oct. 24, 1951, FGP.
[18]Tommie Gipson to Evan Thomas, Oct. 29, 1951, FGP.
[19]Author's interview with Frank Wardlaw, May 2, 1974.
[20]Frank Wardlaw to Fred Gipson, Nov. 21, 1951, FGP.
[21]*Texas Historical Quarterly*, vol. LVII, no. 1 (July 1953), p. 139.
[22]Tommie Gipson to Thomas, Oct. 29, 1951, FGP.
[23]Crain to Gipson, Nov. 24, 1951, FGP.
[24]Crain to Gipson, Sept. 12, 1951, FGP.
[25]Author's interview with Joe Small, May 14, 1974.
[26]Author's interview with Small.
[27]Austin *American-Statesman*, March 1, 1952.
[28]Author's interview with Small.
[29]Gipson to Thomas, Feb. 4, 1952, FGP.
[30]Thomas to Gipson, Feb. 13, 1952, FGP.
[31]Gipson to Crain, March 5, 1952, FGP.
[32]Tommie Gipson to Thomas, May 14, 1952, FGP.
[33]San Angelo *Standard-Times*, May 25, 1952.
[34]Tommie Gipson to Charles Ferguson, June 12, 1952, FGP.
[35]Charles Ferguson to Fred Gipson, June 25, 1952, FGP.
[36]Ferguson to Gipson, Aug. 26, 1952, FGP.
[37]Gipson to Ferguson, October 1952, FGP.
[38]Ferguson to Gipson, Oct. 9, 1952, FGP.
[39]Thomas to Gipson, July 16, 1952 and July 28, 1952, FGP.
[40]Other information in chapter 12 was obtained, in part, in interviews by the

author with: Tommie Gipson North, April 20, 1974 and July 23, 1979; Joe Small, May 14, 1974; Frank Wardlaw, May 2, 1974.

CHAPTER 13.
"You May Someday Come Up With Something Great"
    [1]Maurice Crain to Fred Gipson, Jan. 29, 1953, FGP.
    [2]Crain to Gipson, March 23, 1953, FGP; Evan Thomas to Fred Gipson, Feb. 24, 1953, FGP.
    [3]Fred Gipson, "The Road Leads West," unpub. ms., p. 14, FGP.
    [4]Author's interview with Joe Small, March 9, 1977.
    [5]San Angelo *Standard-Times*, Sept. 6, 1953.
    [6]Fred Gipson, *Cowhand: The Story of a Working Cowboy* (1953), p. 216.
    [7]Annie Laurie Williams to Fred Gipson, April 3, 1952, FGP.
    [8]Williams to Gipson, June 30, 1953, FGP. Before the television contract was signed, Tommie went to New York and met with Charles Ferguson of *Reader's Digest*. The matter of television rights was new legal ground, and Ferguson said he did not want to put anything in writing. But he gave oral permission for the television production based on "My Kind of Man."
    [9]Fred Gipson, *Trail-Driving Rooster*, author's note.
    [10]Crain to Gipson, Oct. 1, 1953, FGP.
    [11]Crain to Gipson, Oct. 22, 1953, FGP.
    [12]Gipson to Crain, Nov. 2, 1953, FGP.
    [13]Crain to Gipson, May 21, 1954, FGP.
    [14]Author's interview with Tommie Gipson North, July 23, 1979.
    [15]Gipson, "The Road Leads West," p. 227.
    [16]Ibid., p. 235.
    [17]Author's interview with North.
    [18]Gipson, "The Road Leads West," p. 331.
    [19]Ibid., p. 249.
    [20]Ibid., p. 250.
    [21]Thomas to Gipson, Nov. 29, 1954, FGP.
    [22]Ibid.
    [23]Crain to Gipson, Dec. 9, 1954, FGP.
    [24]Houston *Post*, Jan. 30, 1955.
    [25]Thomas to Gipson, March 3, 1955, FGP.
    [26]Mary Russell to Fred Gipson, June 16, 1955, FGP; Thomas to Gipson, June 15, 1955, FGP.
    [27]Williams to Gipson, May 13, 1949, FGP.
    [28]Tommie Gipson to Dick Patterson, Jan. 30, 1956, FGP.
    [29]*Variety*, Nov. 25, 1955.
    [30]Author's interview with Small.
    [31]Tommie Gipson to Mrs. Clyde Poore, Nov. 29, 1955, FGP.
    [32]*Variety*, Nov. 25, 1955.
    [33]Corpus Christi *Caller-Times*, June 8, 1955. Other information in chapter 13 was obtained, in part, in interviews by the author with: Tommie Gipson North, July 23, 1979; Joe Small, March 9, 1977.

CHAPTER 14.

A Big Yellow Work Dog

[1]Evan Thomas to Fred Gipson, Nov. 29, 1954, FGP.
[2]Tommie Gipson to Evan Thomas, July 27, 1955, FGP.
[3]Gipson to Thomas, Sept. 22, 1955, FGP.
[4]Fred Gipson to Ursula Norstrom, Oct. 12, 1955, FGP.
[5]Norstrom to Gipson, Oct. 14, 1955, FGP.
[6]Author's interview with Fred Gipson, May 16, 1971.
[7]Norstrom to Gipson, n.d., FGP; Thomas to Gipson, Jan. 23, 1956, FGP.
[8]Maurice Crain to Fred Gipson, Jan. 6, 1956, FGP; Crain to Gipson, Jan. 26, 1956, FGP.
[9]Gipson to Crain, Jan. 30, 1956, FGP.
[10]Crain to Gipson, Feb. 15, 1956, FGP.
[11]Gipson to Crain, March 22, 1956, FGP.
[12]Tommie Gipson to Thomas, May 23, 1956, FGP; Tommie Gipson to Maurice Crain, June 20, 1956, FGP.
[13]Fred Gipson to H. N. Swanson, June 13, 1956, FGP.
[14]Swanson to Gipson, April 11, 1956, FGP.
[15]Crain to Tommie Gipson, June 25, 1956, FGP.
[16]*Book Review Digest*, 1956, pp. 362–363.
[17]Tommie Gipson to Crain, July 5, 1956, FGP; Crain to Tommie Gipson, July 20, 1956, and Aug. 6, 1956, FGP.
[18]Tommie Gipson to Crain, Aug. 2, 1956, FGP.
[19]Tommie Gipson to Crain, n.d., FGP.
[20]Fred Gipson to Erma Mancill, July 3, 1956, FGP.
[21]Author's interview with Tommie Gipson North, April 20, 1974.
[22]Bob Thomas, *Walt Disney—An American Original*, p. 293.
[23]Ibid.
[24]Author's interview with North.
[25]Author's interview with Joe Small, May 14, 1974.
[26]Tommie Gipson to Mrs. Allen R. Baker, Oct. 9, 1956, FGP.
[27]Author's interview with Frank Wardlaw, May 2, 1974.
[28]Crain to Gipson, Dec. 19, 1956, FGP.
[29]Misc. letters, FGP.
[30]Ibid.
[31]Gipson to Thomas, April 29, 1957, FGP.
[32]Fred Gipson to Lyndon B. Johnson, Feb. 22, 1957, FGP.
[33]Fred Gipson to Leonard Shannon, March 13, 1957, FGP.
[34]Memo to Disney Studio, n.d., FGP.
[35]Shannon to Gipson, March 21, 1957, FGP.
[36]Walt Disney Productions, "Disney Animal Actors Get Star Treatment," promotional material, 1957.
[37]Author's interview with Small.
[38]Disney Productions, "Disney Animal Actors Get Star Treatment."
[39]Tommie Gipson to Thomas, Feb. 11, 1957, FGP.
[40]Gipson to Thomas, March 11, 1957, FGP.

⁴¹Other information in chapter 14 was obtained, in part, in interviews by the author with: Tommie Gipson North, April 20, 1974; Joe Small, May 14, 1974; Frank Wardlaw, May 2, 1974.

CHAPTER 15.
"Helpless As a Tied-up Calf"
¹Author's interview with Joe Small, May 14, 1974.
²Tommie Gipson to Allen Maxwell, July 15, 1957, AMP.
³San Angelo *Standard-Times*, June 9, 1957.
⁴Fred Gipson to J. Frank Dobie, Aug. 2, 1957, TGNP.
⁵Fred Gipson to Maurice Crain, Oct. 21, 1957, FGP.
⁶Fred Gipson to Joe Small, n.d., JSP.
⁷Gipson to Small, Nov. 25, 1957, JSP.
⁸San Angelo *Standard-Times*, Dec. 4, 1957.
⁹Tommie Gipson to Evan Thomas, Jan. 3, 1958, FGP.
¹⁰Tommie Gipson to J. Frank Dobie, Jan. 1, 1958, TGNP.
¹¹Ibid.
¹²Dobie to Tommie Gipson, Jan. 25, 1958, TGNP.
¹³Leonard Maltin, *The Disney Films*, p. 292. *Old Yeller* grossed $8 million in domestic sales alone and is credited with having convinced Disney that, if his studio were to prosper, animated films would have to be considered only sidelights in the future.
¹⁴Ace Reid to Fred Gipson, Feb. 9, 1958, FGP.
¹⁵Crain to Gipson, Jan. 11, 1958, FGP.
¹⁶Crain to Gipson, Feb. 20, 1958, FGP.
¹⁷"Mason Writer Determined to Grow Grass," BGP.
¹⁸Gipson to Crain, Feb. 22, 1958, FGP.
¹⁹Tommie Gipson to Maurice Crain, March 30, 1958, FGP.
²⁰Crain to Tommie Gipson, Aug. 25, 1958, FGP.
²¹Author's interview with Allen Maxwell and Margaret Hartley, March 4, 1977.
²²Tommie Gipson to Margaret Hartley, June 18, 1958, AMP.
²³Fred Gipson to Harry A. Harcher, June 26, 1958, carbon copy in AMP.
²⁴Fred Gipson to Tommie Gipson, June 22, 1958, TGNP.
²⁵Tommie Gipson to Martha Wynn, Aug. 1, 1958, TGNP.
²⁶Gipson to Tommie Gipson, July 31, 1958, TGNP.
²⁷Crain to Tommie Gipson, Aug. 25, 1958, FGP.
²⁸Austin *American-Statesman*, Jan. 16, 1959.
²⁹Crain to Gipson, Aug. 22, 1959, FGP.
³⁰Gipson to Tommie Gipson, n.d., TGNP.
³¹Gipson to Tommie Gipson, April 17, 1959, TGNP.
³²Tommie Gipson, "Helpless in Hollywood or How Much Is That Hound Dog?" *Southwest Review*, vol. XLV, no. 3 (Summer 1960), pp. 259–260.
³³Ibid., p. 262.
³⁴Ibid., pp. 259–260.
³⁵Tommie Gipson, Aug. 9, 1959, TGNP.

[36]Tommie Gipson to Edgar Carter, Sept. 9, 1959, FGP.

[37]Austin *American-Statesman*, Nov. 6, 1959.

[38]Other information in chapter 15 was obtained, in part, in interviews by the author with: Beck Gipson, July 28, 1979; Tommie Gipson North, April 7–8, 1977.

CHAPTER 16.
Dreams

[1]Author's interview with Tommie Gipson North, April 8, 1977.

[2]Tommie Gipson to Bernard Brister, Feb. 23, 1960, FGP.

[3]Tommie Gipson to Fred Gipson, Feb. 23, 1960, TGNP.

[4]Tommie Gipson to Maurice Crain, March 17, 1960, FGP.

[5]Tommie Gipson to Evan Thomas, March 29, 1960, FGP.

[6]Tommie Gipson to Crain, July 5, 1960, FGP.

[7]Tommie Gipson to Thomas, May 13, 1960, FGP.

[8]Tommie Gipson to Ivan Bruce, Sept. 29, 1961, FGP.

[9]Tommie Gipson to Alex Louis, Aug. 24, 1960, ALP.

[10]Fred Gipson, notes for address before Parent Teachers Association of Texas, Nov. 19, 1960, FGP.

[11]Tommie Gipson to Crain, Dec. 8, 1960, FGP; Tommie Gipson to Thomas, Jan. 17 and Feb. 19, 1961, FGP.

[12]Fred Gipson to Maurice Crain, April 13, 1961, FGP.

[13]Crain to Gipson, April 7, 1961, FGP.

[14]Victoria *Advocate*, Feb. 26, 1961.

[15]Tommie Gipson to Crain, May 10, 1961, FGP.

[16]John Fischer to Tommie Gipson, June 26, 1961, FGP.

[17]Crain to Tommie Gipson, July 11, 1961, FGP.

[18]Tommie Gipson to Brister, Aug. 28, 1961, FGP.

[19]Tommie Gipson to Fischer, Oct. 9, 1961, FGP.

[20]Tommie Gipson to Bruce, Sept. 29, 1961, FGP.

[21]Ibid.

[22]Fred Gipson to Evan Thomas, Oct. 2, 1961, FGP.

[23]Tommie Gipson to Paul Bolton, Oct. 28, 1961, FGP.

[24]Tommie Gipson to Donald and Beth Day, Dec. 18, 1961, FGP.

[25]Tommie Gipson to Brister, Jan. 30, 1962, FGP.

[26]Tommie Gipson to Thomas, January 1964, TGNP.

[27]*The New York Times Review of Books*, May 13, 1962.

[28]Author's interview with Joe Small, March 9, 1977.

[29]Author's interview with Small.

[30]Tommie Gipson to Maurice Crain and Annie Laurie Williams, July 2, 1962, FGP.

[31]Author's interview with Beck Gipson, July 28, 1979.

[32]Tommie Gipson to Brister, July 30, 1962, TGNP.

[33]Tommie Gipson to Gloria Allen, July 23, 1962, TGNP. Other information in chapter 16 was obtained, in part, in interviews by the author with: Beck Gipson, July 28, 1979; Tommie Gipson North, April 8, 1977.

CHAPTER 17.
Along Recollection Creek
[1]Author's interview with Frank Wardlaw, May 2, 1974.
[2]Fred Gipson to John William Brown, n.d., BGP.
[3]Tommie Gipson to Evan Thomas, Jan. 30, 1964, TGNP.
[4]Author's interview with Tommie Gipson North, July 23, 1979.
[5]Fred Gipson to Joe Small, n.d., JSP.
[6]San Angelo *Standard-Times*, June 13, 1963.
[7]Frel Gipson, unpub. acceptance speech for Young Readers' Choice Award, Washington School Library Association, Aug. 13, 1959, FGP. Other awards given in recognition of *Old Yeller* include the Maggie Award for Western Book (1958); William Allen White Children's Book Award, Kansas State Teacher's College (1959); First Sequoyah Award, Oklahoma Library Association (1959). *Old Yeller* also is on the Newberry Honor Book List. In 1962, Gipson was presented a lifetime membership in the International Institute of Arts and Letters, Zurich, Switzerland.
[8]Mike Cox, San Angelo *Standard-Times*, July 7, 1968.
[9]Bill Walraven, Corpus Christi *Caller-Times*, Jan. 5, 1967.
[10]Corpus Christi *Caller-Times*, March 9, 1964.
[11]Author's interview with North.
[12]Author's interview with Beck Gipson, July 28, 1979.
[13]Author's interview with Carolyn Cook Gipson, July 28, 1979.
[14]Fred Gipson Papers.
[15]Author's interview with Beck Gipson.
[16]Fred Gipson, undated notes, FGP.
[17]Austin *American-Statesman*, May 13, 1973.
[18]Author's interview with Wardlaw.
[19]Author's interview with Wardlaw.
[20]Author's interview with Wardlaw.
[21]Dallas *Morning-News*, March 25, 1970.
[22]Fred Gipson, undated notes, FGP.
[23]Sam H. Henderson, *Fred Gipson*, p. 49.
[24]Frank Wardlaw, remarks delivered at funeral of Fred Gipson, August 17, 1973, tape recorded by the author.
[25]Other information in this chapter 17 was obtained, in part, in interviews by the author with: Beck Gipson, July 28, 1979; Tommie Gipson North, July 23, 1979; Stella Gipson Polk, Jan. 22, 1977; Ace Reid, Jan. 3, 1977; Frank Wardlaw, May 2, 1974.

Sources

UNPUBLISHED WORKS

Berry, Margaret C. Interview with the author, Austin, Texas, March 1977.

Carter, Mrs. Arch. Interview with the author, Mason, Texas, April 7, 1977.

Davis, Norris. Interview with the author, Austin, Texas, March 31, 1977.

Giddens, Eunice Green. Interview with the author, Austin, Texas, Feb. 28, 1977.

Giddens, Eunice Green. Papers (letters). In possession of Eunice Green Giddens, Austin, Texas.

Gipson, Beck. Interviews with the author, Kerrville, Texas, June 2, 1979; July 28, 1979.

Gipson, Beck. Papers (letters). In possession of Beck Gipson, Kerrville, Texas.

Gipson, Carolyn Cook. Interview with the author, Kerrville, Texas, July 28, 1979.

Gipson, Charles. Interviews with the author, Mason, Texas, April 7–8, 1977.

Gipson, Fred. Interview with the author, Mason County, Texas, May 16, 1971.

Gipson, Fred. Papers (letters, notes, unpub. mss., misc. documents). Humanities Research Center, University of Texas at Austin.

Hill, Grady. Interview with the author, San Angelo, Texas, April 7, 1977.

Hartley, Margaret. Interview with the author, Dallas, Texas, March 4, 1977.

Jordan, Miles (Swede). Interview with the author, Katemcy, Texas, April 7, 1977.

Leach, Stanford. Interview with the author, Austin, Texas, April 1977.

Louis, Alex. Papers (letters). In possession of Alex Louis, Dallas, Texas.

Maxwell, Allen. Interview with the author, Dallas, Texas, March 4, 1977.

Maxwell, Allen. Papers (letters). In possession of Allen Maxwell, Dallas, Texas.

North, Tommie Gipson. Interviews with the author, San Angelo, Texas, April 20, 1974; April 7–8, 1977; June 2–3, 1979; July 23, 1979.

North, Tommie Gipson. Papers (letters, notes, misc. documents). In possession of Tommie Gipson North, San Angelo, Texas.
Old Yeller Promotional Material. Walt Disney Productions, 1957.
Polk, Bess Gipson. Interview with author, Mason, Texas, May 5, 1980.
Polk, Stella Gipson. Interview with author, Mason, Texas, Jan. 22, 1977.
Polk, Stella Gipson. Papers (letters). In possession of Stella Gipson Polk, Mason, Texas.
Reddick, Dr. DeWitt. Interview with the author, Austin, Texas, April 18, 1974.
Reid, Ace. Interview with the author, Kerrville, Texas, Jan. 3, 1977.
Seaquist, Garner. Interview with the author, Mason, Texas, April 8, 1977.
Small, Joe. Interviews with the author, Austin, Texas, May 14, 1974; March 9, 1977.
Small, Joe. Papers (letters). In possession of Joe Small, Austin, Texas.
"Vital Statistics on *Return of the Texan*." 20th Century Fox Promotional Materials, 1951.
Wardlaw, Frank. Interview with the author, Austin, Texas, May 2, 1974.

PUBLISHED WORKS
Austin *American-Statesman*.
Berry, Margaret Catherine. *UT Austin: Traditions and Nostalgia*. Austin: Shoal Creek Publishers, Inc., 1975.
The Corpus Christi *Caller-Times*.
Cox, Mike. " 'Old Yeller' Still Author's Favorite." San Angelo *Standard-Times*, July 7, 1968.
The Daily Texan, The University of Texas at Austin, 1935–1937.
"Fred Gipson on Writing for Young People." *Library Journal*, February 1960, p. 832.
Gipson, Fred. Various published and unpublished works listed in appendices and referenced in footnotes.
Gipson, Tommie. "Fred Gipson As Seen by His Wife Tommie." *People's Book Club Newsletter*, vol. VII, no. 9, 1950.
Gipson, Tommie. "Helpless in Hollywood or How Much Is That Hound Dog?" *Southwest Review*, vol. XLV, no. 3 (Summer 1960), p. 259.
Green, A. C. *The Last Captive*. Austin: Encino Press, 1972.
"He Learned the Hard Way." *San Antonio Express Magazine*, Jan. 23, 1949, p. 6.
Henderson, Sam H. *Fred Gipson*, Southwest Writers Series No. 10. Austin: Steck-Vaughn Co., 1967.
Hobdy, Donna Jean. "Trip to Gipson Place Rewarding." San Angelo *Standard-Times*, June 13, 1963.
"Hound-Dog Man." *Book-of-the-Month Club News*, December 1948, p. 6.

Hunter, J. Marvin. *Peregrinations of a Pioneer Printer*. Grand Prairie: Frontier Times Publishing House, 1954.

Hyde, Wayne F. "I Remember One Time." *True West*, January-February 1973, p. 19.

Koehler, William R. *The Wonderful World of Disney Animals*. Berkeley: Howell Book House, Inc., 1979.

"Life Goes on a Coon Hunt Hunt—Two Small Boys Take to the Woods with 'Hound-Dog Man' Fred Gipson." *Life*, Oct. 24, 1949, p. 126.

Maltin, Leonard. *The Disney Films*. New York: Popular Library, 1978.

Mason County Historical Commission and Historical Society. *Mason County Historical Book*, n.p., 1976.

The Mason County *News*.

"Mason Writer Determined to Grow Grass." Publication facts unknown. In Fred Gipson Papers.

Matlock, Cora B. "Fred Gipson at Work on New Book." Austin *American-Statesman*, Nov. 20, 1963.

Norman, Jerry. "Writer Prefers Success." San Angelo *Standard-Times*, Oct. 18, 1962.

Phelan, Richard. *Texas Wild: The Land, Plants, and Animals of the Lone Star State*. New York: E. P. Dutton & Co., 1977.

Polk, Stella Gipson. "The Gipson Churn." *Sheep and Goat Raiser*, date unknown.

Polk, Stella Gipson. *Mason and Mason County: A History*. Austin: Pemberton Press, 1966.

Polk, Stella Gipson. "My Brother Fred Gipson." *True West*, July-August 1974, p. 16.

Polk, Stella Gipson. "A Personal Reminiscence." *The Highlander*, May 6, 1976.

Pope, Harold. "Hound-Dog Man." *The Houston Chronicle Rotogravure Magazine*, Sept. 13, 1953.

"Portrait." *Saturday Review of Literature*, Jan. 22, 1949.

The San Angelo *Standard-Times*.

The San Antonio *Light*.

Shuffler, R. Henderson. "Books Old and New." *Texas Parade*, July 1965, p. 46.

Smith, Cecil. "Gipson Pens Literary Monuments to Canines." Los Angeles *Times*, Sept. 8, 1957.

Thomas, Bob. *Walt Disney: An American Original*. New York: Simon and Schuster, 1976.

Tinsley, Russell. "Maverick Author." *The Alcalde*, February 1961, p. 18.

Vann, William H. *The Texas Institute of Letters, 1936–1966*. Austin: Encino Press, 1967.

Waldridge, Earle F. "Fred Gipson." *Wilson Library Bulletin*, October 1957,

p. 96.

Walvaven, Bill. "A Fred Gipson Out of Texas? Author Will Look for Another Barefoot Boy—But in Mexico." Corpus Christi *Caller-Times*, Jan. 5, 1967.

Warren, Bill. "Books." *Show World* (Austin *American-Statesman*), May 13, 1973, p. 35.

Wiginton, Gail. "A Bullfrog for Bait." *Scene Magazine* (Dallas *Morning News*), April 22, 1979, p. 29.

"Young Readers' Choice Award." *Elementary English*, October 1959, p. 373.

Index

Cowhand: public reaction to and sales of, 125; paperback edition, 126. *See also* Alford, Ed (Fat)

Cow Killers, The: Gipson writes text for, 141; published by UT Press, 144

Crain, Maurice: 98, 118, 133, 144; first meeting with Gipson, 85; reaction to and efforts to sell *Clipped Wings*, 94, 96; excitement over sale of *Hound-Dog Man*, 97; reaction to *the Devil to Pay*, 107; reaction to *The Home Place*, 109, 110; suggests book idea to Gipson, 110; visits Mason to discuss book ideas, 114; reaction to *The Way of Jessie Gentry*, 116; reaction to *Trail-Driving Rooster*, 126–127; reaction to *Old Yeller*, 139; reaction to movie sale of *Old Yeller*, 141; reaction to *Old Yeller* movie, 154; believes Gipson's screen-writing a mistake , 159

Crockett, Sam: speaks for Gipson about man's abuse of the land, 109

Daily Texan, The: Gipson's first by-line in, 41; Gipson stories and columns in, 41–48 passim; staff has farewell party for Gipson, 50

Daves, Delmer: 116

David, Grace: 113

Day, Donald: sends "My Kind of Man" to *Reader's Digest*, 78; suggests book on Zack Miller, 80, 81–82; sells *Fabulous Empire*, 83; buys "The Melon-Patch Killing," 85; resigns from *Southwest Review*, 86–87; reaction to *Clipped Wings*, 94; writes article on Gipson, 99–100

Day, Donald and Beth: reaction to *The Home Place*, 112

deer hunting: Gipson's first trip, 24–26

Denver Post: Gipson works for briefly, 94–96 passim

Devil To Pay, The: reaction to by Crain and Thomas, 107

"Dinner Bucket": rejected by Maxwell, 87

Disney, Walt: 147, 148, 152; buys movie rights to *Old Yeller*, 140; monitors *Old Yeller* scriptwriting, 143; discusses TV project with Small and Gipson, 149, 151; buys movie rights to *Savage Sam*, 171; studio not interested in *Little Arliss*, 193

Dobie, J. Frank: xviii, xix, 121, 194; reaction to Gipson's writing, 46; Gipson visits, 58–59, 151; reviews "Old Sancho" script, 153–154; death, 182

Dobie, S. N.: 30

dogs: Old Ring, 5, 22; Old Misery, 21

drought: effects on Gipson's land, 121, 123, 124, 137–138; break in excites Gipson, 145, 151, 152

Dru, Joanne: 116

Du Pont, Henry B.: 117

Fabian: 159

Fabulous Empire: Gipson works on, 82–83; sold, 83; promotion for, 87, 88, 89; serialized, 88; reviewers' and public reaction to, 89–90

farming: during Gipson's youth, 5, 15–16

Ferguson, Charles: 122; rejects Gipson articles, 121

Fischer, John: reaction to *Clipped Wings*, 96; meets Gipson, 98; writes promotion letter about *Hound-Dog Man*, 100; proposes book idea, 107–108; is promoted, 123; advises Gipson against Hollywood, 171

fishing: Gipson's expertise at, xii; Small's experiences with Gipson, xii–xiv, xvii–xviii; annual trip during Gipson's youth, 22–24; Gipson's attitudes about, 79–80; Gipson suggests book on, 115

Ford Times: commissions Gipson, 184

Franz, Dr. Joe: 167

George, Bevil (Doc): 39

Gerding, Bert: 178

Gipson, Beck (Fred Gipson's son): *See* Gipson, Thomas Beckton

Gipson, Beck (Fred Gipson's father): moves to Mason, 1–2; buys land, 2, 3; as storyteller, 5; devotion to hats, 9–10; disciplines Fred, 19, 86; works as deer guide, 24–25; breaking mules, 10, 35;

131–132, 176; worries about Mike, 130, 159; angered by rejection of *The Road Leads West*, 132–133; article by on Texas talk, 133–134; life in Hollywood working on scripts, 135, 142–143, 157–162, 175–176 passim; works on *Old Yeller*, 138–139; opinions about juvenile books, 138, 169–170, 176; suffers from back pain and ulcers, 140, 141, 142, 143, 163; changes agent for movie rights, 140; starts text for book of drawings, 141; problems with drinking, 143, 148, 165–166, 172, 176, 178, 180; fan letters to, 144–145; writes Lyndon Johnson about govt. programs, 145; comments on *Old Yeller* script, 147; plans TV series with Small, 148; proposes TV series to Disney, 149, 151; attitudes about writing for TV, 151, 156; happy about continuing rain, 151, 152; complaints about *Hound-Dog Man* script, 159–162; angered by neighbor's hog operation, 163, 168–169; undergoes shock treatment, 166–167; works on *Savage Sam*, 168, 169, 170; goes hunting in Mexico, 172, 175; writes article on children's literature, 176; reaction to Mike's suicide, 179

Declining Years: fan letters to, 182; continued drinking, 183; reaction to Mike's death, 183; religious/philosophical beliefs, 184; interviews Peter Hurd, 184; interest in Mexico as setting for books, 185; looks for someone to help with writing, 185, 188, 189; relationship with Angelina Torres, 185–186; reaction of Mason County neighbors to, 186, 190; worries about Beck, 186–187; works on *Little Arliss*, 187; relationship with Cookie Cook, 187; reaction to grandson's birth, 188; growing reliance on Beck, 188; interviewed by Bill Warren, 189; attitude towards aging, 189; visits with Ace Reid, 189–190; friendship with Frank Wardlaw, 190, 192; death and funeral, 193–194. *See also* drought; fishing;

Gipson family; Gipson, Fred and Tommie; Mexico; River ranch; Texas Institute of Letters; writing; entries for individual stories and books by Gipson

Gipson, Fred and Tommie: first meeting, 60; courtship and marriage, 61–63; honeymoon, 65–66; financial situation and worries about money, 70, 76, 88, 123, 127, 141, 158–159, 166–167; build own house, 72; move to Austin, 73; home in Mason, 76, 79; visits to New York City, 98, 171; plans for spending money, 113; trip West, 127–131; marital problems, 153, 176, 180; buy ranch on Llano, 166, 167; plan new house, 172, 183; separation and divorce, 182

Gipson, Jennie: 3

Gipson, Mike (Phillip Michael): 113, 168, 169, 175; birth, 68; early years with father, 72; reaction to Beck's birth, 83; fascinated by Charlie Sanders, 91; goes on coon hunt,106; in movie premier, 119; travels West with family, 127–131; Gipson's worries about, 130, 159; works on book, 171–172; commits suicide, 178–179

Gipson, Mildred: 70

Gipson, Stella: *See* Polk, Stella Gipson

Gipson, Thomas Beckton (Beck): 113, 165–166, 168, 169, 179; birth, 83; fascinated by Charlie Sanders, 91; in movie premier, 119; travels West with family, 127–131; goes to Hollywood with parents, 151; joins Army and gets married, 185; is injured in Army, 187; helps father, 188

Gipson, Tommie: *See* North, Tommie Gipson

Gooch, Ben: 3

Grant, Marcus: 131, 152

Grant, Mildred: 152

Green, Eunice: 30, 31

Grey, Zane: Gipson enjoys stories by, 31

Hal Roach studios: buys "Brush Roper" for TV, 134

"Hard-Pressed Sam": accepted by *South-*

on, 187; Disney studios not interested in, 193
Liveoak Ranch: 34
Llano River: Gipson and Small fish, xii–xiv; description of, 2; Gipson kids swim in, 23
"Long Tom: The Wild Gobbler": in *Southwest Review*, 87
Louis, Alexander: 85, 88
"Luck": Gipson's first published story, 28
Lupino, Ida: takes option on *Hound-Dog Man* movie rights, 125

Manning, Bill: Joe Small's alias, 69; receives letter from *Collier's*, 73
Martin, Rudolph: 35
Martin, Sammy: 168
Mason County: descriptions of, 2, 3; farming in, 15–16; economy in late 1920s, 32; cattle drives in, 34; reaction of residents to Gipson, 113, 186, 190
Mason Grain and Produce: price for skins at, 17
Maxwell, Allen: 93, 157; rejects Gipson story, 87; reaction to *Clipped Wings*, 93–94; buys "Bad Day," 118. See also *Southwest Review*
McAvoy, Tom: 106
McCulloch, H. E.: 152
McGregor, Doc: 55
McMurray Bookshop Award: given to *Hound-Dog Man*, 108; given to *Recollection Creek*, 142
McMurray, Elizabeth Anne: holds autograph party for Gipson, 100, 102
"Melon-Patch Killing, The": in *Southwest Review*, 85–86
Mercer, Tom: 59
Mexico: Gipson's trips to, xiv–xviii, 65–66, 148, 172, 175, 185, 188; Gipson attracted by, 148, 185
Miller, Colonel Zack: 81–83
Mix, Tom: Gipson imitates, 11
"Monarch": in *Daily Texan*, 42
Monterrey: Gipsons visit on their honeymoon, 65–66
Mueller, Captain Hugo: 54

mules/muledriving: 10, 35
"My Kind of Man": accepted by *Southwest Review* and *Reader's Digest*, 78; included in textbook, 99, 105; TV show based on, 125; plagiarized, 157–158

New York Times, The: carries book reviews by Gipson, 184
New York Times Review of Books: Gipson article on children's books in, 176
Norstrom, Ursula: 126, 133; reaction to *Old Yeller*, 138, 139
North, Joe: 187
North, Tommie Gipson: 73–74, 113, 121, 167; first date with Gipson, 60; courtship and marriage, 61–63; on honeymoon, 65–66; first pregnancy and birth of Mike, 67, 68; role in Gipson's writing, 70, 76, 108, 118, 153; takes job, 75; second pregnancy and birth of Beck, 79, 83; suffers miscarriage, 88; reaction to Charlie Sanders, 91–92; experiences in Colorado, 96; *Hound-Dog Man* dedicated to, 102; reports death of Jesse Gentry, 117; becomes pregnant again and suffers miscarriage, 124, 126; trip through West, 127–131; reaction to *The Road Leads West*, 132; searches for subjects for Gipson, 118, 137, 151; visits Gipson in Hollywood, 143, 158, 175–176; handles fan mail for Gipson, 145; goes to Hollywood with Gipson and Small, 151; health problems, 153, 156; reviews *Hound-Dog Man* script, 160–162; settles account with Swanson agency, 162; concerned about Gipson's health, 165–166; reaction to Gipson's drinking, 172, 175, 176; reaction to Mike's writing, 175; reaction to Mike's suicide, 178–179, 180; plans to remarry, 187. *See also* Gipson, Fred and Tommie

"Old Sancho": Gipson rewrites for TV, 152
Old Yeller: Gipson works on, 138–139; reactions to by editors, 139; sales of subsidiary rights to, 139, 141–142, 151;

170; reaction to by Crain and Thomas, 170; Disney buys movie rights to, 171; reviews of, 176
Savage Sam (movie): Gipson works on script, 172, 175–176; premiers in Mason, 183
Scantling, Blackie: based on Sanders, 92
Selby, John: 93
Sigma Delta Chi: 47
Small, Elizabeth: 71, 73, 78, 124, 178
Small, Joe: 78, 141, 154, 183; fishing trips with Gipson, xii–xiv, 80, 148; trip to Mexico with Gipson, xiv–xviii; evaluation of Gipson as writer, xx; first meeting with Gipson, 40; offers to buy Gipson stories, 68; advises Gipson on writing and acts as agent, 69; plans column with Gipson, 71, 72; sends Gipson story to major magazines, 73; visits Sanders, 103–104; organizes premier of *Return of the Texan*, 119–120; starts *True West*, 124–125; visits Gipson in Hollywood, 135; worries about Gipson, 143; plans TV programs with Gipson, 148; proposes TV series to Disney, 149, 151; tells Gipson about Mike's suicide, 178
Snow, Bob: 172, 175
soil conservation: Gipson's advocacy of, 109, 113–114
Southern Sportsman, The: 68
Southwest Review: accepts "Hard-Pressed Sam," 43; publishes "My Kind of Man," 78; publishes "The Melon-Patch Killing," 85; controversy over editorial policy, 86–87, publishes "Hound-Dog Man," "Long Tom: The Wild Gobbler," and "Throwback," 87; publishes "Sad Sam," 88; publishes "Town of Beer and Sorrow," 105; publishes "Bad Day," 118. *See also* Day, Donald; Maxwell, Allen
Southwest Writers Conference: Gipson and Small attend, xviii–xix; Gipson on panel at, 121; Gipson's remarks at, 136; Gipson and Mike attend, 171
Steinbeck, John: 98
Stewart, Georgia: 61

Stover, Elizabeth: 98–99, 105, 107
Swanson, H. N.: 157, 161; becomes Gipson's movie agent, 140; sells *Old Yeller* movie rights, 140–141; arranges screenwriting job for Gipson, 159

Taylor, R. L.: 159
Terrell, Rogers: 69
Texas Book Store: 46
Texas Cowboys: take part in movie premier, 119
Texas Institute of Letters: Gipson attends annual meeting, 93; awards to Gipson books, 108, 142; Gipson chosen as President, 167; Gipson named as fellow, 192
Texas Rangers: 51, 70
Texas Rangers, The: reviewed by Gipson, 42–43
Thomas, Evan: reaction to *Clipped Wings*, 96; meets Gipsons, 98; reaction to *The Devil to Pay*, 107; trip to Mason, 108; reaction to *The Home Place*, 109; reaction to *The Way of Jesse Gentry*, 117; rejects *Uncle Vesper*, 122; promoted 123–124; reconsiders earlier Gipson manuscripts, 124; rejects *The Road Leads West*, 132–133; reaction to *Old Yeller*, 139
Thomas, Lonnie: 116
"Throwback": in *Southwest Review*, 87
Timmons, Paul: interviews Gipson, 113–114
Tinkle, Lon: 192
Tinsley, Russell: interviews Gipson, 159
Toepperwein, Fritz and Emilie: 121
Torres, Angelina: Gipson's relationship with, 185–186
"Town of Beer and Sorrow": in *Southwest Review*, 105
Trail-Driving Rooster: 132, 133; origin of story, 123; reaction of editors to, 126–127; sales of, 134; wins award from Texas Institute of Letters, 142
Travels of Jamie McPheeters, The: Gipson works on script of, 159–160, 162
Trouble in the Hills: 124, 126
True West: 124–125